Alexander Johnstone Wilson

The Resources of Modern Countries

Alexander Johnstone Wilson

The Resources of Modern Countries

ISBN/EAN: 9783744667203

Printed in Europe, USA, Canada, Australia, Japan

Cover: Foto ©Suzi / pixelio.de

More available books at **www.hansebooks.com**

THE
RESOURCES OF MODERN COUNTRIES

VOL. II.

LONDON : PRINTED BY
SPOTTISWOODE AND CO., NEW-STREET SQUARE
AND PARLIAMENT STREET

THE

RESOURCES OF MODERN COUNTRIES

ESSAYS TOWARDS AN ESTIMATE OF THE ECONOMIC

POSITION OF NATIONS AND BRITISH

TRADE PROSPECTS

BY

ALEXANDER JOHNSTONE WILSON

REPRINTED, with EMENDATIONS and ADDITIONS, from FRASER'S MAGAZINE

IN TWO VOLUMES

VOL. II.

LONDON

LONGMANS, GREEN, AND CO.

1878

All rights reserved

CONTENTS

OF

THE SECOND VOLUME.

CHAPTER		PAGE
IX.	ITALY	1
X.	SPAIN, PORTUGAL, AND THE NETHERLANDS	40
XI.	CANADA AND SOUTH AFRICA	95
XII.	AUSTRALIA AND NEW ZEALAND	152
XIII.	MEXICO AND BRAZIL	212
XIV.	THE RIVER PLATE, CHILI, AND PERU	243
XV.	THE WEST INDIES AND OTHER MINOR BRITISH POSSESSIONS	292
	CONCLUSION	309

APPENDICES.

I.	COMPARATIVE STATEMENT OF THE TOTAL VALUE OF IMPORTS AND EXPORTS OF MERCHANDISE, ETC.	357
II.	GENERAL DOMESTIC EXPORTS OF THE UNITED STATES IN TWENTY-SIX YEARS	358
III.	ABSTRACT STATEMENT OF THE DEBT OF RUSSIA	360
IV.	THE FINANCIAL POSITION OF EGYPT	364

THE
RESOURCES OF MODERN COUNTRIES.

CHAPTER IX.

ITALY.

THE rapidity with which the new Italian kingdom has grown out of a congeries of petty States and subject provinces is a good augury for its future. Unless we must yet look forward to a time of social revolutions— to struggles between priestcraft and popular liberties— of which there are at present few seriously disturbing signs, there is little to hinder modern Italy from advancing to the position of one of the most thriving nations of the old world.

There is indeed something very attractive in the progress which Italy is making. It is a progress dashed with errors, and not without dangers of course; but it has for all that been great and admirable. We have but to glance for a moment at the picture which the dismembered kingdom presented before she began to stir for her freedom in 1848. The first stirrings were indeed earlier than that; for Italy, bound hand and foot at the feet of Austria as she was by the Congress of Vienna, which restored and solaced exiled and effete dynasties in all Western and Central Europe— Italy never quite forgot the liberal ideas which the republican armies of the young citizen Buonaparte had carried with them out of France. The dull brutal rule of Austria in Venetia and Lombardy, and the more than Asiatic ruthlessness of the Bourbons of Naples, gave the Italians small chance to forget their dreams of a bright deliverance. Accordingly, there had been risings before 1848; and besides the risings many an effort to persuade the people to stand up like men for their rights, that had seemingly led to nothing. But it was not till 1848 that Italy could be said seriously to bend herself to the task of wrenching her shackles off. That year sent a quiver of dread through the heart of every king and kinglet in Europe. Again the impulse came from France, that country so full of striking ideals in its modern political history—ideals which have been made the pretext of tremendous crimes; but dismembered Italy could have made no headway at all against either Bourbon or Hapsburg, except for the resolution of Charles Albert, the King of Sardinia, to become the champion of national unity and independence. The new generation of to-day forgets these things; but middle-aged men remember the excitement, the hopes, at first even stimulated by the sovereign Pontiff, destined to so cruel a disappointment. Italy was beaten back apparently into slavery in this her first grand dash for freedom, and the dreams of Mazzini and Cavour seemed to be gone as dreams all go. The weak-kneed Pope had turned traitor to the nation, in his greed of temporal ascendency, and had given it his curse. Powers too strong for them were arrayed against the people, the Sardinian armies were defeated, and Italy seemed by 1850 to have lost everything. It was not, however, so to be. The defeat gave a keenness to the national feeling all over the land such as it had not attained to before. Neapolitan and Lombard began to recognise themselves as men of the same nationality. The repression of the foreigners had thus to do its final work in welding the nation, and the conquerors endeavoured to do it effectually, to their own ultimate overthrow.

Louis Napoleon also did something, no doubt, for the liberation of Italy, in a grandiose, histrionic, morally contemptible way, urged as he was by the necessity of justifying his rather despicable existence in the eyes of France; but whether he had interfered or not, the power of Austria was destined to fall before the rising forces of Prussia, and with it that of the Bourbons of Sicily, Naples, and Tuscany, most corrupt of all the corrupt creatures whom England had propped up again for a brief space, to play the part of tyrants and oppressors in mundane affairs. It is not my purpose to follow the history of the Italian struggle for independence, through its Napoleonic and other phases; suffice it that we call to mind some of the cardinal facts. Before 1848 Italy, all except Piedmont, seemed hopelessly crushed. Austria, the Pope, and the Bourbons held her in their grasp. Even the comparatively native sovereign of Tuscany had turned oppressor, and all Italy groaned like a man in the grasp of the torturer. Commerce languished, divergent fiscal laws and arbitrary raids on private wealth choked up the channels of intercourse between one part of the kingdom and another; without shipping, without manufactures or foreign trade of a solid kind, possessed of no political security, Italy was, thirty years ago, more insignificant in the eyes of neighbouring nations than Greece or Spain is now. But, once free, her consolidation was almost as rapid as that of the still newer German Empire; and to-day Italy is a power to be reckoned with in the councils of nations, and possesses a trade that begins to be a distinct element in European prosperity, a trade that we in England cannot too carefully give heed to. The bitter bondage which the country has long lain under has ended in making its mixed population, in a hopeful degree, a nation; and, prudently ruled, new Italy may yet have a remarkable career before it.

Naturally enough, all this progress has not been made without great cost, and it is our duty to look at both sides of the picture; nor should the political and commercial success blind us to the fact that the young kingdom is not free from serious economic and social dangers on more sides than one. The very transition from a collection of petty States to a single power entailed enormous waste of resources and almost irremediable administrative confusion. Jealousies were also engendered between province and province, which it will take some time to heal: so that this transition stage cannot by any means be considered at an end in Italy. Nor need we wonder when we remember that it is barely seven years ago since the crowning act of Italian unity was performed, and Victor Emmanuel entered Rome as King of all Italy, to the disgust of Pio Nono and the corrupt creatures around him.

I must leave the historical part of the subject, however, and trace some of the financial characteristics of this period of transition, before examining the trading capacity and mercantile development which Italy exhibits. These financial characteristics are again so intimately bound up with the administrative machinery of the State, that in noticing the one we must notice the other. Indeed, the first things that strike the observer are the concurrent facts that the Government of Italy has, throughout, been impecunious, and, throughout, comparatively feeble and irresolute, while yet the nation has grown and consolidated. No statesman has succeeded to the seat of Count Cavour;

and, either because the men were feebler, or because the constitutional powers, donned suddenly like a garment, fitted but ill, the remedial measures which society and the State required on all hands have been but tentatively and tardily applied, amid not a little bungling. The new kingdom succeeded to all the debts of the petty States it absorbed, and it also succeeded to their corrupt administrations. The debts made a most serious burden to begin with; and when added to the cost of the wars of independence, so handicapped Italy that few people would have been surprised if she had pulled up short and proclaimed herself bankrupt. In a most valuable report on the financial system of the kingdom, recently made to our Foreign Office by Mr. Herries, Legation Secretary at Rome,[1] we are enabled to trace very clearly the stages of this financial malady; and many of the statements I shall make here will be drawn from this source. Quoting Mr. Pasini, for instance, he gives the total debt of the petty States of Italy just before the consolidation of the kingdom in 1871 at 90,000,000*l.*, or 2,241,270,000 lira.[2] The debt was growing rapidly then, as the expenditure in all cases exceeded the in-

[1] *Embassy and Legation Reports*, part iv. 1876.
[2] Martin, in his *Statesman's Year-book*, states the debt of Italy in 1860, the year before the emancipation, at 97,500,000*l.*, but does not give his authority. It is possible he may be right, however, because the debts being reckoned in different currencies, some of which were of fluctuating values, the best statement which could be given was partly only an estimate.

ITALY. 7

come; but, after the new kingdom was fairly started, the deficits grew worse and worse. In the words of Mr. Pasini it is stated that during this disastrous period the receipts were diminished by 1,280,000*l.*, while the expenditure was increased by 2,280,000*l.*, and the public debt by 30,360,000*l.* Only in the old provinces forming the kingdom of Sardinia was there any elasticity of revenue; in all other provinces the ousting of the old government and the setting up of the new involved almost hopeless fiscal confusion and loss. Income fell off and expenditure increased until the budget deficits, which had nominally been but 520,000*l.* in 1859 for the various States composing Italy, rose to over 4,000,000*l.*, the greater part of which was due to the Neapolitan provinces and Sicily. Taxes of an odious character imposed by the old tyrannical governments had to be taken off and reduced before any regular system of substitutes could be framed to take their place; so that, as pointed out in the report of a finance committee, also quoted by Mr. Herries, and which gives, it would seem, a different estimate from that of Pasini, the income of the States forming United Italy fell from over 20,000,000*l.* at the time of the breaking out of the war to 18,500,000*l.* the following year, and the expenditure exceeded that diminished income by 7,200,000*l.* This defect, however, as others similar, refers mostly, if not exclusively, to the ordinary income and expenditure, and does not include the special outlay incident to the war, which is partially at least represented by the increase of the public debt. In 1860 and 1861 no less than some 370,000,000*l.* nominal appears to have been raised by loans, issues of inconvertible paper, or sales of stocks, only part of which has since been redeemed.[1] There were six separate budgets for the various parts of Italy in 1860, and it was not till 1862 that the Government was able to present a single budget for the united nation; but that

[1] I find great divergencies in the estimates given in various works of the present debt of Italy. For example, Kolb, whom I am disposed to place first as a compiler of statistics of this kind, gives the debt, funded and floating, at the end of 1872 as 10,060,000,000 lira, the interest of which is 460,445,614 lira. In other words, the capital of the debt was 400,000,000*l.* odd, and the interest-charge just under 18,500,000*l.* Martin, on the other hand, in the new issue of his *Statesman's Year-book*, places the capital of the debt at about 380,000,000*l.* at the end of 1873, including of course the paper money, and the interest-charge at just over 15,500,000*l.* Again, the *Investor's Monthly Manual*, a publication usually accurate, and with figures to a more recent date than either Martin or Kolb, places the capital of the debt at only 357,000,000*l.*, and the interest and other charges thereon at 15,300,000*l.* This last estimate appears to me to be an obvious error, because for one thing the deficits on the annual budget have not yet ceased, and these alone for the past four years have amounted to an aggregate of 28,000,000*l.*, which has necessarily added to the debt in some form. If we take Kolb to be correct, therefore, the debt at the end of last year cannot have been less than 430,000,000*l.* all told. This is, it need hardly be said, a very serious burden for so young a nation to carry, and it has been further heavily augmented since by the Italian Government taking over the Italian portion of the old Lombardo-Venetian Railways, as it contracted with the Rothschilds last year to do. This bargain will involve an addition to the debt of at least 30,000,000*l.*, including the extra payments, and should the yearly deficits go on, and the railways not pay—both likely contingencies—the taxation of Italy will have to be seriously increased. By 1880 we may expect to see the funded and floating debt raised to the amount of 470,000,000*l.* to 500,000,000*l.*, and the chances of a redemption of the paper currency almost as remote as ever.

was only the initial stage of the task which Italian financiers had before them. A cumbersome method of account-keeping had to be swept away, which under the old system entailed the mischief of several distinct statements of accounts running alongside each other. The budget passed through no less than seven different stages before it could be considered a finished account, and it was not till 1869 that this was swept away. Now the financial account runs even with each year, and comprises within it only the actual receipts and payments of the year. Further reforms as to the administration of the various departments of the State had still to be carried out, and it was only the other year that Italy could be said to have her finances completely under Parliamentary control. A far more formidable difficulty remains to be noticed—the reformation of the taxes—and that cannot yet be said to be anything like completed, for Italy is still too poor to have a consistent fiscal system. There was a too radical cutting down of obnoxious imposts in the first moment of liberty and unity, when men's hearts overflowed, and ever since the Government has had to struggle painfully to make ends meet. One of the best sources of national income, the property and land tax, has also been most difficult of administration, through the absence of anything like a sound basis of assessment, and it now only yields something like 9,300,000*l.* including provincial and communal surtaxes. In 1874 this was levied upon 5,130,146 proprietors, and the average impost per proprietor for imperial purposes only was almost exactly 1*l*. The amount of this tax which actually goes to the State is thus only about 5,000,000*l*., the rest being devoted to local purposes under the law which permits provinces and communes to levy certain imposts for themselves. The figures as regards the number of people assessed cannot however be depended upon, any more than the cadastral basis of the tax; and there is no reform more urgently needed than the one which shall distribute the burden fairly over the landowners and metayers. At present the tax falls too lightly on some parts of the country and on the tenant classes, and far too heavily on others, and altogether does not yield probably within millions of what it ought to do. Another considerable source of revenue is the income tax, which is not however to be taken as similar in character to the English tax of that name, being a complex and irritating impost which includes licenses of various kinds, and which presses very heavily on small incomes.[1] It seems to vary in character too in

[1] Mr. Herries makes the following comparison between the burden of this tax on the Italians and of the English income tax. His figures were compiled before the date of Sir Stafford Northcote's budget last year, which relieved small incomes up to 300*l*., while imposing an additional penny on all beyond that; but they are sufficiently close to the facts, and illustrate the peculiar irritation of the Italian tax:—'An Englishman having an income of exactly 100*l*. pays nothing. An Italian pays on its equivalent, if in Category A, 13*l*. 4*s*.; if in Category B, 9*l*. 18*s*.; if in Category C, 8*l*. 5*s*. A so-called 'professional man' in London, with an income of just 300*l*., pays on that amount, minus 80*l*., a tax of 1*l*. 16*s*. 8*d*.

different parts of the kingdom. The grist tax should also be mentioned as an old and most oppressive impost on the grinding of corn, which was withdrawn at the revolution, and re-imposed afterwards under pressure of the necessities of the State. In its new form it is vexatious, and that it should be required at all is a proof both of the poverty which Italy still labours under, and of the imperfect manner in which the fiscal reforms have yet been carried out. It gives a gross return of about 3,500,000*l*.

We might pursue this subject further, and find it very interesting; but my object is only to indicate the broad fact that Italy is reforming; is, though slowly, growing solidly together; that she has to all appearance heartily adopted constitutional forms, and is shaping her destiny to good purpose, in spite of the many drawbacks to which she is subject. By means of the changes which have been introduced, the peace and security that have prevailed, and the consequent increase in wealth, the gross income of the kingdom has slowly recovered itself, until in 1875 it amounted to 55,480,000*l*. In 1876 it was rather less, being only 54,800,000*l*., owing to the insufficient harvest, rather than to any weakness in the country. In 1877 the fiscal estimate of ordinary income was about

If he establishes himself at Rome, he will soon find his means of subsistence diminished by a charge of 24*l*. 15*s*.; the sum which in England would be due from a commercial house making a clear profit of 2,970*l*. a year.'

51,000,000*l*., but the total receipts, ordinary and extraordinary, were placed at about 56,000,000*l*. There are still deficits, of course, but they are growing on the whole less alarming; that for 1875 having been only 1,124,000*l*., that for last year 1,160,000*l*., and the estimates for the present year showing a surplus, which will, however, in all probability prove delusive. There is perhaps some reason to hope that deficits may really disappear before long, unless unforeseen events check the gradual development of the community, or unless the imprudent commitments of the Government to railway purchases and administration lead to unexpected loss. I should not be surprised, however, were this to prove the case; and, if so, the small deficits of the last year or two may again increase for a time, but only for a time. Italy has but to push forward her social reformation, to steadily reorganise her finances and her provincial administrations, and there can be no fear that the wealth of the country will not be found in time sufficient to furnish all the Government requires. The only serious elements of financial danger are the funded and floating debt, and the wasteful expenditure of the municipal and district Governments, some of the Italian cities, such as Florence, Naples, and Genoa, being, for example, almost as spendthrift as New York. These therefore constitute grave dangers, which Italian statesmen cannot too deeply recognise. Not only should every effort be made to keep down the national and local expenditure, so that there should be no further increase in its amount, but every effort should be made to reduce the debt also. This is especially necessary with regard to the paper currency, which now forms such an intolerable drag upon the commerce of the people. In amount it seems light beside that of France, being only some 40,000,000*l.*; but then the population of Italy, and the trade of Italy, are both much less. The imports and exports together are under 100,000,000*l.*, or less than a third of those of France. Moreover, Italy has little or no metallic reserve, so that her paper currency is of necessity bound to fluctuate with every adverse movement of the exchanges. As the imports of the country have been stimulated for many years by the issue of such paper and by other loans, so that they uniformly exceed the exports, it follows, of course, that exchanges are often adversely affected. Add to this the fact that a good deal of Italian *rente* is held abroad, in France, Holland, and England, and we have abundant materials for a very troublesome state of mercantile credit. The premium on gold is rarely less than 10 per cent., and it rises sometimes to 12 and 15, or even to 20. During one year the fluctuation is not unfrequently as much as from 5 to 7 per cent., so that the difficulty of adjusting prices so as to avoid ruinous losses becomes most serious. A premium on gold becomes, as I have said before, a universal tax, because no commodity sold or bought can be made exempt from its influences. Of late, however, there has been less tendency to violent movement in this gold premium, and the average is lower now than it was in the years immediately succeeding the national independence. Should the funded debt be kept well within bounds, therefore, it might be worth the consideration of Italian statesmen whether the Government should not make an approach towards a resumption of specie payments by means of an issue of bonds for the purpose of redeeming the currency debt. A measure of the kind, were it accompanied by the exemption of the foreign creditors of the State from an income tax, which is not fairly justifiable when imposed on loans which were raised abroad, would do a great deal to elevate the commerce of Italy out of its fifth-rate position, and to make it solidly prosperous.

There are, as we see, drawbacks in the situation of the country; but for all that I shall miss my aim grievously if, in this rapid sketch, giving the outlines of both sides of the subject, I do not show that Italy has made, and is making, steady progress. She is not standing still, nor going back in either her political organisation or her finances. The nation has vitality as a nation, and through all the drawbacks and difficulties, one can discern the possibility of a new future for the peninsula which once ruled the world. Splendidly situated for doing at all events a Continental trade with Asia and the far East, it is possible that the tide of commerce will partially roll backwards to her long-deserted shores. We must try, then, to find out what Italy is doing in the way of developing her trade—what her capacities are, and what hindrances there may be in her way other than the merely financial or administrative.

In the first place, it may be at once admitted that Italy is not a manufacturing country now, nor very likely speedily to become one. The races which inhabit Southern Italy are ill adapted for the hard incessant labour to which 'factory hands' and 'foundry hands' have to submit in any country, but most of all in a country striving to establish a business for itself at the expense of rivals. In Northern Italy there is much more raw capacity for industry; and the hardy Lombards or Piedmontese—even the Venetians and Tuscans—might, if it depended upon mere labour alone, rise with some rapidity into the position of competitors with other nations for certain kinds of manufactured staples. But, granting everything to be favourable in the character of the people, Italy does not possess the raw materials necessary to a great manufacturing nation in sufficient quantities, or in a form so readily accessible as to make it possible for her to become great in this way. The only industry in which she can be said to possess some advantage over her neighbours is silk-weaving, and in this, I believe, some progress was made up to the time when a change of fashion and failure in the Italian silk crop gave the entire industry a severe blow: but as a producer of textile fabrics generally Italy does not promise to take a strong position. Her exports of silk, raw and manufactured, averaged in value about 15,000,000*l*. in the years 1870 to 1874, according to tables given by Mr. Herries. This was balanced to some extent by imports of the average value of 5,500,000*l*. Besides silk, Italy grows a certain amount of cotton, but not nearly enough to supply her own wants; and although she has an export trade to Austria in cotton tissues, it is more of a transit trade, I believe, than the result of the competition of Italian spinners and weavers. Her industries are, indeed, all—except that of silk—small and of quite local importance. Italy is in nothing more provincial, in fact, than in the isolated condition of her cotton, linen, and woollen manufactures. But, although insignificant, they still increase in a measure, and may well grow very much bigger without interfering in the least with the purchasing power of Italy in other countries, or competing very seriously in foreign markets. With her immediate neighbours, Switzerland, Austria, and France, it is in the nature of things that her trade should grow larger, and that where competition is possible Italian products should in some directions beat ours; but there is as yet certainly nothing alarming in the situation, and we have no cause to be envious of her prosperity. At present the total export and import trade of Italy is, as I have said, well under 100,000,000*l*., and the bulk of the exports—silk, oil, wine, marble, and glass—are of a kind which do not come much within our competing range. As far as the direct trade with Great Britain is concerned, it is on the whole steady and profitable, and amounts to about an eighth part of her entire commerce; Italy buying from us much more largely than we do from her, although the discrepancy is less now than it has been, owing, in part, I fear it must be said, to the more effectual competition of French manufacturers. The consumption of Indian and Egyptian raw cotton is also steadily increasing in Italian mills, although these are in great part still of a primitive kind. Some progress has been made in the establishment of small iron-works, and one work at Venice, belonging to an Englishman named Nevill, has attained to some local celebrity. Italy possesses few iron mines, however, and, as far as we know, has no rich contiguous stores of iron and coal such as are essential to a country destined to lead in almost any branch of skilled production.[1] We must, therefore, after making all allowance

[1] In Kolb's *Vergleichende Statistik* it is stated that the average annual value of the production of iron in Italy in the years 1867-70 was just over 800,000*l*., the product of 11,100 workpeople; that of copper, 53,000*l*., won by the labour of 2,500 workmen. Coal and petroleum together represented the insignificant value of 120,000*l*., and gave employment to 3,450 workmen. Lead was considerably more valuable than copper, but only gave an average of about 330,000*l*., a quantity clearly

for the signs of local activity which are to be met with in the country, come to the conclusion that Italy is not in a position to become a great manufacturing centre. Her people are by preference pastoral; and as in France, although the tenure of the land is not the same, large tracts of the soil are parcelled out amongst small holders, whose position is nearly as secure, if not so independent, as that of the French peasant proprietor, and the attractions of the workshops are not sufficient to draw a comparatively comfortable and by no means crowded population from their fields.[1]
not sufficient for home consumption. Italy is, in fact, a steady customer to England for the metals of manufacture and for coal.

[1] According to the return published in 1861, the latest which seems to be available, about 8,000,000 of the population of 22,000,000 then comprising Italy were employed in agricultural pursuits, and a nearly equal number were returned as 'without calling.' The number engaged in mineral production was less than 60,000, and there were devoted to manufactures about 3,100,000. In this latter would of course be included all the local tradesmen, the shoemakers, smiths, carpenters, masons, and clockmakers, which go to make up the population of the villages, so that the numbers engaged actually in what we should in this country call manufactures would probably not reach half that figure. These figures are not of much value now, however, for Italy has been changed and opened up greatly since then, and in some of the northern provinces manufactures and agriculture overlap each other, so that the same people ought to be classed in both; not only so, but the addition to the population, both by natural increment and through the incorporation of fresh provinces, has materially added to the proportions of certain classes. Instead of 22,000,000, Italy has now a population of 27,500,000, of which, according to Behm and Wagner's last Annual on the population of the earth, issued in Petermann's *Mittheilungen*, 6,900,000, or 25·7 per cent., form the scattered population, the remainder being gathered in the cities, towns, and agricultural villages of the land. I am unable to say, however, what proportion of the entire population may now be actually employed in, or directly dependent upon, the labour of the agriculturist. From an official report lately issued on the state of the Italian agriculture in the years 1870–74, of which copious analyses have been appearing

But, though not a great manufacturing nation, Italy is, as we have seen, advancing in several respects as a producer of articles meant for home use, and her tariff is, like that of other countries we have mentioned, acting as a strong bulwark to protect the home producer against competition. One would imagine, for example, that in the matter of silk the Italian manufacturer would require little or nothing in the shape of protection, seeing that he could set up his

both in the *Economista d' Italia* and in the *Economiste Français*, I learn that 11,600,000 acres of land are devoted to wheat, and yield about 142,420,000 bushels, or, roughly, a little more than twelve bushels to the acre—a very small yield for so rich a country—and the best commentary we could have upon the exceeding backwardness of agriculture. Of maize, rice, barley, and oats, the yield was rather better, as the following table will show :—

	Acres	Total yield in Bushels	Yield per Acre
Maize	4,242,000	85,959,000	20·3
Rice	582,000	27,000,000	46·4
Barley and rye	1,162,000	18,417,000	15·8
Oats	798,000	20,471,000	25·6

Allowing for the difference of grains, this table still shows great variableness in the yield. At the worst, however, Italy compares very favourably with such a country as Russia, where the yield per acre of wheat is estimated in the latest returns at only five-and-a-half bushels per acre. The total yield of wheat in Italy is indeed within 15,000,000 bushels of that of Russia, and leaves a considerable margin for export. Besides these grains and root crops, olives, cotton, and flax, a large acreage is devoted to the vine, no less, according to the table from which I quote, than 4,700,000 acres, the yield upon which was 597,000,000 gallons of wine. Altogether, the agricultural land in Italy included in the official returns extends to 68,000,000 acres. The tendency would seem to be to extend the pasture lands, a good trade offering to Italy in cattle with Austria, Switzerland, and France, which the vegetarian habits of the agricultural population enables it to turn to better account than the mere enumeration of the flocks would lead one to suppose. In horses particularly Italy is poor, and she stands numerically in all kinds of animals behind Austria and Hungary, but for all that she can export to them.

mills in the heart of a silk-growing country, and yet Italy levies a duty on all kinds of silk tissues imported, which, though small, is, like the Indian duty on cotton goods, sufficient to debar foreign imports to a considerable extent, and to raise prices at home. Woollen, cotton, and linen fabrics are more heavily taxed still, as will be seen in the note which I append;[1] and,

[1] The import duty charged at Italian ports on silk tissues is 5 per cent. *ad valorem*, or 1s. 1d. per lb.; ribbons pay from 1s. 10d. to 2s. 11d. per lb. if of silk alone, and 10 per cent. *ad valorem* if mixed. Only silk twist is admitted free. Cotton yarn, on the other hand, pays according to fineness, and to whether it is bleached and dyed or unbleached, a duty varying from 6s. 1d. to 14s. 1d. per cwt., the twists and double yarns and bleached and dyed ditto paying respectively 11s. 9d. and 14s. 1d. On cotton tissues the duty is very heavy, varying from 26s. 5d. on unbleached cotton to 47s. on cotton prints per cwt., while cotton embroidery pays 4l. 14s. 3d. per cwt. Woollen yarn comes off worse still, undyed paying 18s. 9d. and dyed 28s. 3d. per cwt., while woollen cloths pay substantially about the same nominal duties per cwt. as cotton. Blankets and carpets, for example, are charged 23s. 6d. to 32s. 6d., according to quality, per cwt.; tapes and lace of pure wool or mixed 4l. 13s. 6d. Ordinary woollen tissues or cloths pay, however, either a 10 per cent. *ad valorem* duty or 3l. 5s. per cwt. What the incidence of much of this taxation is according to the values of the articles taxed it is of course impossible for any but exporters to tell; but it must vary considerably, and in some instances, when the cloth is of a cheap kind, represent something like 20 to 30 per cent. of its value or more. The same may be said of linen, hempen and jute fabrics, all of which pay heavy duties, which, if nominally less in amount than those levied by France or Russia, are by their rough and ready mode of adjustment probably practically as prohibitory. Measured by the wealth of Italy, compared with France, they must be more so. As to iron and steel, the tariff of Italy is, if anything, more foolish than that of any other country we have had under review, because in this instance there is nothing to be protected worth speaking of. There are no blown-up hectic home industries in iron to pamper and to fine the people for the maintenance of, as in the United States; and therefore these duties have here not even the irrational excuse which the States, France, Austria, and Germany may plausibly advance. Italy charges, for all that, a duty of some sort on every kind of iron except pig-iron and broken scraps. In some cases, as, for example, rails, the duty is relatively low,

speaking generally of the Italian tariff, we may say that, instead of being now light and liberal, as Count Cavour wished it to be, when compared with that of other European countries, it is essentially the tariff of a country devoted to protectionist ideas. Driven by stress of poverty, Italian statesmen not possessed of the political sagacity of Count Cavour, have re-imposed some very obnoxious customs duties, and increased their burden, without, however, adding materially to the yield, while certainly hindering the development of the trade of the nation. Compared with the fragmentary tariffs in force in 1858, the duties are, however, still very low, and Italy should get credit here also for at all events not slipping back into the slough from which she emerged. Still, the present tariff is higher in a good many instances than that in force in 1863 and 1864,[1] which alarmed the short-sighted economists of the country by the smallness of its yield; and it is

only some 5½d. per cwt. or 9s. 2d. per ton; but in others it is very high—steel wire paying 9s. 5d.; rolled and bar steel, 5s. 7d.; tin plates, 6s. 1d.; fine iron wire, 3s. 3½d.; tools for mechanics or agriculturists, 3s. 9d.; knives of ordinary kinds, 20s. 4d.; and with fine handles, 40s. 8d. per cwt. Steam-engine boilers and machinery of all sorts also pay duties ranging from 1s. 7½d. to 4s. 10½d. per cwt., agricultural machines being admitted at the lowest scale. All this indicates an extremely short-sighted policy, because it is hampering the progress of the community, without doing any class in it even a temporary benefit, or bringing the Government much profit. And these are by no means all. Italy taxes the import of food grains, of meats, of sugar (which pays from 8s. 5d. to 11s. 9d. per cwt., according to fineness), and chemicals (such as the alkalis so valuable in agriculture), and yet with it all the gross income from the customs barely reaches 4,000,000l. a year.

[1] See tables in Mr. Herries's *Report*, pp. 597–599.

apparently further beset by vexatious provisions and excess charges which aggravate importers and cumber business, without yielding any adequate return. We may hope then that, when the time comes for a fresh revision of the general and special customs tariffs of the kingdom—as come it speedily must—a step forward will be taken, and that England will be admitted within the inner circle, if Italy cannot find it in her heart to open her gates to all alike. But at present it must be candidly admitted that the signs are the other way. From year to year Italy has been going to revise her general tariff, but hitherto the revision has been postponed. A fragmentary tariff between Italy and France was, however, signed in the middle of July last, and it indicates rather an increase of fiscal obstructiveness than the reverse. Sundry duties on articles specially affecting the two countries, such as wine and silk, have been rearranged mostly for the worse, and Italy has distinguished herself in particular by large additions to her list of export duties. Altogether this treaty augurs ill for free trade, and ill for the reciprocal business of Italy and France, which has lately been flourishing apace. We may rest patiently therefore under the present burdens imposed on our trade, lest a worse evil befall us. A few years' further experience of the mischiefs in the present system may lead to change in the direction of freedom, which Italy is clearly unprepared for now.

 Yet it would be decidedly the interest of Italy to

revise her tariff in a free-trade sense, were it for no other reason than that her wealth is neither mineral nor industrial in the English sense of the terms, but agricultural. How decidedly Italy is a pastoral country is seen best by her actual foreign trade; the staple exports of Italy, beyond her silk and her small amount of silk manufactures, being oil and wine, fruits and seeds, cereals and hides, timber, animals, hemp and flax, some sorts of provisions, and a little wool. She is inevitably, in spite of the development of her local industries and manufactures, much dependent on foreign supply for many necessary articles of clothing, for much of her machinery used in mills, on farms, on railways, and in steamboats. Italy is, in consequence, and in spite of herself, therefore, a customer of growing importance, either to Great Britain or to industrial countries such as France or Germany, and she ought to recognise the fact so as to make the benefits as much as possible mutual. For example, she took from us alone, in 1875, about 2,600,000*l*. worth of cotton yarn and piece goods, besides what may have reached her indirectly, and a considerable amount of iron and iron manufactures, as well as woollen goods and coal. The character of her trade with us is very decidedly fixed by the tariff, however; and we discover here, as in the case of France, a tendency to take from us raw or half-manufactured articles in increasing quantities rather than the finished goods. It is not satisfactory, for instance, from our point of view, to find that the value of the cotton yarn entered for Italy was in 1875 almost as large as the value of the cotton cloths. It shows us that, however unfitted Italy may be by nature and circumstances to become a great manufacturing country, she can at least secure the temporary advantage of being in a considerable measure her own provider. Still less satisfactory is it to find that for some years France has been gaining steadily where we have been losing, and that although our general trade with Italy gives few signs of weakness, but rather the reverse, our cotton manufacturers are being decidedly elbowed out of her market. The following tables given by Mr. Malet in his report to the Foreign Office on the trade of Italy for 1875 will show the position most clearly:

Table showing the Value of Imports from England and France to Italy of Tissues of Hemp or Flax of less than nine Threads of Warp in the Space of five Millimètres, whether Raw or Bleached, during the five Years ending December 31, 1875.

	1871	1872	1873	1874	1875
	Fr.	Fr.	Fr.	Fr.	Fr.
England	1,473,000	1,287,000	1,035,000	978,000	1,145,000
France	798,000	717,000	1,031,000	674,000	1,338,000

Table showing the Value of Imports from England and France to Italy of Cotton Tissues, also mixed with Thread and Wool, Coloured, Dyed, or Printed, during the five Years ending December 31, 1875.

	1871	1872	1873	1874	1875
	Fr.	Fr.	Fr.	Fr.	Fr.
England— Cotton or dyed	6,732,000	6,458,000	6,339,000	4,267,000	5,529,000
Printed	17,778,000	14,020,000	14,475,000	10,633,000	12,696,000
	24,510,000	22,478,000	22,814,000	14,900,000	18,225,000
France— Cotton or dyed	2,620,000	3,727,000	4,497,000	5,566,000	6,649,000
Printed	5,311,000	6,326,000	7,748,000	7,166,000	8,472,000
	7,931,000	10,053,000	12,245,000	12,732,000	15,123,000

Table showing the Value of Imports from England and France into Italy of Tissues of Wool or Hair, also mixed with Cotton or Thread, during the five Years ending December 31, 1875.

	1871	1872	1873	1874	1875
England—	Fr.	Fr.	Fr.	Fr.	Fr.
Paying *ad valorem* duties	16,542,000	15,734,000	12,485,000	9,521,000	10,873,000
Paying by weight	3,170,000	3,103,000	3,533,000	3,204,000	2,074,000
	19,712,000	18,837,000	16,018,000	12,725,000	12,947,000
France—					
Paying *ad valorem* duties	7,231,000	9,225,000	10,500,000	11,015,000	14,471,000
Paying by weight	4,918,000	6,653,000	6,926,000	7,812,000	6,831,000
	12,149,000	15,878,000	17,462,000	18,827,000	21,302,000

Embassy and Legation Reports, Part II., 1877, p. 137.

These figures are of a sufficiently startling kind, and would seem to make good the contention of Mr. Malet, that French manufacturers have now the advantage of us. There is no reason to be alarmed at that fact even supposing it true, and least of all as regards Italy, which is France's next-door neighbour; but I am disposed to think that the importance of this growth of the French trade in tissues might be easily exaggerated, and that were trade to be made free we should regain a considerable part of the ground we have lost. At present both tariff and freight are against us, and the freight probably turns the scale as compared with France more than anything else. And these figures at least tend to confirm the statement that Italy is dependent on foreign supply in most important branches of manufacture. Her tariff may give a certain forced prosperity to some of her endeavours to become a rival of England and France, but she has no other advantage than her tariff gives, for living is not much cheaper for the working classes in Italy than here, and, as a rule, they are less capable, more ignorant, and more disposed to 'scamp' work than our own, so that, with wages nominally on a lower scale, the real cost of production in Italy is probably higher than here. I have not, indeed, attempted to discuss in any adequate way the 'labour element' or the 'wages element' in dealing with the competing capacities of other countries in contrast with our own, because, in my judgment, they are of comparatively secondary importance to the primary forces of reserves of capital, of habit, and above all of geographical and physical adaptabilities. Against the enormous advantage which England still possesses over almost all other countries in most respects, were she free of the markets of the world as the world is free to hers, the labour and wages elements have, in my opinion, little force. It is not labour itself so much as the facilities for applying labour in all departments of manufacture in the most economic manner possible which determines the battle, and in these facilities no country in the world can hope for some time to rival us. So far, therefore, as the policy of Italy tends to fight against this superiority, I hold it to be mistaken; but it is a policy which we cannot immediately hope to see departed from there or elsewhere; and we cannot therefore expect that the present reaction, partly the result of over-speculation, partly artificial, will soon end even in increased demand from Italy for our woven fabrics, although in regard to our general trade with that country we have good reason to be hopeful.

Left unforced, the course which Italy might pursue with most advantage to herself and to the world, as a commercial nation, is very clearly marked out by her poverty, her physical peculiarities, and her geographical situation. To the first we shall refer again presently. As to the second, we need only say that the highly favoured climate and rich soil of Italy render her admirably adapted for the production of wine, oil, sugar, maize, and choice fruits, for which she would find, and does find, a ready market, not in Europe only, but also in the East, and in America, North and South. Already a considerable trade is established with the United States, for instance, and the large flow of Italian emigration to that region, as to Brazil and the River Plate, tends to extend this kind of commerce. But for the backward character of Italian agriculture, which, except in Piedmont and perhaps part of Lombardy, is hardly worthy the name of tillage at all, Italy might to-day be much more prominent as a rival of France in the supply of luxurious nations with dainties, and of physically ill-conditioned countries with cheap food. With Italy, as with France, it is the fruits of the earth which must form the solid basis of all her trade. To much of the rest of the world these fruits are, or might become, delicacies of the most precious kind; and, therefore, whatever Italy does to develop agriculture, is better than the establishment of a dozen unhealthy factories In some measure the Italian Government may be said to see this, inasmuch as they devote a considerable amount of attention to agricultural education, establish depôts of agricultural implements in various districts for the purpose of educating the people, and so forth; but that is only toying with the great reforms needed, which must include a wide remodelling of the fiscal burdens, a new cadastral survey, followed by a revised land tax, and the protection of the tillers of the soil alike from the extortions of their do-nothing landlords and the robberies of the brigand. Recent letters from Italy have shown the Italians to be morbidly sensitive to this last subject; and the curious vanity which they have displayed about their rights and liberties is not pleasant. For certainly this brigand question is more vital to the true settlement and prosperity of Southern Italy than almost any other. Until the nefarious robbers are extirpated, and the so-called upper classes of the towns—the remnant of a debased and corrupt nobility —prevented from aiding and abetting them in their depredations, Italy cannot advance as an agricultural nation. Her peasantry, unable to cultivate the vine, the olive, and the citron in peace, must remain, over almost half the land, degraded, stupid, and wasteful.

Instead of strutting about, talking of national dignity, therefore, Italian statesmen would do well quietly to set about the task of making each man's life and property secure through the length and breadth of the land. Unless they do so, their work may one day be partially undone, and the country, ill-taxed and overtaxed, poor and vexed by thieves and priests, may see itself outstripped on every hand. In vine-growing now it cannot for a moment compete with France or Spain, hardly with Greece; indeed, but for the dishonest trade with France in bad wines, used for adulteration, the export wine trade of the mainland would be of hardly any value at all, and no Italian wine is known widely in England except the Sicilian Marsala. If she does not take care her silk trade will be in like danger from the competition of our Australian Colonies, as well as from that of China and Japan. Italy has done much; but what she has done only brings into most startling relief all that she has to do. And, latterly, not the tariff only, but several acts of internal administration, show signs of retrogression rather than progress, which the best friends of Italy must lament over. Her apathetic deputies are far too disposed to shirk their duties, and would do better to display the fire and hotheadedness of the French Assembly than the selfish absenteeism now so common, which makes the Sardinian again begin to think that he has nothing to do with the affairs of Lombardy; the Lombard indifferent to what interests Venice; and all the North together agree in looking with something like cold dislike on the troubles of Sicily and the South. Ministers, aided by such a Parliament, are hardly to be blamed if they sometimes go backwards in their attempt to keep the State solvent, and not the least unsatisfactory feature is the little help they get from the King, who, but for his family, might ere now have ruined all the fair prospect.

Reverting to the position of Italy as pre-eminently an agricultural country, I may enumerate a few of the clogs which prevent her progress in this direction. The re-establishment of the grist tax was, for example, a distinctly retrograde movement. It costs the nation, directly or indirectly, perhaps five times as much as it yields. The mere irritation to which the millers who grind the corn and those who own it are alike subject must be very dispiriting, and check agricultural progress. Again, Italy copies French fashions a good deal in the manner of her taxation: and we find all the array of succession duties, mortmain dues, stamps, taxes on locomotion, licences, and such like, in full sway. Some of them are wise and fair enough, and might bear increasing, were their incidence fairly distributed; but many of them are obstructive and injurious to the prosperous growth of the national wealth. Italy also has her tobacco monopoly, on the security of which she raised a loan for 9,500,000*l.* in 1868, and who shall say that it is not hurtful to her true interests? But of wider scope for evil, almost unproductive as they are, we must characterise the export duties now levied on many articles of vital importance to Italy. These duties have, like those on imports, been increased in recent years under the plea of necessity, and now act as a serious barrier on free export. A low customs duty on exports may do more harm than a higher one on imports, because it cripples the nation in competition directly, and, as it were, at the sources of its life ; and no country is so exclusively possessed of advantages in the production of any particular article as to be safe under such hindrances. The liberal Sardinian customs law of 1854 was much inveighed against at the time it came into force,[1] and when its benefits were spread partially over the rest of the kingdom of Italy the manufacturing classes looked as usual for ruin. Of course no such ruin took place. On the contrary, Sardinia prospered then, and Italy has prospered always in proportion to the liberality of her commercial policy, and if many branches of her agricultural industry stagnate now, it is because, apart from general causes affecting all trade, she has gone backwards in her fiscal laws. Her small manufactures have ever been benefited by the lowering of her tariff. After the passing of the liberal import tariff, the import of raw cotton rose from an average of about 6,500,000 lbs. to over

[1] Mr. Herries's *Report*, p. 589, *et seq.*

17,000,000 lbs., and in other respects home industries such as these were benefited. What has thus, as always, proved true in the case of imports holds good with still greater force in regard to exports, because a tax on production is of all taxes the most wasteful. Make bread dear and you make life hard; and in like manner put a barrier between the tiller of the soil and a free market in any raw produce, and you strike at the root of the entire national prosperity. This is unfortunately what Italy has in no small measure done by her grain taxes, her grist tax, and her vexatious, barren export duties, to which she has in her special treaty with France lately made large additions. Let her take a lesson from the policy of her greatest statesman and repeal these, and she will have done more to stimulate agriculture than all her schools and exhibitions ever can do. On the whole, agriculture may be pronounced now more burdened than manufactures since the recent tinkering at the general tariff has, in various ways, increased the pressure on this, the all-important source of her prosperity. I give below Mr. Herries's figures, comparing the present export duties charged on a few of the principal articles with those in force in 1863 and 1864, which was the period when the tariff was lowest.[1]

[1] ITALIAN EXPORT DUTIES.

	On August 1, 1863 Lira Cents	At present Lira Cents
Lime, per hectolitre	free	1 10
,, ,, bottle	,,	0 06
Olive oil per 100 kilog.	0 33	1 10

ITALY. 33

Hard necessity may be pleaded for this backward movement as for that in the import duties; but no such plea can be admitted for a moment, inasmuch as taxation of this kind tends to keep agriculture—and all that depends on it—primitive and unproductive. Therefore this policy does also, and necessarily, lessen the tax-paying power of the community, and the coherence of the young State. The whole fiscal system of Italy thus requires to be remodelled, special favouritism in tariffs done away with, and the duties which cannot be dispensed with levied with as little irksomeness as possible on the articles that can bear a tax with the least injury to the country. Till this is done the trade of Italy will not grow as it ought to do now in the directions which nature has marked out for it, and I will even say that the consolidation of the races which inhabit the

ITALIAN EXPORT DUTIES—*continued.*

		On August 1, 1863 Lira Cents	At present Lira Cents
Volatile oil	per 100 kilog.	free	2 20
Lemon juice	,, ,,	free	{ 0 17 { 1 10
Extract of aloes	,, ,,	,,	3 30
Oranges and lemons	,, ,,	,,	0 28
Meat, fresh or salted	,, ,,	,,	2 20
Cheese	,, ,,	,,	4 40
Bulls and oxen	per head	,,	5 50
Hides and skins	per 100 kilog.	,,	2 20
Wool	,, ,,	,,	6 60
Silk, raw	,, ,,	,,	38 50
,, waste	,, ,,	,,	8 50
Unspecified dried fruits	,, ,,	,,	1 10
Almonds	,, ,,	,,	{ 1 65 { 1 30

Report, p. 599.

VOL. II.   D

peninsula cannot be held assured, while their free development is in this manner forbidden.

We may, then, I think, put aside all fear both that Italy will become a rival to England in any of her important branches of manufacture, and that, once unfettered, she will cease to be a progressive customer. The character of the trade between the two countries may vary in some measure, and the competition of other countries may grow, in certain directions, more effective, but I do not think that these will cause our Italian trade to grow less in bulk or value, and a liberal, well-organised and classified tariff in Italy would, I am sure, make it year by year greater, to the benefit of both countries.

But there is another direction in which I think Italy may not only rival us, but become in a great degree, and within well-defined limits, a monopolist, if she goes on as she has done these last dozen years. Her geographical situation peculiarly fits her to become again the distributing and carrying maritime nation for Central Europe and the Levant. I do not dream of a revived Venice. Venice may indeed flourish again in a modest way, but not as a great port and mart for the civilised world. I mean, rather, that the sea-borne trade of Italy and of the neighbours of Italy along the Greek archipelago, in Egypt and Syria, and possibly even in the Black Sea and the Danube, seems likely to be carried on more and more in Italian ships, and that her merchant marine may in time come to be no mean rival of that of England in those regions of the South and East. The progress of Italian shipping since the establishment of the kingdom is evidence that in this direction she has already taken considerable strides. Italian vessels not only nearly monopolise the coasting trade of the Adriatic and Mediterranean ports near her borders, but the Rubattino line of ocean steamers, sailing from Genoa and other ports, compete successfully with the Austrian Lloyd's and the French Messagerie Maritime lines in the Eastern seas, while two other important lines, the Florio and the Pierano, are fast sweeping into Italian hands the heaviest share of the trade of the Mediterranean and the Levant. Moreover, the fact that our own mail company, the once unrivalled Peninsular and Oriental, is compelled to make a depôt at Brindisi, is itself a sign of change in the position of the Eastern trade. As yet, this depôt may be said to exist only for the convenience of overland passengers and fast mails, but goods will be sure to follow in time this overland route to some extent, and a certain portion of the carrying trade of England become diverted to Italy. The Suez Canal has hitherto been almost an English waterway, and will, no doubt, long continue to be used in a predominating degree by English ships; but it obviously makes competition by a country situated as

Italy is much easier than it was before, and that competition is being even now felt, fostered as it is by the postal subsidies which the Italian Government, in imitation of our own, gives to the Rubattino Company. Looking at the map, we see that the harbours of Italy are, as it were, placed directly in the way of ships coming westward through the Canal, and the Asiatic trade which the discovery of the Cape passage threw into the hands of the Dutch, the Portuguese, and the English, to the ruin of Venice and Genoa, may not unlikely tend now to revert in some measure to its old channels. Steam, no doubt, neutralises the altered circumstances somewhat, but not altogether. Once let Central Europe get consolidated into peaceful communities, Turkey become pacified or obliterated as a separate State, to be replaced by, at worst, less devastating governing agencies, and we may expect the trade of Italy as a common carrier on the seas to be greatly extended in that quarter. The cotton mills which she possesses, or that may exist in Austria, Hungary, and Bavaria, are likely to draw their supplies of Indian cotton direct from the ports of shipment, or by Italian ships, almost direct, instead, as heretofore, through England. Marts for the raw produce of India and China are thus not unlikely to spring up in Genoa and Leghorn, if not in Venice and Naples, just as a wool mart is now rising into importance at Antwerp; and London will then no longer occupy the exclusive position which the wars and follies of her neighbours have maintained her in for so long.

Nor need Italy halt with the Eastern trade. Her connections with the Brazils and South America, as well as with the United States and the islands in the Spanish Main, are extending, though comparatively insignificant now, and, unless emigration from her shores ceases, are likely to extend, for a large Italian population is now scattered over the fairest regions of South America.

Therefore, although I do not think that, as manufacturers, we have much cause to look on Italy with any dread, as a competitor for a portion of the European carrying trade which has been so long in our hands, in all its most valuable departments, I think we have good reason to have misgivings. Italy is, in my opinion, destined to make a more marked impression on our monopoly in her own immediate neighbourhood than almost any other European nation, and may yet become a far-reaching rival. Even at present Italy stands forward amongst the nations of the world as a great ship-owning nation. The only European country that is ahead of her besides ourselves is Norway, which has always been prominent with its seafaring population, who have much of the carrying trade of Germany, Russia, and Denmark in their hands. Year by year, until the last two years, when depressed trade has produced some slackening, the tonnage of foreign vessels entering our ports has been on the increase, and of this increase Italy bears its full share.

We must accept Italian competition on the sea as a factor of growing importance therefore, and, instead of being jealous of it, seek to utilise it where it can serve our ends, just as we allow other countries to use our shipping for theirs. There must be free trade in ship freights as in everything else, and in the meantime we need have no fear that Italy will, for a long time to come, drive us from the markets for our manufactures, if she ever does it. While her budgets show an annual deficit, while her paper currency is always at a discount which seldom sinks much below 10 per cent., while her population remains pastoral, and while her internal administration is but half organised and her taxation oppressive, she cannot run far in the race with us, or with any manufacturing country; and for ourselves, free trade is, after all, our great stronghold. When we recognise how far behind us in this respect all other nations yet are, we may be easy in our minds, provided always, of course, we continue to work as heretofore. Free trade will do nothing for a nation of sloths. At present I see no signs anywhere that other countries are in the least likely to be more diligent than we are. Italy, at all events, gives no such indication, and against her competition we can not only pit superior and freer industry, but a higher order of agriculture, a system of internal taxation on the whole less oppressive, and natural and acquired advantages such as it takes generations to bring into play. For the rest, if on the high seas her ships should threaten to rival our own, we can only hope that the trade of the world will become large enough to afford them plenty to do without lessening the employment of ours.

CHAPTER X.

SPAIN, PORTUGAL, AND THE NETHERLANDS.

THE three countries with which I now propose to deal have one characteristic in common. They all possess colonies which are more or less wealthy and important. At one period in their history, too, they have each taken the lead amongst the maritime nations of the old world. Spain in particular stands forth as the country which has made more extended geographical discoveries, and at one time ruled over a more extended territorial empire, than any other nation which the world has ever seen. In the high days of Spanish glory her sovereigns were dominant not merely in Europe, but over all the discovered portions of the New World. They governed almost a continent and a half in the two Americas, and appeared to grow, year by year, in power and dominion, till their might was broken by the slow attrition of stubborn Dutch resistance, and the defeat of the Armada. Since then Spain may be said to have settled down gradually like a vessel which has sprung a leak, until she now lies a wreck at the mercy of every movement of the waters.

Less in might, but in its day of a towering ambition, and no mean dominion, ranks the little kingdom of Portugal, which, stimulated by the precept and example of 'Prince Henry the Navigator,' crept southwards along the then unknown coast of Africa; westwards to the Brazils; and gradually eastwards through the Indian seas, until at one time during the end of the sixteenth and early part of the seventeenth century its prospects of possessing Hindostan were far greater than our own. Less in its greatness, its decrepitude is also less than that of Spain. The little kingdom is, indeed, now busy with efforts at self-improvement, with schemes of colonisation in Mozambique and elsewhere, and may be said to thrive in a modest sort of way in its old age.

Last comes the Netherlands, a country full of the memory of brave conflicts and long-suffering persistence, out of which it emerged to be the main inheritor of the commerce of its ancient oppressor. The ports of Holland were for long the busiest and most enterprising little corners of Europe, and its naval power dominated that of England at the time Dutch William came to the English throne. But the might of the Netherlands has also sunk out of sight, and since the devastating energy of Buonaparte swept it into his mad Continental system, causing England to destroy its fleet, Holland has ceased to be a recognised Power in Europe. There is still a busy, prosperous population in the country, and still a considerable trade, but politically Holland is almost completely effaced, and when the new German Empire again troubles Europe with its ambitions, may possibly sink into one of its provinces.

In thus referring to familiar facts, I have no desire to do more than recall the history of these countries. My object is to impress on the reader this dominating idea—that there can be no question of competition with England stirred by the present state of any of these countries. They have had their day, and they have either lost the best opportunities it gave them or have abused them; and there is, I believe, no hope or chance of a return of dominion for them. Spain will not again rule in America; no fleet of hers will alone, at least, ever again terrify the people of England. Portugal is no rival to us in the East, or appreciably in Africa, and the carrying trade of Western Europe shows no signs of passing back again into the hands of the Dutch. There is, consequently, no use in treating these countries from the point of view of possible rivals in any branch of trade. They can only be galvanised into an attitude of rivalry by a foreign motive force such as annexation, and so far, at all events, as Spain and Portugal are concerned, can compete only by the help of an influx of English and French capital. But because we cannot treat any one of them in this light, it does not follow that a study of the commercial progress and capacities of these countries is of little interest to us. We are, or ought to be, as anxious to find out customers as rivals; and in the position of customers, or as aids to custom elsewhere, each of these countries possesses a peculiar interest. They are all interesting also in another way, although I cannot travel far into that branch of the subject. Their fallen greatness, their colonisations, their mercantile policies, are full of most important lessons for us, and by drawing out to view some of the causes of the failure which has followed the attempts of each of these Powers to build up a great empire, we might be able to form some idea of what the chances are that the Empire of England will not soon be wrecked and fall to pieces like that of Spain or the Netherlands.

Confining, however, the attention chiefly to the capacity of these countries to be our customers, I will first of all deal with Spain. And I may as well say at once that I do not know of any general statistics regarding Spain and Spanish trade that are of the least value. Spain is a land where Chaos has held rule for many generations, and one has to grope along in darkness and confusion towards any conclusion one wishes to reach. What figures there are only help, as a rule, to mislead, and it is therefore as well, perhaps, that they are few. Take Spanish budgets as an example. No more imaginative creations exist. The Spanish Finance Minister fully equals the Turk or the Egyptian in framing an illusory national balance-sheet, and one recent minister boldly justified the subterfuge. But, quite apart from habit and disposition, the truth is really almost beyond the reach of a minister. Señor Salaverria is considered an upright man, and his budget for 1876 was to all appearance moderately framed, and with a more honest purpose than most of those which had gone before. Yet it has turned out just as false as its predecessors. Instead of a surplus, or merely a small deficit, there was an empty Treasury, and in order to meet the much curtailed interest on the debt, borrowing, more or less secret, had once more to be resorted to. This result has been reached, too, in spite of an increase in the revenue of about 3,700,000*l.*, due mostly to increased receipts from import duties, from the tobacco monopoly, and from direct taxation; but this increase is only an inadequate set-off to Spanish extravagance, and under the new fiscal laws it may be partially lost. Spain had last financial year a revenue of only 28,700,000*l.* all told; and to meet all her engagements, to carry on her foolish Cuban war, and re-establish her credit, would have needed something like 45,000,000*l.* Such a sum there is not the least hope of her getting under the present *régime*, and her ministers have therefore wisely determined to cut down to the lowest possible limits the amount claimable by the creditors of the State —the creditors, that is, who hold her funded debt. Those who lend to the Treasury for short periods fare better. Señor Salaverria last year made strenuous efforts to arrange the huge debt of his country, and seemed to succeed, so carefully limited were the obligations which the State undertook. The arrangement was not just, nor what a country penetrated with any sense of common honesty would care to propose; but it was tolerable in that it left the Government with not the shadow of an excuse for further defaults. The debt charges were pared down so as to be well within the apparent means of the country, taken at their soberest estimate. Yet what do we find? No sooner is the arrangement carried than the old curse starts up again. Not only has Spain to borrow in order to pay 1 per cent. on her debt, but in order to carry on her insane war with Cuba, and to support the crowds of *fainéants* produced by successive revolutions she raises special loans on Cuban securities to preposterous amounts and drains at the same time her home resources. These needs, in short, added to the peculation and dishonesty of all kinds haunting every branch of the public service, threw the Government back into the hands of Jew money-lenders of Paris and Madrid, before a month of the reformed era had expired.[1] The progress of Spain is treadmill

[1] There is nothing more difficult to determine than the amount of the Spanish debt. All sorts of estimates have floated about regarding it, most of them inaccurate. Some attempt was made, however, to get the real truth out at the time when arrangements for the payment in paper of the coupons overdue were being discussed; and a statement appeared in the *Times* of March 21, 1876, based upon official figures, which is probably as nearly accurate as can be got at. According to this the total debt of Spain was just over 700,000,000*l.*, of which nearly 300,000,000*l.* had been incurred since 1868. This estimate is in one sense misleading,

progress. Instead of a surplus she will this year again show the usual deficit; her creditors on bonds will get nothing but paper and promises or borrowed money, and only the usurers of the capital will grow fat on the spoils of the land. The budgets of Spain are therefore false on all grounds, and not the least false when their framers are passing honest. The corruptions, pride in thieving, and general political and social debility which thus permeate the Government, necessarily affect every department of the social fabric. The trade of Spain is therefore also cumbered by the impossibility of conducting it with fair honesty. The onerous customs duties are evaded on all hands, taxes are left unpaid, and the spectacle stands out before Europe of a population comparatively well-to-do con-

however, inasmuch as it represents merely the nominal amount at which the debt would stand did it all or nearly all figure as 3 per cents. As a matter of fact, a portion of this total is arrived at by taking the 3 per cent. bonds issued as security to lenders for money advances at 17 per cent. of their nominal value. And since the date of this return the new debt caused by the payment of the overdue coupons in 2 per cent. bonds has been issued, bringing the nominal total of the debt up to nearly 800,000,000*l*. In point of fact, however, the money assigned in the budget for the sum of the debt is about 7,000,000*l*., while at its nominal value in 3 per cents. the debt would require for its sum about 22,000,000*l*., more than the entire revenue of the country in recent years. Judging the funded debt by its assumed burden, therefore, it only stands for some 300,000,000*l*. at the outside. From all this it will be seen that any idea of the cash actually borrowed by Spain is quite beyond reach, especially as there have been borrowings and borrowings, as well as compoundings and compoundings, till Spain must have wiped out her indebtedness by a simple nonpayment several times over. The debt of Spain is as old as the days of Ferdinand and Isabella, and were the history of it to be written it would form the most marvellous record of usury, theft, and credulity which the world ever saw.

spiring, as it were, to keep its Government impotent, to cause impecuniousness, and thereby to subject itself to periodic deluges of anarchy and partial spoliation. The ordinary Spaniard would seem to glory in the national bankruptcy.

The more one studies the Spain of to-day, in fact, the more profoundly is it borne home to one's mind that we English did that nation an everlasting wrong in delivering it from the grasp of the French at the time of the Revolutionary wars. Had there been true stuff in the fibre of the people, a period of subjection to that arrogant race would have brought it out. The impracticable, dishonest, and utterly incapable creatures who held the controlling power in Spain then, and who gave us lessons in number sufficient to convince the most stupid that we did no good, and were not wanted, would have been swept away perhaps to make room in time for better men. But we propped them in their place, and, like patient oxen, bore with their crimes, their buffets, and insults, as if they had been the dispensation of Heaven. The world saw the spectacle of a military hero, with a foreign army at his back, delivering a reluctant nation from an oppressor whom many in it welcomed as a deliverer from the anarchists and effete tyrants at home. The Peninsular campaigns of Wellington have thus proved almost a pure curse to the people of the Spanish Peninsula. What true life is in them has never yet got its opportunity. Without statesmen, without patriotic zeal or cohesive force of any kind, buried in a corrupt officialism, Spain hurtles on her way to what goal I dare hardly venture to think. Held in the steel grip of France for a generation or two, she might to-day have emerged as Italy is emerging, and with even a grander prospect of future growth than Italy. I confess I see small prospect of that resurrection to-day. The short gleam of hope which followed the advent of Castelar has vanished, and Spain has entered anew on a career of miserable anarchy, which the tinsel of a restored monarchy hides only for a little while. The day has long gone by when any offshoot of Bourbonism can purify a people from its administrative and other corruptions. The only result of the restoration of Alphonso has hitherto been reaction and the deepening of the shadows which hang over Spain. Old ideas are clung to; wealth and precious lives are lavished to retain Cuba; priests come back like crows to settle on the doomed land; and liberties are narrowed or altogether proscribed. There is a nobler Spain, it is true, than what we thus see, but it is feeble, scattered, and helpless against the hideous official and hereditary corruption which we English, as it were, picked up out of the ditch whither the French had thrown it, and with measureless expenditure of blood and money, toil and endurance of sufferings, set again on the necks of the people. There is at the present day no more melancholy spectacle for Englishmen on the earth than Spain, when we contrast what she is with what she has been, and when we add to the contrast the thought that our hands have, beyond all others, destroyed, perhaps for ever, her chance of self-deliverance.

But I must leave this tempting subject to speak of her trade, which, like her wealth, is considerable, and, like her Government, ill regulated. Spain has a magnificent sea-board, and, next to ourselves, possesses what ought to be the most valuable aid to foreign trade in the shape of her colonies, and of the countries founded on what were her colonies in America and the Eastern seas. Her trade with these dependencies and offshoots is, of course, very small compared to our own, but it is an important element in her wealth, and, with a more enlightened Government, might raise Spain once again into the position of a second-class Power at no very distant date. I do not look for this resurrection any more than I look for any of the South American Republics to rise into the position of a respectable State while dominated by people of Spanish blood. I only note what might be in other circumstances, while the actual facts compel me to say that there seems every probability that Spain will in the near future lose at least a portion of such trade as she now has. Her recently promulgated tariff will, unless modified, have, at all events, the effect of seriously lessening Spanish trade with England and France.

This has been hitherto no small part of her total trade if we may judge by the figures published in our own or in French official documents, which are indeed the only reliable guides in the matter. The total of our own trade with Spain is about equal to that with Italy. The two sides of the account are, however, significantly reversed. Italy buys from us much more than she sells to us, but Spain is comparatively a very poor buyer. In her revolutionary years, following the expulsion of Queen Isabella, her purchases from us fell in value below 3,000,000$l.$ a year—about a fourth of the imports of Belgium. At present Spain buys of us between 4,000,000$l.$ and 5,000,000$l.$ per annum, or, at all events, goods to that value are sent from here to her ports; but even this is little more than a million in excess of the imports of her little neighbour Portugal, and will now most probably be again diminished. On the other side of the account we find that our purchases from Spain have been as high as 11,000,000$l.$ (in 1873), and that they average from 8,000,000$l.$ to 8,500,000$l.$ We buy from her, in other words, nearly double what we sell to her, and may soon do much more unless Spanish folly closes her markets against us by the operation of the new tariff. This is not a large trade, although much larger than that between Spain and France, and on the whole, perhaps more healthy, as it indicates a stronger hold upon Spanish products by English capitalists than the French trade does. It is not 9,000,000$l.$

altogether, and the imports of France are larger than the exports. Still our trade with Spain is small and far from satisfactory, considering the positions of the two countries, and their mutually helpful capacities. This smallness is by no means to be taken as implying that Spain is poor; only that its wealth is ill regulated or mismanaged; and the fact that we import so much more from Spain than we export thither is not, on the other hand, to be taken as implying that we have helped to make Spain rich.

For this divergence of the account apparently so much in Spain's favour the causes are various, but chief among them is the amount of English private capital invested in Spain in wine-culture and mines. The iron region of Bilbao, of which Defoe speaks in his 'Captain Carleton,' has long attracted the attention of the English, and was the seat of a prosperous English mining company before the outbreak of the last Carlist war, and there are several important copper and sulphur mines also in English hands. The wine cultivation in the south, again, has long been stimulated, and in a good degree sustained, by English money and English-governed labour, which has also, although to a small extent as yet, been put into several of the other industries of Spain, the quicksilver loan being, for example, another cause of a flow of Spanish products to this country in a small way. Natural causes would, however, and independently of these mortgages, tend to draw towards England a still larger portion of Spanish raw produce, were the country well opened up and in anything like decent order. The mineral wealth of Spain is enormous. It has been nibbled at and scratched, as it were, for at least two thousand years, and is practically inexhaustible still. I am told that the veins of ore possessed by the Tharsis and Rio Tinto Mining Companies are capable of yielding for many years enough sulphur, and almost enough copper, to supply the wants of the whole world; yet these mines had been worked by the Romans; and the latter company, at this very time, extracts a considerable amount of metal from the refuse that these old miners left in heaps on the ground. Coal, iron, lead, copper, zinc, silver, all are found in abundance in Spain.[1] Being thus provided, and having no powerful manufacturing capacity either in population or in organised productive machinery, Spain is thus, as our near neighbour, most admirably adapted to be a storehouse from which we

[1] A return of the production of the mines of Spain, and of the motive power and manual labour employed in mining operations, in 1870, is given by Mr. Consul Wilkinson in his report for 1872, from which we learn that the total quantity raised was as follows:—Iron, 436,586 tons; lead (soft and argentiferous), 352,193 tons; copper, 395,695 tons; zinc, 113,583 tons; and manganese, 16,873 tons. The total numbers of workpeople employed were 33,277 men, 1,508 women, and 6,225 boys. There were also 148 engines of 3,711 horse-power in use. I am disposed to regard this return as very imperfect, however, as, for one thing, no account is apparently taken of the large export of pyrites of sulphur and copper, and the quantity of manganese mined seems to be obviously understated. We can only take these figures, therefore, as a sort of dim indication of the facts.

can draw many raw materials at little cost, and to the great saving of our own more limited and sometimes overstrained resources. I have not the least doubt that, were Spain in the position that Italy even now occupies, we should find this tributary supply of ores and raw produce much greater than it yet has been; and, in any event, it is likely to make rapid progress when the world's business takes a new start, unless Spain, under the guidance of her purblind and reactionary royalists, deliberately locks her doors. The conditions of crude labour are such in Spain that we can probably, for a long time to come, procure her minerals cheaper than the United States can do out of their own mines; and we have thus a reserve of competing power which we should seek to preserve with infinite solicitude and pains while we can. The more we can husband our home resources the stronger we shall continue to be. It is not at all probable that Spain will become a large buyer from us for many a day. The tenacity of the fixed ideas burned into the minds of the race by the fanatic semi-insane kings that followed the Emperor Charles V.—himself power-mad—is still illustrated by the policy of such statesmen as Spain can boast of; her whole fiscal system is framed on the basis of the old notion that it is good to sell, but bad to buy, and that gold and silver are the only real wealth; and the pernicious character of these ideas has been well exemplified in the new tariff which was promulgated in July last. The tariff makes some modifications of a favourable character in certain imports, but does not permit these modifications to benefit England or the United States. The result of this exclusion is that the exports of these countries to Spain are likely to be curtailed by perhaps one-half. So important has the question of the Spanish tariff suddenly become, that I am constrained to turn aside and deal with it at more length than the old blindly obstructive state of things would warrant, and I give in a note the main features of the tariff charges extracted from a summary lately printed in the 'Times.'[1] Here I

[1] The following is extracted from the *Times* of August 21, 1877. I include only the more important articles or those showing the greatest divergence in duties:—

'British trade with Spain in 1876 showed imports from that country amounting in value to 8,763,146*l.* and exports valued at 4,796,498*l.* The general history of the last ten years disclosed a gradual increase of trade. The imports had increased by 50 per cent. and the exports had doubled. An exceptional movement in 1873 made the imports greater than in any other year. This gradual development will now be rudely interrupted by the step, taken with unwonted promptitude, of the Spanish Government in raising the customs tariff. A reduction of duties has been fixed in favour of countries which have commercial treaties with Spain. England, which admits to the benefits of free trade merchandise arriving under any flag, is excluded from fiscal advantages. France and the United States suffer the same exclusion. The favoured nations are Austro-Hungary, Belgium, Germany, Italy, Morocco, the Netherlands, Portugal, Russia, Norway and Sweden, Switzerland, and Turkey. The Budget was passed on July 11. On July 17 the tariff received the approbation of the King. On the 21st the King fixed the date on which it should come into force. It was published in the *Madrid Gazette* on July 22, and came into operation on the first of the present month. Three classes are established by the new regulations. One set of duties (*a*) applies to the nations which have no 'most-favoured nation clause,' the second (*b*) to nations which have treaties, the third (*c*) is for articles specially provided for. The extraordinary charge (*c*) is a mysterious

THE NETHERLANDS. 55

need scarcely observe that on some of the most important manufacturing staples, such as machinery or extra duty, which is cumulatively imposed for the 'protection' of Spanish industries upon the favoured and the unfavoured nations alike. The differential duties run throughout a great part of the tariff, and apply to a vast list of the most heterogeneous articles. Our largest exports to Spain are in textile fabrics and in iron; and it will be observed that considerable differential imposts are levied in these respects. Rectified petroleum, mineral oils, and benzine are charged 5 pesetas 50 centesimos per 100 kilogrammes when they come from nations in class *a*, as from Great Britain, for example. From nations in class *b* they pay at the rate of 5 pesetas. The special or extraordinary charge is 12p. 50c. The peseta is worth 10*d*. Iron in pigs and scraps (*a*) 2·50, (*b*) 2p. 31c., (*c*) 37c. per 100 kilos. Iron, fine manufacture, polished or with porcelain coating, or ornamented by other metals, (*a*) 17·50, (*b*) 13·75, (*c*) 2·20. Iron and steel in bars, (*a*) 8p., (*b*) 7·59c. (*c*) 1p. Iron in plates above 6 millimètres in thickness and rivets or returns, (*a*) 9p., (*b*) 8·10c., (*c*) 1·08; ditto in bars, plates up to 6 millimètres, axles, tires, plates, and springs for carriages and hoops, (*a*) 13p., (*b*) 10·50c., (*c*) 1·40c.; ditto in fine work or polished, with porcelain coating or ornamented with other metals, and steel manufactures not otherwise mentioned, (*a*) 27·50c., (*b*) 25·50c., (*c*) 3·40. Wrought tin (*a*) 62·50c., (*b*) 62·25c., (*c*) 8·30c. Copper in pig and old, (*a*) 12·50, (*b*) 12, (*c*) 4·80 per 100 kilos. Copper and brass in bars and ingots and old brass, (*a*) 22·50c., (*b*) 19p., (*c*) 7·60c. Copper and brass in sheet, nails, and copper wire, (*a*) 50, (*b*) 44·20, (*c*) 10·40. Copper and brass in pipes and in pieces partly wrought, (*a*) 70, (*b*) 52, (*c*) 10·40. Brass wire, (*a*) 30p., (*b*) 26, (*c*) 10·40c. Bronze, unwrought, (*a*) 10p., (*b*) 9·50, (*c*) 1·30. For the above metals wrought, and all alloys of common metals in which copper may form a portion of the hardware, (*a*) 125p., (*b*) 100, (*c*) 16p. For the same, gilt-plated, nickelled, and varnished, (*a* and *b*) 250p., (*c*) 40p. For all other metals and alloys wrought, (*a*) 37p. 50c., (*b*) 16p. 50c., (*c*) 4p. 40c. It has not always been thought worth while to quote small additions in class (*c*). Raw cotton is charged to (*a*), 1p. 50c., (*b*) 1p. 20c., per 100 kilos. All other cottons are charged per kilogramme. Cotton spun, twisted in one or two threads, unbleached, bleached, or dyed, up to No. 35 inclusive, (*a*) 1p. 25c., (*b*) 1p. 5c., (*c*) 12c.; ditto above No. 35, (*a*) 1p. 75c., (*b*) 1p. 35c., (*c*) 18c. Cotton—twisted in three or more threads, bleached, unbleached, or dyed, (*a*) 2p. 50c., (*b*) 2p. 25c., (*c*) 30c. Textile goods are charged by the kilogramme. Cloths, pressed, plain, unbleached, bleached, or dyed, in piece or handkerchiefs, up to 25 threads inclusive (in warp and woof in the square of 6 millimètres), (*a*) 3p., (*b*) 2p. 10c.; ditto, above 26 threads, (*a*) 2p. 70c., (*b*) 2p. 25c.; ditto, printed and textile fabrics, we shall now be called on to pay from 50 to 100 per cent. more than the favoured nations, who, most of them, have little or no competing power at all.

As regards the cause of this singularly hostile movement against England, Spain is said to be prompted by two motives—disgust at our conduct in Gibraltar —which is notoriously a smugglers' nest—and dislike

worked up in the loom to 25 threads, inclusive, in warp and woof, (*a*) 4p., (*b*) 3p. 15c.,; ditto, printed, &c., and containing more than 25 threads, (*a*) 3p. 70c., (*b*) 3p. 15c. Quiltings and pinked goods, (*a*) 4p. 50c., (*b*) 2p. 70c. Cloths for socks, gloves, stockings, and other like purposes, (*a*) 5p. 25c., (*b*) 3p. 50c. Corduroys, velveteens, and other double stuffs, (*a*) 3p. 50c., (*b*) 3p. 30c. per kilogramme, are the only goods in which differential duties are charged in this class. In hemp fibre, rope, &c., the differences are but few and slight, plain woven fibre up to ten threads being charged (*a*) 1p. 25c. per kilo., as against 1p. to class (*b*), and of 25 threads 4p. 25c., against 4p. 20c. In woollens, in the class of unwashed wool, the class (*b*) benefits by 4p. in common unwashed wool for 100 kilos., and by 5p. in the higher wool and that fit for yarn, the latter being (*a*) 12p. 50c., (*b*) 7p. 50c., (*c*) 2p. 50c. Worsted, spun rough or with oil, per kilogramme, (*a*) 1p. 85c., (*b*) 1p. 20c., (*c*) 32c.; ditto clean or washed, (*a*) 2p. 60c., (*b*) 1p. 80c , (*c*) 48c.; the same dyed, (*a*) 3p., (*b*) 2p. 10c., (*c*) 56c. Carpets are charged to (*a*) 175p., (*b*) 125p. per 100 kilos. Felts, 75p. to (*a*), 65p. to (*b*) per kilo. Blankets (including rugs) per kilo., (*a*) 2p. 25c., (*b*) 2p. Cloths, and all kinds of woven goods of wool only or of wool mixed with cotton, (*a*) 8p., (*b*) 5p. Horsehair cloths, (*a*) 2p. 50c., (*b*) 2p. per kilo. Silk is charged per kilogramme, raw or spun, but not twisted, (*a*) 1p. 50c., (*b*) 75c.; twisted, (*a*) 6p. 25c., (*b*) 4p., (*c*) 80c.; spun untwisted floss silk, (*a*) 50c., (*b*) 30c.; ditto, twisted, (*a*) 4p. 50c., (*b*) 2p., (*c*) 50c.; plain or worked silks woven, (*a*) 17p. 50c., (*b*) 15p. Velvets and plush, (*a*) 26p. 25c., (*b*) 22p. 50c. Tulles, laces, and points of silk or floss, (*a*) 22p. 50c., (*b*) 21p. The only differences in paper worthy of notice seem to be in wall papers, printed with gold, silver, wool, or crystal, and charged to class (*a*) 200p., (*b*) 150p., (*c*) 24p. for 100 kilos., and a general impost on papers not enumerated of 40p. against (*a*), 35p. (*b*), and (*c*) 14p. Class (*a*) is charged for each piano a duty of 250p., (*b*) 160.' *Vide* also Sir J. Walsham's interesting report on the new tariff presented to Parliament last session (Parly. Papers, C. 1836).

to our wine duties. The revenge which is sought to be taken has not, it seems to me, any justification in our misdeeds, if these are all the faults which can be urged against us; but I nevertheless think that we ought to remove even these pretexts for such treatment. It ought to be a matter of no difficulty for us to stop smuggling at Gibraltar, especially as the Spaniards find abundant opportunities for defrauding the revenue elsewhere, and if we must retain that rock, by all means let us abate the nuisance. Probably nothing that we can do short of giving up the place will satisfy the proud-stomached Spaniards, but we can, at any rate, do our best.

The wine-duty question is to my mind perhaps the more simple of the two. The present scale of duty, which levies 1s. per gallon on all wines below 26 per cent. of proof spirit per gallon, and 2s. 6d. on all over 26 per cent., is a cause of gross injustice to the strong natural wines of Spain, practically shutting the cheaper among them out of the market: it ought therefore to be altered. What intelligible grounds there were for the imposition of so absurd a scale I never could make out. It affords no protection whatever to the distillers in this country, and is no adequate equivalent for the 10s. duty levied on home-made spirits. To approach fairness the scale should have been much more fine drawn. Nor is it any help to the consumer, who, we are told, always is in some mysterious way sure to be endangered by the importation of vile 'fortified' compounds if the duty is lowered. It is distinctly my opinion, therefore, that this is a real grievance to Spain, and if we can procure admission into the position of the 'B' class of nations by removing it we shall have done our excise no harm and our trade a possible good.

I say possible, for I confess that I do not hope much for trade with Spain while this invidious and capriciously variable tariff continues in any shape to exist. Other nations will not gain much by being 'favoured,' nor shall we perhaps lose a great deal beyond what we otherwise might, should we continue to be excluded. France has had special grace in the matter of import duties from Spain since 1865, yet Spain ranks as a buyer of French goods below Switzerland, Belgium, Italy, and Algeria, and as an exporter to France below even Turkey in the trade account of France for 1875. Although now favoured as against us more than ever in nearly all staple manufactured tissues, by the new arrangement which at once gives advantage to nearly all Europe except ourselves, I am nevertheless disposed to think that French exports to Spain will fare little better than they have done. The truth is, the lowest tariff which Spain now exacts on imported manufactured goods is sufficient to prevent the entry of such goods in any quantity. The Spaniards are as violent protectionists as if they had something to protect. One might suppose Spain to be toiling along a mistaken path with the energy of the United States, and fiercely combative for what her manufacturers say are her interests. Nothing of the kind. Hence, taken in connection with her capacity of consumption or her manufacturing power, the Spanish tariff is simply monstrous. As a result, it will minister, as it has always ministered, more to the gains of the smuggler than to the national revenue, and will continue to prove a fruitful source of the national curse of dishonesty in trade and politics. This dishonesty and smuggling go on everywhere, and the latter is, as I have said, a constant source of annoyance to us at Gibraltar, as the traders who run the gauntlet of Spanish Guarda Costa boats and posts find the Rock a most valuable means of entering Spanish territory; and, had the nation been stronger, we might have been drawn into a war with it on this score long ago. On the French side across the mountains, and all along the coast from Barcelona southwards, the same illicit trade goes on, to the great profit of the individuals who engage in it and the serious loss of the revenue.

It is this smuggling which, more, perhaps, than official chaos and incompetence, makes all general figures relating to Spanish trade quite delusive. Such as they are, they give evidence that the disturbances incident to the irruption of Carlos caused a sharp diminution in Spanish production in everything except wine. In the official figures quoted by Mr. Phipps, in his report for 1874 on the trade of Spain,[1] the total outward and inward trade of that year was stated as only 31,500,000*l.*, which was less by 13,700,000*l.* than that of the previous year. The decrease was entirely on the export side, the imports showing an increase, owing to the bad harvest in the eastern provinces necessitating an import of corn. At the highest of fiscal reckoning the foreign trade of Spain is not much more than half that of Italy ; and, did we suppose the figures published represented the facts, we should say that Spain is miserably poor. As we have said, they do not represent the facts ; but her recent attempts at improving her fiscal legislation will certainly not tend to increase her wealth or to draw to her shores much of that foreign enterprise and capital for which she has, with all her pride, no little necessity.

Undoubtedly the trade of Spain is rudimentary and her resources ill developed ; else she is wealthy enough to be a much larger buyer than she is now. She might also be a large exporter of other things besides wine, fruits, oils, merino wool, and ores, and a large importer of manufactured goods, were she politically alive.[2]

[1] *Legation Reports*, Part III., 1875.

[2] According to Kolb, the weaving industries of Spain gave employment in 1861 to about 100,000 people, of which about half were cotton-spinners and weavers. Since that time there do not appear to have been any reliable statistics published. It seems probable, however, from the decrease in the totals of Spanish trade during the Carlist war, that the prosperity of the nation in this respect has not recently increased. At the beginning of the sixteenth century the same authority tells us that in Seville alone there were 16,000 silk looms, giving employment to 130,000

There are, indeed, few countries in the world more adapted than Spain for the judicious outlay of capital in improving the land as well as opening mines; but we can hardly hope to see the capital forthcoming while the existing superstitious dislike of everything not Spanish holds sway with the purblind and corrupt rulers attached to a court whose existence in Spain is itself a hollow sham and a mockery of the people. Spain needs but capital and honest government, and is likely to get neither: with both, what might she not do in agriculture alone!

The cultivated area of Spain was estimated some years ago at 66,355,000 acres, and the waste land at 56,000,000 acres. Making allowance for the moun-

people, but by the end of the seventeenth century the looms had dwindled to 300, and now French and Italian competition has driven it partially if not entirely out of existence. The trade system of Spain from the first made solid manufacturing prosperity impossible. Consul Pratt, in his report on the trade of Barcelona for 1874 (*Consular Reports*, Part IV., 1875), gives a list of the cotton, silk, and woollen factories in and around that city, where the manufacturing industries of Spain now chiefly centre. According to this, the total number of hands employed was over 16,000, and the value of the annual production of the spindles, looms, and printing presses used in the cotton and mixed cotton and silk industry was more than 700,000*l*. The value of the outturn of the woollen mills was over 400,000*l*. At a moderate computation we may say that the production of these industries altogether represents an annual value of about 1,200,000*l*., which for a country like Spain, and with the foreign relations and dependencies which Spain has, is a remarkably poor result. This is substantially about all that protection has done to develop the country, for the manufactories to be found elsewhere are of no great importance. There are a number of small woollen manufactories at Alcoy, in Alicante, where also the famous cigarette paper is produced to the extent of 600,000 reams a year, and elsewhere throughout Spain, more or less, local manufactories are to be found. But there is no national manufacturing industry.

tainous regions and the stripped arid plains of Estremadura and other portions of Central Spain which are capable of reclamation, this shows a very large margin of ground unoccupied that might be well worth cultivating, and would, no doubt, be cultivated, did Spain give the land into the hands of the peasantry. At present a large amount of the property taken from the Church is waste or in the hands of land speculators. It would form an admirable investment for agriculturists, and might be made to produce a great surplus of food, that could be exported every year, instead of fitfully abundant harvests which never get Spain a steady hold on the grain markets of Europe. But there is little chance of either the men or the money being forthcoming for such development. At all events, England will not lend freely, although there is still a lingering idea amongst holders of Spanish bonds that one day the country will become orderly and solvent. The French have been, perhaps, wiser than the English in the matter of lending money to Spain. They hold many of her national bonds, no doubt, but chiefly in pledge for advances at high usury, which have long ago paid themselves. The finances of the nation are always in the usurer's grasp, and he perpetrates all sorts of impositions on the Treasury because of the fools and rogues that keep it; he lends at 20 per cent., defeats all schemes of reform, and, in one way or another, keeps the country always deep in his debt—always in need of new loans. It is so now. It has been so since Spain attained the position of a Catholic monarchy, and became a fair quarry for the much-kicked but able, unscrupulous, and politic Jews. In fairness to these Jews, and also to the French public, it must, however, be said that they have done something more for the country than help it to drown itself in anarchy and debt. But for French Jews' assistance Spain would never have had half her present railway system, which, in spite of all drawbacks, is doing a great deal for the country in opening the natural wealth of the interior to foreign trade. This has been good work, not unwisely done.[1] But the manner in which capital will now be infused into Spain is rather through undertaking to work mines than by loans for large public works, and even these channels have been temporarily nearly dried up by the events of the last half-dozen years. I do not wish to write despairingly of the future of any country for which hope is discernible, but it would be easy to accumulate evidence tending to prove that Spain may now be where she is for a generation yet for

---

[1] Spain possesses about 4,000 miles of railway in active operation, most of them doing very well, especially those in the south and in Catalonia, where the lines belong exclusively to Spanish capitalists, chiefly Spanish Jews. Other parts of the system have been constructed for the most part with French money, but some, I believe, with English. There are about 2,000 more to construct, and when they are all in working order they will hardly prove too much for the necessities of the nation. In nothing has the foresight and prudence of the financiers who organised the companies and made the railways been more conspicuous than in the manner in which they for the most part have avoided foolish competition.

all that foreign capital will do for her, so much has it been scared away. I shall content myself, however, with saying that I see no evidence that the trade of this country with Spain is destined to any large or rapid expansion. The broken character of the nation, its internal race antipathies and zones of sloth and industry, its feeble Government and bad fiscal laws, combine to make a prospect gloomy enough. Spanish statesmen do nothing but obstruct the nation, and when a storm sweeps one swarm of corrupt officials away another settles in its place. There is no honour, no plain dealing, no truth; only chicane elevated to a science, and superstition glorified into a faith, till contact with Spanish officialism in any form is itself a corrupting thing. In one direction, where we might expect progress from mere force of circumstances, we find next to none. Spain has no great hold on her own carrying trade. English ships bring cargoes of goods to her ports from all parts of the world, and from South America particularly. I am told that her mercantile navy is declining.[1] The late civil war had a pernicious

[1] Almost the only Spanish port which can be said to show signs of advancing prosperity in a marked degree is that of Huelva, which lies on the west coast north of Cadiz. Its prosperity is entirely due to the mining enterprise of Scotch, French, and Anglo-German companies, which have opened up such mines as Tharsis, Rio Tinto, and Calañas. They have also built railways to the port, and the line belonging to the Rio Tinto Company is to be extended to Seville. Huelva is therefore a very busy port, whence copper, copper ore, pyrites, manganese, are sent in great quantities to Great Britain, Germany, and France. There are also large quantities of very good wine made in the neighbourhood, most of

influence upon it, and the long-continued disturbances in Cuba have also driven a good deal of the valuable trade of that island into the hands of the English and other foreign carriers.

The mention of Cuba brings before us a very striking example of the manner in which Spain has flung away her great opportunities. For some nine years now that island has been a scene of miserable civil strife; waste and devastation have gone on, tens of thousands of Spanish soldiers have been sacrificed— all for what? Just merely that the Spaniards of the military and official classes might retain a rich plundering ground against all native Cuban interests. There is of course the usual element of Spanish vanity and childish pride helping to maintain her endeavours to recover the island; but beneath these lies the hard, matter-of-fact inducement of vulgar rapacity which uses the sentimental reasons as a cloak for its base designs.

which has hitherto passed through the hands of the monopolists at Xeres, to be shipped there or at Cadiz and Port St. Mary, but which will find a channel of its own by the new railways. The port of Malaga is also fairly prosperous, having, besides its great fruit trade, a large export business in minerals. Since 1873, however, the latter has been depressed, and, dependent as it is on foreign capital and enterprise much more than native, it cannot at best be taken as a sign of Spanish revival. At these ports, as well as those of Barcelona, Valencia, Carthagena, and Cadiz, however, it is foreign shipping which obtains the bulk of the increased trade Spain has a few steamers and a considerable fleet of sailing vessels, but they are not able to compete for a moment with those of England, or even with those of Italy and France. Heavy port dues, official exactions of the black mail order, and the difficulty of obtaining cargoes out as well as in, prevent the development of an English or of any foreign shipping trade, yet the native craft are getting beaten.

Cuba is rich; her annual foreign export trade is valued at from twenty to twenty-four millions sterling a year; and so fertile is the land, so abject the condition of the colonial population, slave and free, that on this trade the Spaniards are able to levy all sorts of oppressive fines. Cuba is a mine of wealth to the emigrant Spanish official and planter; and because it is so he will not let it go. The treatment which the 'Pearl of the Antilles' now receives is just what Spain has meted out to all her great possessions, and with this result that, when she has been compelled to loose her grasp from them one by one, she has left them a prey for the most part to political rowdies or petty tyrants; all manhood being beaten out of them, all truth forgotten in the hollow baseness of a country which was one huge lie. Not one of the colonies of Spain which have asserted their independence has done any good as a State in the world as yet—is other than a sort of curse to the earth. Cuba, liberated, will most likely fall into the same slough. Tyranny breeds civil incapacity everywhere, and the creoles of the island are too well schooled by tyranny to belie the rule.

Of course the imports of Cuba from England, as from all foreign countries, are heavily taxed; and although with this island, as with its neighbour Porto Rico, our trade is considerable, it is nothing like what it might be did the owners know fair dealing. We buy probably nearly a fourth of the produce of these islands, and the United States alone takes perhaps a half of the remainder—70 to 75 per cent. of the Cuban sugar crops going there [1]—but everything that purblind selfishness can do to obstruct the return flow of commerce is done. The marvel is not that Cuba cannot buy in return, but that she can continue to sell, and no doubt the fruit of all this obstructiveness will, by-and-by, appear in successful competition and a ruined colony. Had Jamaica recovered sooner from her internal troubles, and had Haiti been in the hands of a competent population and government, there is little doubt but that Cuba and Porto Rico would have been distanced and partially beaten ere now. Their situation would have been as that of Mexico and the United States of Colombia. The fact, however, is that these islands have profited by the confusion and impotence which has prevailed around them and on the mainland to an extent that could never have been possible had good government and settled institutions existed elsewhere. Their possession of slaves had also a powerful influence in their favour. With slaves and an inexhaustible soil a cultivator may do almost anything, be the exactions to which he has to submit what they may.

The state of affairs in the Philippine Islands, also and unfortunately a possession of Spain, is only a few degrees better than in the West Indies, because there is no insurrection in them, and no troublesome slave

[1] Consul-General Dunlop's *Report on the Trade of Cuba for* 1872.

question. The State is the sole entity that has any life there beyond that of a machine, and the common population is only of use to keep the Government in life. The history of Spanish foreign dominion is, however, summed up in that one description. A more heart-saddening story than that of Spanish conquest and Spanish rule in many of the fairest portions of the world is not to be found in the records of any nation that has ever risen to empire since articulate history held the deeds of nations up to judgment. No wonder, therefore, that the trade of Spain is weak, that her mercantile navy languishes, that corruption and venality sit like cormorants on the heads of the people. Spain and her colonies are almost incapable of themselves rising into a better phase of national existence; and although sections of the populations that inhabit them are growing rich, the riches do not conduce to civilisation and progress, nor are they in many instances altogether the product of Spanish foresight and industry. The ordinary Spaniard prospers best now, as he has always done, where rapacity, falsehood, and selfishness yield the highest returns at the lowest risk.

Much might be said about the little kingdom of Portugal, to which I must now direct attention; but the importance of actual British trade, or trade prospects, with that country would not warrant a wide discussion here. For some five years past the total trade accounts of Great Britain with Portugal have averaged about 7,500,000*l*., and, as might be expected from the high Portuguese tariff, the heavier portion of this was imports from that country. There has been an increase in the total business of nearly 3,000,000*l*. a year since 1860, and there is, therefore, a certain amount of prosperity visible in the recent history of the trade between the two kingdoms. But it is partly of a forced character. Like other countries, Portugal has gone into great public works, labouring thereby to increase the productiveness of the country without at the same time acting liberally towards trade. Until last year Great Britain, although the best customer and best friend in all ways that Portugal has, was treated worse than France in the matter of commercial facilities and freedom. France has enjoyed since 1866 a special tariff, which has imposed duties on the average only about half what England has to pay; and the wonder is, that our manufacturers, so heavily overweighted as they have been, were able to make headway at all. The tariff is still very high on many articles, but so much lower by comparison with the past that English exports to Portugal will no doubt receive considerable impetus, unless the state of the country prevents it. This is just the point of doubt. Portugal has unquestionably made progress in recent years; railways have been built, roads made, banks established, and much done to open the inland valleys to trade. The result has been a large increase in the exporting capacity of the country, which has told, especially in the north, in an increase of the wealth and resources of the people. But against this has to be set two very serious elements of danger—the steady growth of the State debt and the extravagant height to which speculation has pushed institutions of credit. It will scarcely be credited that whereas a quarter of a century ago banking was almost unknown in Portugal, there should now be thirty-six or thirty-seven banks in a country possessed of only two large towns, and the total population of which is only some 4,000,000, mostly agricultural people; but such is the fact. There is, of course, no legitimate business for most of these banks, which are often started by returned emigrants, who have made their fortunes in Brazil or in Africa, and who, finding no ready outlet for investing their means, amuse themselves by starting high-sounding lending institutions in the small towns, and even villages, of the country. Having no legitimate business for these, they either, as a matter of course, engage chiefly in the business of bolstering each other up, or in tempting a needy, left-handed, and rather stupid Government to borrow for this, that, or the other loud-sounding 'public work.'[1] There would have been a

[1] The capital of these Portuguese banks appears to aggregate about 11,000,000l., and the deposits do not amount to much more than 3,500,000l. This includes the paid-up capital and the deposits of the London and Brazilian Bank at its branches in Lisbon and Oporto. Such

crash among these banks last year that would have swept half of them out of existence, crippling the country for years, but for the interference of their chief debtor, the State, which decreed a suspension of the power of creditors to enforce payments, and borrowed money of the Jews and others in London with which to back up their credit. Of course this money could only be repaid by raising a new funded loan here and in Paris, and accordingly the funded debt of the kingdom was increased this year by four millions sterling. Originally the loan was to have been for 6,500,000*l.* nominal at 3 per cent., and to be issued at 50 per cent., but it took so badly, although issued here by the house of Baring, and in Paris by a highly respectable finance and banking company, that the Government withdrew, or said it withdrew, 2,500,000*l.* Of the remainder the greater part lies in the hands of

a swollen amount of capital as this, compared with the smallness of the resources lent by the public to the banks, indicates better than anything else the mushroom character of this banking speculation. In fact, as I have said in the text, the banks lend each other their available means in order to enable the whole to float, and they are thus, with three or four conspicuous exceptions, in whose hands the mercantile business of the country centres, a sort of mutual pawning clubs. Fortunately, their issues of notes are rather limited, most of them having none at all, so that their collapse is not likely to have that universally paralysing effect on the trade of the nation which followed the destruction of the English mushroom banks in 1825. None the less are they a source of much present mischief and fufure danger, because they inflate credit most outrageously, and also because they have drawn in the Government to sustain the inflation. They are also centres of wild gambling in many instances, so much so that the crisis of last year was brought about, not by the state of trade, but by a severe fall in Spanish 3 per cents., which these so-called banks had been speculating in heavily for the rise.

the contractors, and the temporary advances which the loan was to meet have not been all paid off. It is stated that the monetary public here and in France has not taken 250,000*l.* nominal of the loan, and already the agents of the Government are endeavouring to negotiate further advances. Be that true or not, it is certain that the Government must soon again borrow, were it for no other reason than that half the banks in Portugal will want propping, and must soon be propped by the Government or not at all. This method of keeping enterprise afoot is highly dangerous at best, and one can easily see that amid such a muddled confusion of public and private interests, it has become a serious question whether the ever-growing burdens of the Government, or the increased yield of the land, will win the day. I am inclined to fear the former. That the resources of Portugal have expanded greatly since the 'progress' fever took hold of her is proved by the reduction in the deficits, which used to be often a million or more a year on a revenue of little more than 3,000,000*l.*, and are now dwindling, till, according to the budget estimate for the present year, there is an anticipated shortcoming of only some 400,000*l.* Last year the deficit was about 600,000*l.* These results, too, are inclusive of the charges for the Public Works outlay. With the large increase in revenue, however, Portugal ought not to have any such deficit at all. By keeping her works well within the increased means, and avoiding paternal support to every little speculation which crops up in the country, there should be no necessity to recur every few years to a fresh loan, and no such partial collapse in raising a loan as has lately occurred. The income of the country is now about 5,500,000*l*., an increase of more than 2,000,000*l*. since 1870–71, due principally, it is said, to increased trade, and this should have sufficed to keep Portugal out of the market as a borrower and something more.

The new Ministry, which is said to be more economical than the last, ought accordingly to prove its superiority by putting an end to deficits, and finding a surplus for the reduction of debt. The country is at peace, and, by comparison with Spain, is securely governed. Were her agricultural resources in the south developed more by the subdivision of land amongst small cultivators, as in the north, and the railways finished, Portugal might possibly pull through by retrenching. It would be a heavy task, but it is possible, and I do not wish to be too pessimist in the view I take of the situation. Her new administrators will, however, have to remember that a portion of the prosperity of the past half-dozen years has come from exceptional causes, among which are to be reckoned these very public works themselves, which have entailed large imports, upon which duties have been levied ; also that a good deal of the prosperity of Brazil, from which Portugal still derives no small benefit in one shape or another, has been due to the same exceptional causes. Were either Portugal or Brazil to be pulled up short in their credits or their trading facilities abroad, therefore, a collapse would be almost certain to follow in both, which would, at least, do great temporary injury, and which might upset the rather rickety credit of Portugal altogether. For it must not be forgotten that many of the public works created are a source of direct loss to the Government every year, and likely to continue so for some time to come, so that the burdens of the State are increased in two ways—by the debt charge, and by the cost of maintaining works which the debt has paid for. Hence, whatever the ultimate outcome of the present not unpraiseworthy efforts of Portugal at home and in her African colonies to run abreast of the new habits and ideas of the day, I think a balancing of these considerations will prevent any sanguine hopes for the immediate future. The best we can say is, that on the whole the country seeks to move forward, and that her pace is not an alarming one, although it may none the less be rather beyond her strength, as certainly her financial methods are radically bad, and her mercantile credit deeply undermined.

It must not be forgotten either that the debt of Portugal is enormously heavy, reaching now well upon 80,000,000*l.* ; that it has been defaulted on more than once ; and that, except Brazil, her connections and dependencies abroad are of very little value to her, commercially or otherwise. The colonies of Portugal are not indeed overshadowed by the gross tyrannies that have torn the life out of those of Spain, but they are feebly administered, far scattered, and poor. The island of Madeira is perhaps the richest possession which Portugal has. Her territories along the north-west coast of Africa, and in the south-east of Africa, at Mozambique, and Delagoa Bay are not very profitable. There are efforts made at extending their productiveness, no doubt, especially in Mozambique and at Delagoa Bay, which has only just fallen to Portugal, but if they are not more profitable than those which have gone before, they will do little good. The truth is that the Portuguese Government, under a seeming solidity, is considerably worm-eaten with a venerable traditionary sort of corruption unfavourable to healthy colonial development. Robbery prevails nearly everywhere, and the management of a colony is merely more or less a big job. Hence the manner in which Portuguese rule in Africa still shelters the slave traffic, although the complete abolition of slavery has long been decreed to cease in 1878. It is quite notorious that along the coast of Mozambique haunts of slavers are to be found, and that these often trade under Portuguese colours, and find shelter and tacit encouragement in Portuguese harbours, although doubtless the Government at Lisbon may be horrified at the fact. That Government can do little against officials who have purchased posts from it in order to make for themselves fortunes, and who therefore farm the colonies to their own profit rather than the general good. Absurd customs regulations also prevail in most of these colonies, seriously impeding their prosperity, and the Portuguese, though a better colonist than the Spaniard, has not succeeded in planting anywhere, except in Brazil, settlements which may grow into new nations, and of Brazil itself my hopes are not high.

Once more, on the brighter side of the picture it is to be noted that a certain progress in agriculture seems to have been made in Madeira, in Portuguese Guiana, and elsewhere. Cotton has been grown to some small extent in Angola, and it is said to be of good quality. And there can be no question that Portugal still possesses territories capable of becoming valuable possessions were they administered for the public weal. No more desirable district is to be found in Africa than some of those on the south-eastern side which Portugal now holds. Her possessions in India are insignificant territorially, but might be of some importance as centres of trade; and the same may be said of Macao, Portugal's solitary foothold on the coast of China. As matters stand, all of them are good only for what Brazil is still good to Portugal—they are places where the few make fortunes, perhaps, but which the parent country, as a whole, keeps up at a loss, and they are not, even in the fortune-making light, taken in a lump, at all comparable in value to Brazil. In some of them, such as the Azores and Madeira, the development is due to British enterprise and capital much more than to Portuguese, and it is to British ships that Portugal is indebted for her best mercantile facilities with nearly all her possessions. Two lines of fine steamers run from the English colonies in South Africa to London, carrying no inconsiderable portion of the Portuguese African trade, and English, French, and German vessels do almost all the business with the Brazils.

To sum the matter up, then, Portugal is a country where English capital has done much, where our trade is increasing, and would increase faster did it get fair play; but the policy of the Portuguese Government, alike at home and in its possessions, is backward and improvident at the same time. There has been some abnormal stimulus of business here, as elsewhere, and the backward swing to which all trade is subject cannot be prevented here more than anywhere else. Portugal has little to depend on, after all, but her colonial trade, her wines, and her other agricultural produce, and the last has not been increased much in amount by her efforts at improvement. The increase in the wealth of the country and its dependencies is as yet unimportant against the inflation of credit with which it has been accompanied, and that inflation may yet sweep the Government into the chaos of bankruptcy. That, however, is not necessarily a condition which would destroy our trade with the nation. On the contrary, if the nation have the elements of order and stability within it, a collapse of the State might actually unshackle trade and increase it.

It is time now to turn to the Netherlands, which is, after all, for us the most important of the three countries I have included in this chapter, alike in its trade and in its foreign dominions. I have not left space to treat it according to its importance; but fortunately the points of doubt and difficulty regarding it are very few. Holland, like the other two, has had her day of conflict and of triumph, and it is past. She is now settled down into the position of a peaceful nonentity amongst the big Powers, still vexed by their greatness. Her possessions some may covet, but her might now makes none envious. Holland is free to pursue her industries and commerce without much fear of molestation, and nothing could well be more in contrast than her condition compared with that of Spain, whose sovereigns once spent the energies of nations and the wealth of a continent in efforts to bring the stubborn Dutchmen under their heel. Few countries are perhaps more substantially comfortable than Holland, and, except France, no country that I know of has a population more industrious and thrifty. Although the population is only some 4,000,000, including the Grand Duchy of Luxembourg, or about 300,000 less than that of

Portugal, the Netherlands are not only able to export large quantities of agricultural produce, but to maintain a considerable manufacturing industry in connection with their East Indian possessions. The trade of this little kingdom with England alone is more than five times that of Portugal, exclusive of direct colonial trade. To be sure, a good deal of this is transit trade, the ports of Holland having gained steadily in importance of late years, as *entrepôts* for the ingress and egress of the trade of Western Germany. Rotterdam is in this respect no mean rival of Antwerp, and now that the new North Sea Canal has opened the port of Amsterdam to ships of large tonnage, that city also promises to become more a centre of solid transit business than it is now. But, allowing for this through trade, the fact remains that Holland itself does a very large business with England. We import thence cattle and vegetables, and all kinds of agricultural produce, in increasing quantities every year. One of our railway companies has a regular line of steamers plying between Harwich and Rotterdam three times a week for the purpose of carrying on this trade, and there is also a Dutch line, which runs between Dutch ports and London.[1]

[1] Some thirty-seven steamers ply between the port of Rotterdam and various ports of the United Kingdom, nearly the whole of them under the English flag, during the busy parts of the year. One English line— that of the Great Eastern Railway Company—is rapidly opening up an admirable new tourist route to the Continent, the steamers being both well appointed and well managed. Two steamers trade between Rotterdam and Dublin and Belfast, and there are five run between that

Busy and prosperous as Holland is, however, she has never recovered, in any substantial degree, her former position as one of the leading seafaring nations of the Old World. Dutch shipping is on the whole being pressed hard and run down by English and German; and were it not for the manner in which her East Indian commerce is fenced in for the benefit of the Netherlands Trading Company, and the Netherlands India Steam Shipping Company the carrying trade of Holland would probably now be much smaller than it is. The number of foreign vessels which enter the ports of Amsterdam, Rotterdam, and Flushing is on the increase, that of Dutch vessels rather on the decline; and there is little difficulty in accounting for this. Amongst minor causes is the disadvantage which Holland is placed in through possessing none of the materials necessary to construct the modern iron steam-vessels at home. She buys most of them from Clyde builders. Her attempts to keep abreast of the requirements of modern trade are therefore met by difficulties at the outset, and she has so far less chance of success. In point of fact, I believe only the Netherlands Trading Company—a huge monopolist concern headed by the

port and Leith, Grangemouth and Dundee, besides occasional sailings from other places. This is, of course, independent of the trade of Amsterdam, which, till the opening of the new canal, was a declining though important one. A Dutch company has lately begun to run a line of steamers between Flushing and Sheerness in connection with the Chatham and Dover Railway, but hitherto its success has not been encouraging.

King—has made any serious attempt at competing with English ship-builders, and the attempt has not been successful. Other things being equal, the country that has to buy its ships from foreign builders will be very likely to find the trade pass into the hands of its neighbours who make the ships. In other words, the nation that builds ships cheapest and best for itself must, as a rule, be the nation that can run them with most success and profit. The Netherlands have had no success, for example, in competing with England for American trade, and only make their East Indian lines pay through incorporating them as, in a manner, a part of the colonial system.

Another cause of perhaps even greater force acting to produce the decay of the foreign carrying trade of Holland is the rise of Germany, and the pushing endeavours of the Germans to get a good grasp upon an extended foreign trade. This resuscitation of the German Empire is threatening to Holland in several ways, and, should nothing come to upset the ambitious edifice, may lead by-and-by to the extinction of this little kingdom as a separate Power. Holland and Denmark would form but two morsels to the giant. In the meantime Germany overshadows Holland in matters of trade in some important channels. The ports of Bremen and Hamburg struggle for the mastery over Amsterdam and Rotterdam, and show abundant signs of prevailing so far as general over-sea business is concerned. However much use the Germans may make of Dutch railways and Dutch ports for the local export- and import trade of their Westphalian provinces, it is to their own ports that they seek more and more to draw the staple over-sea traffic of the Empire. And thus it is bound to be, till Dutch ports become German. While, therefore, the North German Lloyd's line of ocean mail-steamers prospers fairly in the American trade, the Dutch American has been unable to reap a profitable return.[1] It is, consequently, fair to assume that Holland, though much richer, and a much more extensive trader than the other decayed nations which we have noticed, is certainly in no position to interfere, if left to her own resources, with the predominating position of England as an over-sea goods carrier for all nations.

This conclusion is, I think, quite consistent with the belief that the prosperity of Holland may in other ways continue. Industrious populations cannot become, under any ordinary circumstances, reduced to abject poverty; and while England continues to be a great manufacturing, seafaring nation, Holland is bound to have a large trade with her. In spite of herself she must buy of us manufactured goods of all kinds, but particularly machinery and agricultural implements; and, in spite of ourselves, we must be in some measure dependent on her agricultural produce for food. Her

[1] Consul Turing's *Report on the Trade of Rotterdam for* 1875.

meat and fruit and vegetables are most invaluable to us. On the whole, this interchange of products is at present nearly as unfettered as we could expect with the trade ideas still current nearly everywhere. The Dutch tariff for our manufactured tissues is, as a rule, only 5 per cent. *ad valorem*, which is fairly liberal, and permits of a considerable consumption of English manufactures within the country. It is true that we have the sugar grievance in a mitigated type against Holland as against Belgium; but were it not that France has hitherto used the pretext which these countries give her as a justification for the maintenance of her own more onerous system, we should have little cause to grumble. Holland will, of course, endeavour to keep a strong hold of her Java production of sugar, whatever happens; but beyond that her trade has not hitherto extended much, nor does it seem likely to extend. The quantity of raw sugar which we import direct from Holland is quite insignificant as a rule, and the import of refined, though very much larger, is to some extent counterbalanced by the increasing hold which we are obtaining over the raw produce shipped direct from Java. It is probable, moreover, that the revision of the treaty between France and this country, and the new convention entered into by the three Powers— France, Belgium, and Holland—with our Government over this miserable sugar dispute, will soon practically remove the grievance altogether, although one cannot predict this with certainty, and the draft proposals of France, lately made public, are not all that one could wish.

Holland herself cannot, unfortunately, be a very large consumer of English goods in any case, so that the liberality of her tariff does not count for a great deal while she so jealously preserves for herself the trade of Dutch East India. Her management of Java and the adjacent islands is indeed a curious subject for the study of the political economist. From a humanitarian point of view the Dutch policy stands almost at the antipodes of that professed, but not always practised, by England. Idealism in government, and the tutelage of subject races in the art of self-government, form no part of the Netherland programme in Java and Sumatra. All Dutch colonies are held for the purposes of gain, and to these purposes native population and the Government are alike bound to be subservient. From such a prosaic method of viewing their foreign possessions, it is natural that the Dutch should come to treat their colonies as huge farms or private estates. Commercially this system has its advantages for the owners, who are not only able to draw all possible profit from the sale of the produce of their possessions, but to command almost the entire supply of the wants of the subject population. The profits of this closely guarded trade must amount, at the very least, to several millions sterling a year, on an average of years, independently of surplus State revenues, and this is unquestionably of more pecuniary importance to Holland than posing before the world as a philanthropic power. In her Indian provinces she rules over a population of more than 20,000,000, that of Java and Madura alone being about 18,000,000; but no attempt is made to 'develop' the natives, nor are they admitted to any share in the government, however humble. Their duty is to produce either for the privileged Dutch trading corporations, or for private persons of the dominant race intent on fortune-making, and consequently Holland is not bothered with the dynastic and other troubles which disturb our rule in India. She might not be able to hold her possessions if she were. It is not my purpose to discuss otherwise what is to be thought of this policy; I merely note the fact. The dependencies of Holland are not governed as those of England are, but hitherto they have been more obviously profitable to her than ours. For many years after Holland obtained the complete mastery of Java, the annual surplus of revenue drawn from it by her came to between 2,000,000*l.* and 3,000,000*l.* a year, and sometimes exceeded the latter sum. Recently, however, a rather more enlightened system of taxation has prevailed, monopolies have been partially abolished, and the direct results of Government estate overseeing have fallen off, but the indirect gains of the trading company and private merchants have probably increased. There have indeed been rather severe losses suffered in Java sugar lately, owing principally to the effects of the French bounty system, already noticed; but Java tea has been growing in favour, and the production of rice has been growing in quantity. On the whole, the profitableness of the island to its owners has not seriously lessened. Java cannot fail to be a most profitable investment while governed as it now is, for it is an island whose fertility is not yet half developed; and did the Dutch abstain from wars in Sumatra, which they do not seem very well able to conduct, and give themselves earnestly to arts of peace, they might year by year increase its productiveness. Cotton, tobacco, tea, coffee, cereals of various kinds, wool, fruits, almost every product of value to mankind, can be produced by the island with an abundance that should, under a more liberal trade policy than yet obtains, enable its owners to command a much wider market than they do. The Straits tin, for example, marketed by the Netherlands Trading Company, regulates the European tin markets now, and under the present system of sales, which resembles that of our Indian Government in the case of opium, it forms a favourite medium for gambling amongst metal brokers.

The competition of such a possession as Java with our Indian Empire is a danger which it might be easy to find a plausible colour for; but I do not think it affects us at present to any appreciable extent, except, perhaps, in spices and indigo. There is none of the eager, feverish desire for advancement in modern arts and sciences to disturb or impel the Dutch into hot competition. They go quietly on in their old-fashioned ways, adopting improvements and opening up their possessions with slow, cautious circumspection, intent chiefly on keeping the profit to themselves with the least possible risk. Although near neighbours, the trade between Java and British India is indeed very restricted, compared to what it might well be were the former in the hands of a pushing people. Probably certain consignments of goods find their way to the Netherlands India through the English free port at Singapore ; but, granting that to be so, the total intercourse between the two countries is not worth counting on, and since the war broke out between the Dutch and the Atchinese there has been a decrease on both sides of the account.[1] We have, therefore, about as little to hope for as to fear from the Dutch in that quarter of the world, which is in several senses a pity.

It is much the same with regard to the direct trade of England with these possessions. For the last year or two it has shown some increase through the competition which English steamers carry on against the Netherlands lines, and the eagerness with which speculative merchants have striven to push goods against the Dutch ever since the import duties were somewhat reduced.[2] But, at its largest, the direct trade between

[1] *Vide* Mr. J. E. O'Connor's introduction to last year's issue of the *Statement of the Trade of British India.*

[2] Consul Fraser, in his report on the trade of Java for the year 1874

this country and the Dutch possessions has not exceeded 3,300,000*l.* in any one year, and usually it has been about from 800,000*l.* to 1,500,000*l.*, taking exports and imports together. Of course, as I have already said, a considerable indirect trade is done through Holland, whose traders buy of us to send to the Indies on their own account in their own ships; but this indirect trade has not been very satisfactory lately, I suspect, to any of the parties concerned, any more than the recent push of English merchants for direct business, which has resulted in a glutted market and ruinous prices. Besides, the indirect trade is, so far as English exports are concerned, to a large extent limited to half-manufactured articles, such as yarns, which the Dutch make up themselves for their Eastern market, and sell there at higher prices than English merchants ask for their fabrics. Their control of the market

---

(*Consular Reports*, Part IV., 1876), makes the following observation on the alteration in the Dutch colonial import duties. It lets a flood of light into the failures of Dutch government in these regions :—' At the opening of the year, when the modified scale of duties came into force, considerable difficulties were caused to importers by the irregular and inconsistent taxations imposed by the customs authorities for the 6 per cent. *ad valorem* duty. The taxations are revised every three months; but in some early instances valuations far exceeding market currencies were imposed, and the liberal spirit which induced the Home Government to abolish differential duties thus neutralised. The attention of the customs authorities was called to the matter by the Chamber of Commerce, and, backed by a protest from the Batavia Exchange, through the medium of their price current, resulted in a material improvement, although complaints are occasionally heard regarding exaggerated values being placed on goods.' An *ad valorem* scale of duties, revised arbitrarily every three months, must be the height of torture to a trader.

probably enables them to exact these higher prices with a certain impunity.

Except as a source of gain, the Dutch East Indies are of little value to the mother-country, to whom they give hardly any political importance, and might pass out of her grasp almost with as little noise as Ceylon, once so bright a jewel in the crown of the Stadtholder. The same assertion holds good of all other Dutch possessions. They may be more profitable to her than those of Portugal and Spain are to those countries; but they do not make their owner a great State. Nor has Holland, any more than these others, ever made a mark as a coloniser, pure and simple; her most successful effort in that line being the settlements in South Africa —almost the last direct memorial of which has again fallen into the hands of the conqueror of all the rest, a conqueror by whom, a quarter of a century ago, it had been abandoned because the Dutch people refused to become English. How the Transvaal will fare now under the rather anomalous philanthropic despotism which Lord Carnarvon has inaugurated is a question which I shall not now try to settle. The Dutch boers, at all events, have not prospered alone, except at cattle-herding, and seem unable to knit themselves into strong self-governing communities with success.

It would take me too far out of the range of my subject to discuss this question at length; but, I think, one remarkable feature can be distinguished in the failures of all efforts on the part of these three nations to found great colonies, which, apart from the distinctive race characteristics, marks them off from our later colonisations. They all governed their dependencies over-much to begin with, and sought to make them merely a source of material aggrandisement to those left at home. And the worst of it was that they succeeded for a time in this endeavour, through various causes, until all *verve* and independent life was in a manner squeezed out of the offshoots. We tried that plan ourselves in America, but, fortunately, too late to do any harm except to ourselves. We had lazily suffered the existing states, planted there by independent adventurers, to go too far alone before asserting forcibly the current kingly ownership doctrine about colonies, and they accordingly beat us, as we deserved, when we tried coercion. Since then England has let well alone. Her colonists have had almost complete liberty to order their ways from the first, England only lending them an ornamental head, with maternal advice good or other on occasion. A vigour has thus been communicated to most of them which promises to carry them far, and such as all other colonies appear to want.

But though a failure, like Spain and Portugal, at the art of colonising, Holland has not been so to the same degree, and she still preserves a dominating power over many spots on the face of the earth which would start anew into importance, did the little kingdom fulfil its 'manifest destiny,' and become a portion of the German Empire. That consummation may not come perhaps, or before it does the dependencies of Holland may not exist in their present condition and shape, and, whether or not, the English race and English power have spread too widely over the world, let us hope, to be easily driven back or overtaken by the greatest inheritor of the old Empire of the Netherlands.

As a general conclusion we may say that with Spain and Portugal our trade is not very promising, much hampered, and, without a great change in the mercantile policy of these countries, likely to advance very slowly, and to suffer heavily in depressed seasons. The same may be said about the dependencies of Holland; they do good well-nigh exclusively to Holland. But with that little kingdom itself, and through it with its great continental neighbour, we do a good solid trade which is reasonably free, and which we may therefore hope to see increase.

I ought not, perhaps, to close this essay without a word about Denmark, which is another kingdom, once famous, now rapidly sinking into oblivion. Its general trade is too insignificant, however, to call for much notice, and it is too surely enclosed by German influences to possess great interest for us. Its business is, however, still considerable with this country, and we derive a supply of raw sugar from the small West

Indian islands still in Danish keeping. But there are no features in this trade worth commenting upon. It is steady, and so far as regards imports to this country from Denmark has increased considerably, but the exports thither are nearly stationary and hardly likely to expand much. Since Prussia reft away Schleswig-Holstein, Denmark has been steadily sinking into a Prussian province and may soon become extinct as a separate State. Whether it does or not, it is of less account by far in all that relates to statecraft or to trade than the Swiss Cantons.

The trade of Scandinavia might also be considered worthy of some analysis, but there is little in its present aspect that is unfamiliar or that calls for remark. Sweden and Norway have not partaken much in the economic revolutions which have changed the face of so many regions of the earth except in so far as their commerce has been thereby increased. There has been augmented demand for Norwegian timber, and for certain food products of the peninsula such as fish, oats, and oils, and the shipping trade has been enormously benefited by the great increase in the carrying trade of other nations and especially of England. The total tonnage of Swedish and Norwegian shipping is the highest of any in the world except our own and that of the United States, and much more than half this tonnage may be considered as auxiliary to that of England. Norwegian ships carry a great deal of the timber and corn which comes to us from North America, especially from Canada, and the trade between the two countries, as also between the Baltic and England, is to a great extent carried in Scandinavian bottoms. The profits of this trade are visible in the continued power which Norway and Sweden have to import more than they export, and between their steady quiet commerce and their international carrying trade these countries are fairly prosperous. There has been less wild speculation, more of quiet prudent money-getting, in them than in any other country in Europe except perhaps Holland. At the present time these countries have together nearly 3,000 miles of railway in operation, which have for the most part been cheaply constructed, and of which about 1,000 miles belong to the State. Yet even this moderate mileage has proved more than the country could use by a good deal, and there has been a considerable sum of money lost in some of the lines by English people; but they do not seriously burden the country, and to a certain extent offer indirect compensation by the facilities which they give for commerce. Should the two kingdoms continue their quiet course importing manufactures and exporting such raw produce as they possess, they will continue sound and healthy commercially, and as auxiliaries to the trade resources of England must always have a high value to us.

At the present time considerably over 40 per cent.

of the entire direct trade of Sweden and Norway is with Great Britain. We send, in addition to textile fabrics, coal, hardware and machinery materials, and get back their raw produce, including a considerable quantity of Swedish iron, which is of very fine quality. Altogether the aggregate trade between England and Scandinavia last year came to nearly 17,000,000*l.*, and there is nothing that I can see which tends materially to lessen its volume except the probability that we shall want to buy less. The competition of Germany has not yet told sensibly upon our hold in the peninsula, and there is no reason why it should do so to any injurious extent. And no other country except Germany has any appreciable chance of diverting a stream which has flowed between England and Scandinavia now for many generations.

CHAPTER XI.

CANADA AND SOUTH AFRICA.

Two things strike one at the very outset regarding the English Colonial Empire—its newness and its rapid expansion. Three hundred years ago England did not possess one of her present numerous colonies. Her greatest offshoot of all—now the United States—was not in any part peopled by Englishmen before the beginning of the seventeenth century, and, except the small colony of Newfoundland, no territory held under the British Crown to-day was ours so early as the old State of Virginia. We did not begin to lay our grasp on the French possessions in Canada till 1623, and it was not long anterior to that date that adventurers from Virginia first wrenched the peninsula of Nova Scotia from the same colonisers. And we may say that all the colonies which are now inhabited by English-speaking people began their career as self-governed States only, as it were, yesterday. The Dominion of Canada was organised only in 1869, and cannot be said to be yet a completely homogeneous State. Compared with the extended sway of the Romans over Gaul, Spain, and

Britain, of the Phœnicians in Carthage, or of the Spaniards themselves, under one guise or another, in South America, the colonial empire of England is, indeed, a thing of yesterday, and this should not be forgotten in speaking of the success of our efforts at colonisation. In many respects that success has yet to be proved.

The success, as far as rapidity of growth in the population is concerned, has, however, been very great. Before 1845 it may be said that none of the colonies were of great promise. Canada languished beside her prosperous independent neighbour. New South Wales —then including Victoria and Queensland—was a feeble settlement, still troubled by the *residuum* of those importations of criminals from the mother-country, from which she had been but just relieved; and the Cape of Good Hope was almost Dutch in its European population and its absence of enterprise. The total English population of the whole of our foreign possessions, including the Crown colonies so-called, such as Jamaica and the other West Indian possessions, did not, in 1850, exceed 2,000,000. Only Canada and the United States, previous to 1845, attracted anything like a steady stream of emigrants, and it was small compared to the rush which broke out after the Irish Famine in 1847. That, and the gold discoveries in Australia and California, led, however, to an exodus, which was at its highest in 1852, when nearly 369,000 people left our shores, and the flow has never but once or twice fallen below 100,000 a year since—the average being from 150,000 to 200,000. Of this great emigration British North America has received latterly a much less portion than it did when there was no attraction in the Southern hemisphere; but the numbers going to Australia and New Zealand have, with the exception of the six years 1867 to 1872, been uniformly very considerable. Altogether, since 1845, at least 6,000,000 British-born people have left the mother-country for the colonies and the United States ; and, besides these, there have been large emigrations of Dutch, Germans, Norsemen, Italians, and French, many of whom have settled permanently in the British colonies, and are becoming absorbed in the Anglo-Saxon race. From all these causes, and in spite of occasional return waves of immigration, due to temporary pauses in the headlong pace at which the colonies have developed themselves into communities and states with a great trade of their own, the English population of British North America has risen to nearly 3,000,000, that of Australia and New Zealand to about 2,100,000, and the English and Dutch population of South Africa to more than 250,000. We may say that the population of these colonies has at least quadrupled in thirty years, and in some cases it is now tenfold what it was in 1845. This is a most remarkable fact, and, in estimating what our colonies are or may become, must be constantly borne in mind. They are, indeed, creatures of a generation.

There is another general observation which I should like to make here, and it is this. Nearly all the colonies which are of any importance, and on which Englishmen can live and multiply more or less as in their native land, have been formerly in the possession of another European Power.[1] As a mere instance of the backwardness of the English as geographical discoverers, or ocean marauders, in the Middle Ages, this would be a remarkable fact, but that view of the subject does not concern us. Of more interest is the effect which this previous occupation is likely to have on the future of those colonies which, like Canada and the Cape, still contain a large population descended from the original conquerors of the territories. In a lesser degree the same question would, of course, be interesting as regards the Crown colonies of Jamaica, Mauritius, Ceylon, and the settlements on the north-east coast of Central America, taken from the Spaniards, French, and Dutch,

[1] It may be useful to call to mind the history of our acquisition of these possessions by a brief enumeration of them. The chief sufferer by our habits of appropriation has been France, from whom we have taken Canada, Nova Scotia, Newfoundland, Louisiana, Mauritius, and the small settlements of Dominica, Grenada, St. Lucia, Tobago, and St. Vincent. Besides portions of the United States which became English-governed, either before or since their independence, we have taken from Spain: Jamaica, Trinidad, Honduras, and Gibraltar. Holland has given us the Cape of Good Hope, Ceylon, and Guiana. Portugal alone amongst the seafaring countries of the seventeenth and eighteenth centuries who were large owners of territories in various parts of the world has escaped without paying tribute, except in India.

but I do not intend to deal with these at any length. They are not colonies in any true sense of the word, but merely territories held for gain in regions where, as a rule, the English race could not permanently settle and propagate itself. Their trade is, therefore, entirely what we make it, and their condition also. But in our great colonies it is altogether different. They live and grow, and found institutions, which must exercise a most important influence on the future of the world, as well as of our mere trade prosperity, and we must consequently examine this race element amongst others which come before us in dealing with them.

The most important questions which we have to determine, however, affect the material progress and well-being of the colonies. We have to see how their populations live, how their trade is developed, and in what it consists : and also to endeavour to value the character of their institutions, the wisdom of their commercial policy, and their wealth. For example, at the very threshold of the subject, we find that one characteristic common to all the colonies is debt. Their growth in population has in some cases hardly kept pace with the accumulation of their public burdens, and obviously this debt element must have produced the same results in their case that we have found it doing in the case of foreign nations. The questions which meet us on the threshold of our inquiry into colonial progress and prosperity are therefore many and complicated, and must make one very cautious in the use of the language of unlimited enthusiasm and panegyric which is so common. Beginning now with Canada, I will endeavour to indicate the salient features of the situation of our leading colonies on the lines thus laid down, with impartiality, and as comprehensively as the narrow limits of my space will permit.

The modern Dominion of Canada embraces, as everyone knows, a number of provinces which were formerly separate colonies.[1] In some respects portions of the united country are highly favoured, and in time may rise to be important portions of a great nation; but there can be no question that the situation of the Dominion as a whole is, in the meantime, not satisfactory. Numerous drawbacks are to be met with, of which not the least is the manner in which the blundering heedlessness of the English Government has caused its inhabitants to be cooped up almost entirely in the bleak north in such a fashion that the best province of all—that of Ontario—is, from a trade point

---

[1] The present Dominion of Canada was formed in 1867 out of the old Provinces of Upper and Lower Canada, Nova Scotia, Prince Edward's Island, and New Brunswick, and the new district of British Columbia. On the cession of the Hudson's Bay territory to the Dominion in 1870 part of the northern territory was erected into the province of Manitoba and incorporated with the Dominion. Newfoundland is still under an entirely separate organisation. Although united under one central Parliament, consisting of several Houses of Representatives, each province has still a separate legislature and separate internal administration. The franchise is on a different footing as to property qualifications in different provinces, and only New Brunswick appears to have the ballot.

of view, at the mercy of the United States for a considerable portion of the year. If the reader will take a map of North America he will see this at once. By reason of the manner in which the boundary line, running from the sea to its interior, is carried northward from the St. Croix River to the St. John's River, an immense tract of territory is taken away from Eastern Canada, and the whole of the western part of the Dominion is thereby shut up in winter by ice and snow. This boundary was not settled till 1842, and by its settlement on the present lines Canada has undoubtedly been most seriously injured.[1] Owing to the manner in which Canada is squeezed up on the east side, for example, the Intercolonial Railway has been driven northwards through a comparatively useless and waste territory, causing not merely an enormous increase in the mileage, but an almost complete stoppage of business during five months of the year. Had the boundary originally intended been settled on, this line might have run straight across a fertile country, open all the year round from Quebec or Montreal to St. John's, or even to Portland, and the trade of Western Canada might thus have been kept as independent as the country itself wishes to be considered. Now, however, as I have said, the west is cut off from the east, and the traffic of Ontario benefits the United

[1] For a clear account of this boundary bungle see *The History of the Intercolonial Railway*, by Sandford Fleming, published in 1876.

States more than the eastern provinces of the Dominion. The coal of Nova Scotia is placed 200 miles farther from Montreal by railway than it need have been, and that province is also by this means thrown, as it were, into the arms of the American Union, which promises to be its best market. Great ports and large trading centres on the coast of New Brunswick or Nova Scotia are thus, to my thinking, rendered impossible; while the magnificent waterway of the St. Lawrence is in the open season of much less use to the Dominion and the cities on its banks than it would have been had no United States railways tapped the traffic of Western Canada at Buffalo and Detroit, and, by offering a cheap comparatively short direct route to the sea, drawn the trade away to the south-east. No railway system which Canada could now construct would ever be able to remedy the mischief that has been done, and the trade battle which she tries to wage in her existing condition is beyond question utterly hopeless.

I dwell on this point at the outset, because it appears to me to concern vitally the whole future of the Dominion. The hearts of the people will in time go the way of their interests, and the union so recently formed between the various provinces may be broken one of these days by the secession of Ontario to the United States. For, unhappily, the chill which intercourse between the parts has received is further aggravated by miscellaneous causes, all tending to separate the east from the west. First of these we may place the fact that the large province of Quebec (formerly Lower Canada), which interposes between Ontario and the maritime provinces of New Brunswick and Nova Scotia, is inhabited mostly by a poverty-stricken and unenterprising French population. We have in that territory more than a million of people, chiefly French Canadians, who live still for the most part in the primitive superstitions of three centuries ago—a people who have not been moved by the tide of civilisation and material progress surging around them, who, with a railway running past their doors, as it were, refuse to use it, and creep along in the ways of their fathers. These, therefore, form a race barrier between the east and the west which makes free intercourse between the purely English parts of the Confederation very difficult, which prevents community of interests from being realised, and generally tends to complete the mischief that the boundary muddle began. Add to this that the soil and wealth-producing capabilities of Quebec province are about the poorest in all the Union, and that it is overladen with debt at the instance of reckless speculators who appear to have bribed its legislature, and we have reasons enough for doubting whether the different parts of the Dominion are likely long to cohere. What was necessary to give the country a chance of becoming homogeneous was, in short, the northern portion of

Maine, handed over to the States in 1842, where a race of Anglo-Saxon and German settlers might have grown up to unite the east and centre.

Passing to the west coast, we find still more serious difficulties in the way of the development of a great State, and there also the mischief has in part been done by the stupidity of English officials, who surrendered without necessity or warrant vast regions of magnificent country to the United States. The superficial area of British North America has never been accurately ascertained, but on the map it looks to be about the same as that of the United States, and probably is somewhat larger. The physical condition of the two countries is, however, altogether different; and while almost the whole of the United States is habitable, and capable in time of sustaining a population as large as that of China, the greater part of the Dominion is a forbidding land of frost and snow, whose brief summer is barely sufficient to permit a scattered Indian population and a few Hudson's Bay trappers to find the means of subsistence. There is indeed a possibility that settlers from Europe may reclaim portions of the central and western territories of Canada, and some of the valleys of Manitoba are capable of cultivation, in a certain fashion. Possibly also the introduction of a vigorous race and the reclamation of the land might have a favourable influence on climate, driving the zone of frost farther north. But at present the prospect of any such change is remote indeed. Canada is shut up, separated into isolated communities all winter, and the free intercommunion which would enable all the parts to grow into a great whole is utterly destroyed. To have conquered the icy north she ought to have had more of the south and west, parts of Ohio, Indiana, Michigan and Illinois, and the whole of Oregon. All the magnificent territory which we flung away to the Union, from first to last, should have been hers, and then, westward as well as eastward, there would have been a basis upon which a mighty empire might have been reared. British Columbia would not then have been a miserable settlement cooped up between a lonely sea and forbidding mountains, vainly hoping that a railway across the trackless continent will unite it with the east, and set it free from all its troubles. With the western regions now called Oregon and Washington uniting it with more favoured lands southward and eastward between the southwestern shore of Lake Superior and California there might have been scope for its growth, since there could have been ready intercourse through magnificent lands, capable of being quickly peopled. Instead of God-forsaken groups of struggling settlers dotted here and there over the vast area of the Dominion, numbering altogether not a tenth of the population of the United States, there might have been a powerful confederation capable of taking its place amongst the leading nations of the world.

It is useless to regret these 'might-have-beens' now. I only allude to them in order to illustrate the more forcibly what I consider the initial, and, I fear, insurmountable, difficulties which stand in the way of Canadian progress. The Dominion is to me a hopeless congeries of provinces which have little community of interest, and the best parts of it can only have their full development when united to the greater Union of the South, or to the northern half of it. We have tried to make a united whole of what we by our own folly everlastingly divided, but there could be no task more hopeless than that which seeks to produce a single State from provinces like Nova Scotia and Quebec, Ontario, British Columbia, and Manitoba.

The worst of all this blundering is that it continues to be so expensive. We have spent millions upon millions of money on Canada, chiefly in a vain endeavour to accomplish the impossible, and Canada appears to have been deluded by these spendings into a belief that we should succeed. She has got her Parliament, her Vice-King, her Ministers of State, and her huge debt, and complacently calls herself a new empire—the brightest jewel in the English crown. 'Loyalty' is, in fact, the one article in which Canada repays the English people for their lavish endeavours to overcome the follies of the past, and when one talks of the probable dismemberment of the Dominion, this loyalty is always flung in one's teeth. 'Look how enthusiastic Canada is for the Queen and the old country; *she* will never revolt.' This is the purest nonsense, to my mind, for Canadian loyalty is, and has always been, a very mercenary affair. Let the country once get into the depths whither it has been hastening under our leadership, and let the various provinces begin to feel their individual burdens—as they only can do when British money ceases to flow in—and we shall then see what this loyalty means. Will it hold Ontario when Ontario is in dread of having to pay the debts of Quebec or any one province when the burden of imperial taxation becomes over heavy? I doubt it; nay, I more than doubt—I utterly disbelieve it.

We must take this geographical question, then, as a cardinal factor of the problem in dealing with Canadian progress. At the very outset it reveals to us how very mistaken that 'progress' has, in many cases, been in its aims. The legislators of the Dominion have sought to accomplish the impossible. Take, for example, the Canadian Pacific Railway scheme, and judge it by the dry facts of the situation. Conceive what a railway means—what it needs to maintain it in order—and imagine a line built across vast plains, through almost impassable mountains, along the greater part of whose track there would not be 10,000 inhabitants; which would be subject in winter to enormous falls of snow and intense and destructive frosts, that would not only stop all traffic probably, but necessitate constant repairs; and having realised in this fashion how very mad the scheme is, ask yourself why it was conceived; why England came forward with a guarantee for part of its cost, buoying up British Columbians with visions of the good the line was to do them, till, not getting the promised boon, they threaten to secede from the federation. Who can avoid the conclusion that the whole scheme is a wild attempt to retrieve the past— to try and bind together with a band of iron lands irrevocably separated, we having lost for ever the opportunity of uniting them by filling first a fertile southern continent with a numerous and thriving population of Englishmen! The provinces thus separated may thrive after a fashion, but there can be no united nation built up by such means. For all that, this railway is being pushed on, and last year the Government of the Dominion spent $2,390,000 on its construction and survey. As many as 681 miles of the line are now definitely located, and 227 of these are contracted for. It appears that the intention is to penetrate into British Columbia by the Yellow Head Pass and the gorges of the Fraser River, where portions of the line are also surveyed. Here the engineering difficulties are enormous, and will involve quite incalculable expense, so that the chance of the road ever becoming other than a burden on the Dominion would be remote even were conditions as to trade more favourable than they are ever likely to be. As things are, the line will be in ruins probably within five years of the date of its completion, and it may yet be the instrument which will rend the Dominion asunder. Trade it cannot produce, for the line will be 2,000 miles long, reckoning from the head of Lake Superior only ; and what can British Columbia produce that will bear a land carriage of 4,000 miles if carried by rail to the east coast, or of nearly 3,000 if transhipped at Quebec ?

The railways which have already been carried out in the Dominion are almost all financial failures, and ought to be a constant source of wisdom to those who now seek to hurry the country into still more grievous disasters. The Grand Trunk Railway, for example, is in a state of utter bankruptcy, and has very little prospect of ever being anything else. It may pay ultimately on one or two more millions of capital than it does now, though that is rather doubtful; but it does not seem to me to have any chance of ever becoming a great 'through' road. Along its eastern half it has little or no local traffic; and, although it leases a road down to Portland, in Maine, it must always be beaten by the railways of the States, which are much shorter, in any competition for the traffic of the west. Almost equally disastrous is the history of the Intercolonial Railway likely to be. It has been built by the Government with money partly guaranteed by England. It is another part of the iron bond of union, and is a failure for its primary object, whatever it may come to do for

New Brunswick alone. What with Government business paid for out of loans, and the mails, it has a share of traffic now which the condition of the country and its route prove to be of a quite misleading kind.

But perhaps the most signal example of the loss and ruin which has been the result of all Canadian efforts at material development is afforded by the history of the Great Western Railway of Canada. Formerly this line earned large dividends and was very prosperous. Not content with this, Canadian speculators—of whom there are many—backed, it is said, from New York, built an opposition road, which was almost at once seized upon by Vanderbilt, of the New York Central, and forthwith the Great Western was ruined. Its prosperity had been based, not upon Canadian traffic pure and simple, but upon the traffic connection with the Great New York line; and when that was taken away the collapse was almost instantaneous. Thus almost the only prosperous railway undertaking which Canada had was prosperous through foreign help; and the Canadians themselves made haste to destroy this prosperity. Such is their patriotism. Whether a union of this bankrupt line with the bankrupt Grand Trunk would mend matters now is doubtful; but that is, at all events, the only remedy left for English investors to dream about.

The truth of the matter is, that Canada has neither population nor trade of a kind capable of sustaining great railways. The trade consists mostly of lumber, corn, and flour, none of which can bear heavy overland freights. Nova Scotia possesses minerals, and exports a good deal; but it is so favourably situated for water carriage that it has little need of railways. The inland provinces of Canada have also good water carriage all summer; and it is so much better fitted for the kind of raw produce which they have to move that the railways would get beaten for a portion of the year, even were there no short overland carriage through the States to the sea. Then the population of Canada is not only thin—the Dominion altogether containing little more than 4,000,000 souls—scattered in unequal groups over, territory larger than all Europe, thickest and poorest in Quebec provinces; more scattered, but richer, in Ontario, Nova Scotia, and the other eastern provinces; —not only is this population thin, but it does not travel extensively. And even were it to be rushing about continually, it would not be able to keep the present railway system in a flourishing state.[1]

[1] Canada possesses altogether nearly 6,000 miles of railway; but some of the lines are not in operation yet, or have been closed, so that actually there are not more than about 5,000 miles which can be described as earning anything. The Grand Trunk Company owns, leases, and works about 1,390 miles, the Great Western Company about 797, and the Intercolonial system represents 844. Not one of these corporations yields a net revenue of 1 per cent. on its capital, and many of the branch lines do not earn their working expenses. The total capital involved is, in round figures, about $300,000,000, or say 60,000,000*l*., of which nearly $50,000,000, or say 10,000,000*l*., has been contributed by the Dominion Provincial and Municipal Governments. Of course, much of this capital has been issued at a serious discount, so that the actual cash spent has not been so much as this represents. This

In respect, therefore, of the heavy outlay which Canada has incurred on railways, I think there has been a huge blunder. The credit of the colony has been strained to breaking for a very inadequate gain. A certain amount of progress has no doubt been made, population has increased, and trade has extended; but in no instance has the progress at all justified the pace at which the colony has gone ahead with its railways—a pace which has been the ruin of thousands. The Dominion debt, for public works of all kinds, has, I fear, been incurred with almost equal recklessness. In the matter of debt, indeed, Canada is not peculiarly or pre-eminently a sinner, for all our colonies have plunged more or less recklessly into it; but her powers of expansion are, in my opinion, so small that she stands in more danger from her burden than any other colony, except perhaps New Zealand. Exclusive of the provincial and municipal requirements, the Dominion Government alone requires a payment of from 5*l*. to 6*l*. per family every year in the shape of taxes,[1] and has now to face deficits. These taxes represent well nigh a month's labour to the working man—a most serious

is of little consequence, however, in judging of the results of investment in these railways. We find then that in 1875 the actual net earnings on this capital were just $3,700,000, or little more than 1 per cent. Last year the yield was less, and it could not well be otherwise with declining traffic and keen competition. The whole system carried in the twelve months about a fifth of the number of passengers carried by the English Midland Company.

[1] Budget speech of the Hon. R. T. Cartwright in the Canadian House of Commons, February 1876.

drawback on prosperity. Thus, although the total may seem a small one, compared with the burdens which we shall find that some of the Australian colonies have taken upon themselves, it is for Canada a very heavy item, because at least a fourth of the population of Canada is excessively poor. And this is not all; every province has its own budget, and in some of them it is very heavy. Quebec, for instance, is crushingly overladen, and has a budget of its own which from the growing deficits it displays ought to alarm all prudent citizens; yet it rushes into fresh loans for railways, projected by speculators for their own profit merely, with a levity which strikes one with positive amazement. What the actual individual burden of imperial and local taxation, taken together, in Canada may be per head, I have not been able to ascertain with exactness, because the accounts of the various provinces are not regularly obtainable; but, as near as I can estimate, I should say that, speaking moderately, it is not less than 3*l.* per head. The country has, in short, been forced and overdriven to a degree in all directions, and will now suffer from it severely. A false step was taken when the Dominion assumed the debts of all the provinces that joined it without restricting them from borrowing again on their own account, and we now find burdens increasing on all hands, municipalities being steeped in debt with the rest. In the aggregate I estimate the liabilities of this sort which Canada bears at about

30,000,000*l.* to 35,000,000*l.* besides the debt of the railway corporations. The present debts of the Provincial Governments of Canada incurred in England amount to nearly 3,000,000*l.*, and the four cities— Montreal, Ottawa, Toronto, and Quebec—have borrowed here about 2,500,000*l.* Their united population is not more than 250,000. These figures may seem tedious, but they suffice to give a better idea of the position of Canada than a very long argument. Everywhere we find debt. The whole fabric of the State hangs upon it, and the pettiest municipality in the country thinks itself hardly constituted unless it can boast of an issue of bonds. The result of all this of course is, that the country lies under burdens which we at home here, patient as we are, would almost rebel against, and which must, I fear, prove before long a great deal too much for Canada.

For a time, of course, trade has been inflated by the inflow of money, and there is no doubt that some of this inflation may prove to be permanent gain; but the danger of all such movements is, that they put trade upon a false basis, which sooner or later gives way and causes widespread ruin. It becomes a thing resting on credit and bolstered by credit, instead of a solid fabric well grounded on national wants, and expansive by reason of the growth of these wants. The primitive character of the industries which such a country as Canada possesses, and its almost complete dependence on good harvests, make an ample margin of solid resources absolutely necessary when reverses come; but she has practically left herself with none. Moreover, as I have often insisted, feverish progress always tends to defeat itself. Fresh taxes have to be imposed, and these hinder trade. Protectionist theories find currency in order to give plausible justification for these taxes, and so matters go on till irreparable mischief is done to the real advancement of the community. At present the import taxes of Canada are light, compared with those of the United States, but they are distinctly protectionist, nevertheless.[1] We in consequence hear a good deal of the necessity of developing native manufactures, of the excellence of Canadian cloth, its cheapness compared with English, and so forth, as if it were a real gain for such a country, needing, as it does, every energy to battle with climatic difficulties and win bread and clothing from the soil, to turn itself into a woollen factory. The result so far of the effort of Canada to force business, and of the blown out credit

[1] The Canadian tariff is not in itself a heavy one, many articles of manufacture paying no more than 5 per cent. *ad valorem*, and never more than 25 per cent., while the free list is pretty extensive. The duty on cotton, woollen, and silk goods is 17 per cent. *ad valorem*, and on iron 5 per cent. There is, indeed, strong complaint on the part of some classes of Canadians that the duties are so low, and only very recently a strenuous effort was made in the Canadian Parliament to get them raised further than the Government desired. Exigencies of the exchequer have compelled the Finance Minister to augment several duties, but the languishing manufacturing interests are not yet enough protected in the eyes of those who are engaged in them and ambitious of rivalling other countries in the production of clothes and machinery.

on which her trade is based, is pretty clearly set forth in the following extracts from Messrs. Dun, Barlow, and Co.'s excellent summary of the Canadian trade outlook for the year 1877 :—

While the failures in the year just closed are over two hundred less in number than in 1875, with a decrease of three millions of dollars in liabilities, both number and amount continue to be exceptionally large, especially as compared with the preceding years. In 1873 the number of those who failed in Canada in proportion to the number engaged in business was one in every 47. In 1875 there was a failure to every 28 names reported in business; while in 1876 there is one failure to every 32. In the United States in 1873 the number was one in every 108; in 1875 one in every 83; and in 1876 the number is one in every 69. The average liabilities in Canada for 1875 were $14,656; and in 1876 the amount varied only very slightly, being $14,767. The results of the year's business do not encourage the belief that the conditions of trade in the Dominion have much improved. The number of traders who have added to their capital is comparatively few; those who have held their own are to be congratulated; while those who have diminished their surplus are not inconsiderable. The disease from which the commercial body politic has been suffering for the past three years has, it is hoped, well nigh spent itself. But the signs of improvement, which it was thought the past year would bring, have not been fulfilled. Had we been favoured with good crops of agricultural produce in the year just past, a great stride would have been taken towards the return of prosperity. But in this, the fine promise of the first half of the year was unfulfilled, and notwithstanding lessened imports, restricted sales, and reduced indebtedness, the improvement which all these would help to create is without effect, because the amount of wealth produced in the last year is far below that of the average of years. Seldom in the history of the country was a good crop of cereals more needed: rarely has the failure in the crop been more general. The manufactures of the Dominion, which in late years have assumed a growing importance, are struggling against a variety of adverse conditions, the chief of which is the competition from the United States. The decline in values in greater proportion to that of gold in that country, in the early part of the year, and the lessened home demand in the face of enormous productive power, have caused competition from this quarter to be unusually severe, against which Canadian manufacturers have deemed themselves insufficiently protected. But all these unfavourable symptoms of disturbed trade—whether the result of poor crops, limited lumber demand, or depressed manufactures—all indicate no organic trouble, but are temporary in their character, and time alone is essential to a recovery. Farmers, though the crops of 1876 were a failure, were never so wealthy as a class. While many of them may not have the ready money at hand to promptly pay the yearly account for supplies furnished by their country merchant, they nevertheless are in a much improved condition as compared with former years. A much larger area of land is in a higher state of cultivation, and they are in possession of facilities, in the shape of implements with which to economically and rapidly perform work that years ago was not near as well accomplished with much greater expenditure of time and labour. The development of large areas of country, under the influences of local railways, has been most remarkable, and throughout the Western Province the increased purchasing and debt-paying power amongst the vast majority of consumers is undoubted. It is safe to say that no country in the world possesses a population more industrious, economical, thrifty, and prosperous than the farmers of Canada. Then, with regard to the lumber interest, the present depression can at worst only be temporary, while it has even compensating advantages that the future will disclose. This particular asset in the nation's wealth is gaining in value with a rapidity hardly dreamed of, and the realisation of which is only a question of time. So scarce has accessible and marketable lumber become, that it is alleged that plots of land, now cleared farms, with all appliances, are really less valuable than if the trees stood in undisturbed majesty thereon. Even certain towns in former lumbering districts would bring less than if the land they occupy were covered with pine forests. Over-production has cheapened this great staple, and the waste of years may well be atoned for by a few years of cessation and depression. Nothing will eventually be lost by this delay in realisation ; indeed, the yearly gain in value of this valuable product will more than compensate for what appears to be loss and disaster at the moment. . . . The failures in Canada in the last two years number nearly four thousand, which, occurring among fifty thousand traders, is a proportion indicative of something radically wrong in the trade of a rich country. At this rate, in ten years, every second business man in Canada may succumb! The gross liabilities of failed estates during the two years are over fifty millions of dollars, a sum barely equalled by the entire exports of grain in that period ! Of this fifty millions, at least thirty millions have been irrevocably lost, and when this amount is divided among the limited number of first hands which comprise the merchants, manufacturers, and bankers, the marvel is that they have stood these calamities with so few signs of distress. It is time to adopt some policy that will lessen these disasters. A lessened number of traders, and a higher standard of credit, are the first essentials. Active and available capital, instead of real estate, should be the basis of credit, in addition to capacity already developed and character already tested. Credit based mainly on real estate is a delusion and a snare, for it is not capital available but locked up.

These extracts give a curiously chequered picture,

the 'lights' of which I am disposed only partially to approve. No doubt the farmers in Canada, just as in the Western States of the neighbouring Union, have been prosperous, and are comparatively rich, but they are not so all over the country. It is only in Ontario where farming is at present, and in bad times even, a good occupation. Elsewhere the wealth is not nearly so apparent, and even in Ontario the farming is carried on to an enormous extent on money borrowed from land mortgage companies. This is not in itself a bad thing, but coupled with the manifest bankruptcy of the general trading community and the toppling loads of Government and local debt, it offers a serious warning against congratulation. As to the general trade of the country, nothing could, it is indeed obvious, exceed the reckless speculativeness of its character. Almost every man has gone into business on the neck-or-nothing basis, and the result is failures, losses, and almost every conceivable mischief. The bigness of purpose which characterises colonial traders is, however, a marked feature in the history of all our colonies, and one great cause of their frequent recklessness in getting into debt seems to me to be unquestionably the inflated ideas which the possession of enormous tracts of country has engendered. The mind expands before infinite possibilities; the man feels that he has room, and he straightway launches forth into the most imprudent courses possible.

As with the individual so with the State. It has

been intoxicated by its wealth in real estate, and much of the wild efforts at development and progress which have marked the history of our colonies in the last generation are due to the free manner in which they felt at liberty to trade on this presumed wealth, to mortgage it, to sell it outright, or to give it away in slices large enough sometimes for the wants of a moderately large nation. The land of all the colonies theoretically belongs to the Crown, and has been by it handed over to the communities as they took to themselves parliaments, and became self-governing, and this land these communities have all dealt with in the most reckless fashion possible. I shall have to notice this in connection with every colony, but a brief detail of the habits of unthrift common to them all, though subject to minor variations, may, if given here, save a good deal of repetition. The rational and simplest way of dealing with vast territories owned by a State would be to lease them for, to begin with, a nominal rent to tenants for purposes of reclamation, the State retaining the fee simple and power to revise rents at stated periods of, say, thirty years. By such a course every one of our great colonies would, in course of time, have become possessed of a splendid revenue, which might have taken the place of all other forms of taxation, and the incidence of which would never have been seriously felt, for the increase of rent would probably have fallen far short of the real increment in the value of the land.

This simple plan did not, unhappily, suit the colonists. Their ideas were framed on the familiar lines of English feudalism, and it was impossible to dissociate their minds, therefore, from the notion that the state or community was a big landlord who had almost limitless stretches of spare ground to sell; so, instead of leasing the land, all haste was made to dispose of it outright, at any price it would fetch. Nay, the State would almost give it away, rather than that it should not be got rid of, and in many cases good land has actually cost the colony something considerable to put tenants upon it, rather than realised any substantial sum to the community. In most colonies a good deal of land is always selling, however, at one price or other, and as a rule according to the briskness of immigration is the nominal amount which the State annually pockets under this head.

In Canada, the provincial governments draw the major portion of their revenues—other than the imperial subsidy—from the land sales, which are conducted, to some extent, on the principle of an English building society—failure to pay instalments involving foreclosure. There is also a certain amount of land leased, of course, and there are royalties exacted from mines, but, on the whole, take away the proceeds of sales pure and simple, and every province in Canada would have been in distress ten years ago. And very soon trouble from want of means is certain to come upon them all, for the land will not last for ever, and supposing it did, emigration is not at present working at all satisfactorily. People go to Canada, indeed, but they do not stay there as a rule, and the demand for land is, in consequence, insignificant. Moreover, with the recklessness of spendthrifts who thought of nothing but the pleasures of the hour, large tracts have been passed over to land mortgage companies and to other land speculators, who reap the benefit of such demand as there is, and not the Government; such has been the haste in Canada and elsewhere to fling away for ever the most valuable source of permanent revenues.

It is the uniform custom of the colonies to treat the money obtained from land sales as revenue, in the ordinary sense of the term. Our colonies, in fact, do with the proceeds of the land sales precisely what an Englishman at home would be guilty of if he sold off his estate acre by acre, and spent the proceeds as income. But the vastness of the territories to be sold, and the apparent endlessness of the income which their sale would produce, have blinded people to the true nature of this proceeding, and in the meantime colonial legislatures have been tempted to go heavily into debt because their resources looked so fabulous. There could be no more dangerous mistake, at all events in the case of Canada, who has decidedly outrun her tether, and in doing so is compelled to levy taxes which seriously detract from the value of the land unsold, and retard its sale, which hamper her foreign trade, and reduce her to unthrifty ways of making ends meet. Canada may pull through it all, and, in one way or other, become prosperous, but it will be at a very fearful cost. At the very moment when I write, her mercantile convulsion is staring her in the face. The Hon. Mr. Cartwright, in his budget speech delivered last February, dwelt with great force on the evident spread of wealth which had taken place in Canada during the last few years, and adduced, in evidence, the increased deposits in the banks. It would seem that these have swollen enormously, notwithstanding the mercantile depression and the general state of debt into which Government and people have fallen. A curious commentary on this pleasant picture is, however, afforded by the rapid fall which has lately taken place in all Canadian bank shares—a fall induced by the feeling that many of their assets were not solid, that much of the credit given—which has helped, of course, to swell the total of the 'deposits' at times—has been a source of loss, and that there is danger of a sudden collapse of the whole fabric. Canada may pull through, but till her windy inflations of false credit are all swept away, she must live in a daily dread of a tempest of ruin.

In the meantime her foreign trade is not flourishing in proportion to the demands of the country, or in accordance with this wonderful flow of wealth; on the contrary, for the last three years at least it has decreased in amount with almost every other country with which the Dominion does business. Such as it is, England derives, and has always derived, great benefit from it. Canada supplies us with quantities of timber to the value of from five to six millions sterling a year, with nearly a million and a half's worth of the various kinds of grains and flour, besides considerable quantities of bacon, butter, lard, and other animal products. Her fisheries, especially those of the unabsorbed province of Newfoundland, are also of considerable service to us, and might be more, both to us and to Canada, but for the inroads of United States fishing-boats on Canadian waters. Canada, like all our colonies, in short, supplies us with a certain amount of food at a comparatively cheap rate, and a good deal of raw produce, which are just the things we want. In turn she gets from us all kinds of manufactures which it is for our benefit to sell. The total annual yield of her fisheries alone is, I believe, about 3,000,000*l.*, most of which goes to the United States; but the trade of the Dominion is with England in a preponderating degree, both as regards her imports and exports. On the whole, too, her trade with this country has not suffered quite so severely as with the States, for the simple reason that we are better able to buy than they. The imports of Canada are not, however, drawn from English sources, so much as our large purchases from her might lead one to expect, and it is rather in buying cheap from Canada than in selling dear to her that England prospers. She does not allow us even the privilege of being her sole ocean carrier, for her own shipping is considerable, and, although for the most part engaged in lake, river, and canal traffic, it also carries on the bulk of the business done with the United States, outside which and ourselves Canada has but little trade.

Canadian trade figures, taken generally, have for long given unmistakable signs that her business on the whole was not following its natural course. Canada has been importing beyond her means year after year, or at all events much beyond her exporting capacity, and no doubt she has been able to do so by reason of the money which we have so freely lent her. A new, raw, unopened country can have no margin to trade upon in this fashion except by borrowing, and it follows therefore that, so far as our business with Canada has been based on money lent beyond the true capacity of the country to pay the loans, it has been unsound, and must be reduced. Since 1873 a process of reduction has been going on, which is, therefore, so far healthy; but the limit is, I am persuaded, not yet reached, especially as the exporting capacity of the Dominion has, at the same time, been on the decline.[1] What the healthy basis may be, it would be hard, in

[1] The following official table gives at a glance the export and import trade of the Dominion for the past nine years. It will be seen that the

view of the facts I have indicated, to predict; but it is quite clear, when we consider the large sum which the country has yearly to find for interest on Government loans and on dividends on companies working with foreign capital, there can be no safety till the export figures are in excess of the import. So many things are against Canada, her debt, her disjointedness and isolation, her raw undeveloped condition, the difficulty of keeping population in the wintry north—Manitoba has but 12,000 to 14,000 inhabitants, most of them either trappers or Indians—and her foolish though feeble efforts at protection, that we can never count on her ability to go on working on extended credits, till gradually the country develops up to a capacity great enough to cope with its swollen liabilities.[1] All these

imports uniformly much exceed the exports, a most dangerous and unhealthy occurrence for a new country which is every year increasing its foreign debt. The figures do not include the returns of British Columbia, which are quite insignificant, as in the case of such an out-of-the-world territory is to be expected:—

Fiscal Years ending June 30	Total Exports	Total Imports
1868	$57,567,888	$ 73,459,644
1869	60,474,781	70,415,165
1870	73,573,490	74,814,339
1871	74,173,618	96,098,981
1872	82,689,663	111,430,527
1873	80,789,922	128,011,282
1874	89,351,928	128,213,582
1875	77,886,283	123,070,283
1876	80,299,834	95,056,532

[1] The inhabitants of the new province of Manitoba are mostly halfbred Indians, the descendants of French and Scotch fathers and Indian mothers, and form a race of varying qualities, amongst which industry does not prominently figure. The extremes of heat and cold to which

obstacles stand in her way, and not a few besides these. The customs barrier set up against her by the United States has also, no doubt, prevented any healthy expansion of her trade in that direction, and the accumulated disasters of a forced and unprofitable business have yet to fall upon her before we can say that we know what the country can stand. 'Canada is on the gravel' is a cant saying of her admirers, meaning that she has reached the very foundation of her trade, and cannot sink further; but no dream could be more delusive. Canadian trade has to sink a long way yet before the 'gravel' is reached, and, in common with the rest of the North American Continent, it must pass through a fire which it is but ill able to endure. 'The farmers are wealthy' is another favourite saying, which affords much comfort to many who do not stop to ask how they have become so. These persons forget that bolstered credit, inflated prices, borrowed money, and hectic industries, all tend to raise the cost of living, and by this farmers profit while true

the climate of Central British America is subject, the pest of flies which infest it during its brief summer, and the exceeding difficulty experienced in establishing communications between it and the outer world, must all tend to make it difficult to people with emigrants from Europe. At present it is an almost inaccessible region from Canada, and can only be got at through the States, by which it naturally tends therefore to be absorbed. Indeed, the priest-incited rebellion amongst the French Canadians and half-breeds in the district, which led to the Red River Expedition of 1870, sought a colourable excuse in a professed desire of the malcontents to join the American Union. No railway can for many a day to come open up this region through Canadian territory. It is madness to think of it.

prosperity is being sapped to the core. Wait till the tide has well turned, and then we shall see what the wealth of the farmer means. He stands to be ruined by a big crop in Europe and America. What Canada has most of—beef, pork, corn, wood, and wool—the United States has a great deal more of herself, and what the United States seeks to supply in the shape of manufactures Canada wants to make at home. There is hence no good scope for a large development of reciprocal trade between these two countries at present, least of all a good outlook for the farmer in the event of a succession of splendid harvests. The truth is also, that both the States and Canada have gone on the foolish plan of practically limiting the farming class during the time of seeming manufacturing prosperity. Railroad finances and company speculation, anything but honest tillage of the soil, has become the occupation of a large part of the population, which has thus been drawn into fields of labour which yield no permanent subsistence. By-and-by, when the country becomes crowded with numbers of these people in need of bread, the present farmers may have to face the double danger of low prices and over-competition. And should this same reaction take place, as is probable, in other lands, we shall have the spectacle presented to the world of an agricultural population in many countries temporarily greatly in excess of human necessities, fighting with each other for a market.

At present, therefore, the trade of Canada appears to me destined inevitably to decline further, and considerably, even supposing that the Government and the banks are together able to stave off the day of reckoning. So many other countries are competing with her for the supply of corn, that she is being distanced in the race; and the heavy demands for her pine, which of late years have done something to balance the account, is not likely to continue. Exceptional influences have been at work, at all events in England, entailing an enormous consumption of timber, but these are passing away. Building has been overdone amongst us, and for our permanent demands in respect of railway timbers we have other countries besides Canada to depend on. Australia is capable of taking her place to no small extent in this as in other things, and the forests of South America are gradually opening to our traders. Besides, the administration of the Canadian forests has been of a piece with her other wastefulness. There has been little or no fresh planting, little careful nursing, and it therefore becomes year by year more difficult to get the timber to market in some districts. There has been a belief current that the cleared land would be at once wanted for corn, and it has been left barren. For this mistake, also, Canada will now pay. The wants of the world have not nearly come up to the level of her ambition, and she will have to sink again into the quiet plodding ways which characterised her long before English statesmen egged on her vanity to ape the neighbouring empire. This is not a very satisfactory summing up of the position of this old English settlement, or group of settlements, and I wish heartily that I could make it more cheerful ; but the facts are too many for me. Canada has gone ahead far too fast ; her prosperity has been a delusion, and her reckoning will be heavy. It may rend the new-fangled Dominion to pieces, and will, at all events, seriously disturb the gushing flow of its rather blatant loyalty. England has herself much to blame for this state of affairs, alike by the manner in which she has neglected Canadian interests in the past, and by the foolish measures which she has taken to try and retrieve her errors. There might have been a grand colonial empire in the north acting as a stimulating rival to, and a healthy check on, the overgrown agglomeration of states in the south, but that can never be now. We have spent one way or another nigh 100,000,000*l.* of good English money to prove that it is impossible.

Taken according to population and wealth, Cape Colony, to which we shall now turn, is by no means next to Canada in importance amongst English colonies. New South Wales and Victoria at least are far more wealthy and fully more valuable ; and had I been bound to go by order of wealth I should have taken these now. But not being thus bound, I cannot pass by the Cape. Our settlements there and in Natal are important enough to call for some detailed notice, and at present, when a momentous political question is still agitating the whole of the settlements, English and Dutch, a review of the position ought to be peculiarly interesting, since I cannot deal with their economies without taking note of their political condition. What strikes one at the outset is that most of our dependencies in South Africa have not been peopled in the first instance with Englishmen. As in Canada the French were before us, so at the Cape the Dutch held possession for 150 years before the country passed into our hands, and to this day the majority of the European inhabitants of the colony are of Dutch descent. In some places, and particularly in the newly added Transvaal territory, the people are nearly all Dutch, just as the French in Lower Canada or Quebec almost exclude every other race. From the earliest time of our possession of the Cape this difference in race between the governors and the governed has given us a great deal of trouble, and coupled with the constant bickerings and wars with the native tribes of Kaffirs, Bushmen, and Hottentots, has led to the gradual extension of British territory northward until, exclusive of the still independent Orange River Free State, mostly inhabited by Dutchmen, but including Griqua Land, the Transvaal, and Natal, the Cape Colonies now embrace a territory nearly as large as France and Germany together. This territory is very diversely endowed, some of it being nearly uninhabitable, and a great part of the inland portions of it being as yet fit for little except pasturing; but, on the other hand, there are near the coast and in the river valleys splendid tracts of country capable of the highest agricultural development, and adapted for the cultivation of every description of semi-tropical product, of fruits and vines, which latter can be carried to high perfection. The wines of the Cape are full of promise as articles of European consumption, and might be better known now in this country than they are, did not the 2s. 6d. duty hinder importation. With a larger European population there is thus nothing to hinder the South African settlements from becoming most thriving communities, having the possibility before them of growing into a nation. As it is, many districts which in former years were considered waste and almost barren have been brought into a promising state of fertility, and have proved capable of sustaining large flocks of cattle and sheep. At the present time the quantity and value of wool exported from South Africa to the mother-country are greater than from any part of the world, except the Australian colonies. 'Cape wool' is an important factor in our trade, therefore, and the south-eastern town of Port Elizabeth has through the expansion of this trade become an important centre of business. The flocks of sheep which the Cape and Natal possess exceed those of Canada by some eight millions, including African sheep; and year by year their general trade increases as well as their revenue. In 1870 the revenue of Cape Colony alone amounted to but 735,000*l.*, in 1875 it had risen to 1,015,000*l.* The least prosperous of our South African possessions is Natal, which has somehow never become a favourite resort of emigrants, in spite of its natural advantages. It requires to discover diamonds or gold in order to obtain the raw material which it wants to subdue the land. Yet Natal is not quite standing still. Its exports were smaller last year than they have been since 1873, but they were three times as much as in 1867, and her total trade is now about 1,700,000*l.* a year, which is not amiss for some 20,000 Europeans or less, and a total population of little over 300,000, mostly Zulus. Natal has, of course, borrowed money—no British colony could live otherwise—but it has not yet betrayed any wild extravagance; and, could it only get Europeans of a good stamp to emigrate to its unoccupied lands, might in time become one of the most flourishing provinces of the dreamt-about South African Confederation. Its soil is capable of producing sugar of good quality, and will also grow coffee and most excellent cotton, although the frequent rains in some districts rather hinder the successful cultivation of the latter. For a long time Cape Colony itself was most wretchedly provided with population, but the diamond discoveries in the territory of the half-breeds—in Griqua Land West and the Orange River Free State—and of gold in the Transvaal, have given a little fillip to immigration. The population is still, however, very sparse, and were it not that a certain amount of labour is got out of the natives, particularly in the inland districts, there would be little or no progress made. Behm and Wagner, in their admirable compilation already cited,[1] estimate the total population of British South Africa at 1,339,000, of which 720,984 fall to Cape Colony proper, including British Kaffraria. Cape Colony has, however, only 236,783 inhabitants of European origin. All the rest are either Kaffirs, Hottentots, or other native races, except about 11,000 Malays. And throughout South Africa the state of things is the same. The Transvaal territory just added to the British dominions has a population of about a quarter of a million, of which only some 50,000 to 60,000 are whites, mainly Dutch; and round its borders or between them and Natal it seems probable that native tribes numbering over two million souls are to be found, with whom there may be many difficulties before the hold of the English is assured all over the land. These are important figures to bear in mind in judging of the position of this extensive country. They reveal to us at the very outset how much our vaunted success as colonists has here also to be proved. South Africa is, as yet, a nation only in embryo. Not only that, but it is a nation in which the British element amongst the whites is greatly

[1] *Die Bevölkerung der Erde:* No. 49 of Petermann's *Mittheilungen.*

in a minority. So much so, that in the event of a confederation of the various states and provinces into a South African Republic, where all provinces would have equal rights, it is open to question whether the English influence would remain paramount in the country. I am inclined to think that it would not, and therefore do not feel disposed to accord that unmeasured praise to the federation policy of Lord Carnarvon which it is customary to give Mr. Molteno, the Cape Prime Minister. at the time of the agitation started by his Lordship, appears to me to have had sound reasons for doubting whether the states and provinces were yet ripe for such federation. Before it takes place, as it probably will some day, there ought to be a larger influx of English settlers, so as to secure the due preponderance to the English tongue and English ideas in the future administration of the country. This has become more necessary than ever since Sir Theophilus Shepstone annexed the Transvaal. It should never be forgotten, as Mr. Froude has so forcibly pointed out in his memorandum to Lord Carnarvon on this subject,[1] that the Dutch have not many reasons for loving us. Throughout our connection with the colony we have subjected them to many injustices, some inflicted wantonly, some in ignorance. The unlucky Boers have been held up to the reprobation of

---

[1] *Vide* Correspondence on South African Affairs, *Commons Papers*, No. 1399, 1876.

English sectaries as monsters of cruelty to the natives, and under the force of gusts of missionary zeal we have often done them, there can be no question, grievous wrong. So little have they relished our rule, therefore, that for a time they may be said to have become almost nomadic, wandering northward and eastward to escape from us, until, at length, we forced them, in a measure, to constitute themselves into two free republics in the very heart of South Africa, shut out from the sea, surrounded by natives, many of them hostile, and capable of giving unpleasant effect to their hostility, and all of them treacherous and thievish.

By thus driving the Dutch outside the pale of English dominion, we, as it were, confessed our inability to govern them, and we certainly helped to increase their abhorrence of us. This isolation has also tended to sink them in ignorance, and to produce many complications on their frontiers, although they have governed themselves and their surrounding natives in, many respects much better than we anticipated. Their disputes with these have plunged them into debt, however, and their trade isolation has left them little opportunity of growing richer so as to be able to bear their increased burdens. Thus, altogether the quarter of a century or so of their existence has been a time of decadence and gradual approach towards almost helpless subjection to the bolder among the native races. And thus we are, in self-defence, compelled again to step in and take one of these states into British keeping, profiting territorially by the very antipathies which sent the Dutch settlers of the Cape on their wanderings.

Once independent in name, our injustice to these Dutch might have been considered at an end, but it was nothing of the kind. We have hampered their dealings with the natives, not yet at all events capable of being anything but subject and governed; and we have annexed territory to which we had no clear right, directly it became, by the discovery of diamonds upon it, a worthy object of cupidity. To my mind, there can be no doubt that the Dutchmen have been right in many of the disputes they have had with us. We have maligned them and abused them, not once or twice, but dozens of times. If they should, therefore, get control of the Cape by their voting power, there is fair reason for supposing that they may seek to cast off all allegiance to England; and the true way, the only way open to us, to prevent this is to encourage Englishmen and Scotchmen to emigrate to this overlooked but splendid South African territory. There is room for millions where there are thousands in that land, and the more go-ahead qualities of the English would form an admirable set-off as well as stimulus to the steady, quiet, slow, and unprogressive Dutch. At the same time the granting of self-governing institutions might, after this nation had been thoroughly made, nearly put an end to the chances of renewed irritation between the races over the wrongs which the conquered have had to suffer from the conquerors. There has been no greater mistake in our South African policy than our ostracism of the Dutch, only we need not cap that mistake by rushing now to the opposite extreme and giving them the control of the entire territory.

But there is another reason for the strong encouragement of emigration to the Cape to be found in the remarkable stability of some of the African races in the presence of the stronger European. As the figures show us, South Africa may be said to swarm with natives where the European is absolute master. The Bechuanos and Hottentots form his servants and the Kaffirs his dangerous, treacherous, and often openly hostile neighbours. Without a large supply of European settlers there seems to be danger that those already there may prove unable to hold thorough control over these confused native elements. Natal and British Kaffraria, the Orange River Free State, and our own more northern settlements, are all threatened more or less seriously by this race difficulty, which is aggravated rather than lessened by the numerous mixed breeds which the loose habits of the European immigrants have called into being. It was the threatening aspect of the native tribes which more than anything else offered a colourable justification for our summary absorption of the Transvaal; and the responsibility we have thus assumed, although it may have taken away the immediate danger, is of the gravest possible character. What shall we do with all these blacks in the event of our succeeding in keeping peace? How shall we control them, and what position will they hold in the future within British territory? The annexation has perhaps lessened one or two dangers that immediately threatened us, but others more serious still loom in the near future. And while all these difficulties beset our territories in South Africa we can hardly call them a great possession or cite them as a sample of successful British colonisation. Territorially, South Africa is great, and its natural resources are magnificent, but we have not yet stamped it with the genius of self-development and made its people the father of a mighty nation. It remains to be seen whether the Transvaal will prove an acquisition, and whether the native tribes will settle down there or in Natal and the Cape, like the negroes in Barbadoes or in Maryland and New Orleans, in moderately peaceable juxtaposition to the whites.

Thus the need of the Cape to my mind is not at present federation, but emigrants, and I cannot but regret that so much is done to puff up some of our other possessions while the Cape is comparatively neglected. If the Government would only encourage the transplanting from this country of farmers oppressed with rack rents and the competition of cheap-producing lands, to such regions as are to be found in South Africa, where landlords and game laws flourish not, it would do infinitely more good than by preaching peace, unity, and concord amongst sections of communities not yet ready for that gospel. The race difficulty may be made an insurmountable one by the premature enunciation of this evangel, whereas, left to work its way to a natural solution, it might in time lead to the creation of a nation possessed of admirable unity and great qualities. The French, German, Portuguese, Dutch, and English elements which are to be found amongst the people ought to be capable of producing this result, and of making South Africa one of the greatest monuments of English aggression and race vitality in the whole world. But there must be less management from home, more latitude allowed to Governors in dealing with these natives—always hitherto a fruitful source of trouble and strife—and far more sincere endeavours made to get the colony peopled so as to make the English dominant in numbers both over the Dutch and the warlike blacks within the pale. However grand in the abstract or profitable in the concrete a pastoral life may be, it is none the less a primitive one, and no colony can become a great nation which does not cease to be merely pastoral. Nay, more, under modern conditions a good part of the apparent prosperity of such a community is waste. The best is not made of the land; it is not husbanded or tilled, hardly cleared, only wandered over, with tame flocks substituted for wild beasts, and its substance eaten up.

Since we have possessed South Africa it has grown, but the growth has been more in size than in substantial development towards a true permanent settlement of the country and such progress as we have made has cost us many miserable wars with miserable barbarous tribes, some of which a more uniformly stern policy might have mercifully prevented. The recent prosperity of European countries, and especially of England, has, however, reacted favourably on the trade of the Cape, and it has fortunately escaped in some measure the 'progress' fever which has swept over nearly every other colony. It was not till 1872 that self-government on its present basis was finally settled for the Cape and Natal, and before that date South Africa stumbled on in the hands of the Governors more or less busy with the inland Boers and the everlasting Kaffir or Bushmen disputes, making the Imperial Government pay what it could towards the cost of the perpetual bickerings and occasional flashes of war. Since the Colonial Government became possessed of taxing powers, however, there has been a considerable advance made in more respects than one, and the Cape, like our other possessions, now borrows freely, in token of its right to be considered civilised. The position is still very favourable compared with most of those, and the aims of the new State are thoroughly practical and good. The increase in her revenue also amply justifies so far the outlay of money.[1] At the same time it appears to me that without more population it is dangerous even for the Cape to push the borrowing system much further. There is a great deal of what I may call superstition about the value of railways and costly public works to such an undeveloped new country. They are not alike valuable even in different countries which may be classed as settled, and before pushing them far eastward or northward in South Africa it should be well considered whether good waggon-roads would not serve instead. The experience of the United States and of Russia is so far decidedly against the profitableness of expensively-made railways far inland in a sparsely peopled agricultural country, and few of the States of the Union are now more thinly populated than the inland districts at the Cape. There is no passenger traffic to speak of, and the raw produce of such territories cannot bear remunerative freights. Until there is a

[1] The trade of the Cape has made very satisfactory progress, as well as that of Natal. According to the official document lately issued along with the prospectus of the last instalment of the Cape debt, the average annual exports for the five years ended 1870 was 2,332,000*l.*, and for the five years ended 1875, 4,012,000*l.* The exports of 1875 alone amounted to 4,088,000*l.* Equally remarkable has been the growth of the imports, which, of course, latterly betray the usual effect of borrowed money—the figures for 1875, for instance, showing an excess of about 1,500,000*l.* over the exports. The total trade of South Africa, outward and inward, is estimated at about 15,000,000*l.* to 17,000,000*l.*, the greater part of which is carried on between the Settlements and the United Kingdom. The trade of Holland with her old possession is, and has always been, extremely insignificant.

varied and heavy trade both ways, the less expensive roads, with their bullock-waggons, would therefore appear to be undoubtedly the best.[1] Roads the Cape unquestionably needs, for it has no navigable rivers; but railways, except inland in one or two directions, for short distances, would only prove a wasteful folly. There is no town in South Africa possessed of 10,000 European inhabitants, except Cape Town; and, without inhabitants of a kind given to movement, how can railways pay? At present the railway projects of the Cape are, as I think, very ambitious, though modest compared with those of Canada, which run over certain almost unpeopled districts with a network reminding one of the labyrinth around Clapham Junction. There is a line from Cape Town to the north-westward by Wellington and Worcester to Beaufort near the Nieuveldt hills, a distance of over two hundred miles; and lines start from Port Elizabeth and Port Alfred, running to Graaf Reynet and Cradock, by Uitenhage and Graham's Town; while yet another system proposes to penetrate towards the Orange River from East London. To some extent this plan of running lines for certain distances inland, from good

---

[1] These bullock-waggons seem to me to be a peculiarly valuable institution. They are of great capacity and strength, and travel at the rate of from twelve to twenty miles a-day, according to the nature of the road. For conveying the produce of the far interior and supplying the wants of farmers, there could not be a better medium in the present state of South African Settlements.

seaports may, as I have said, be justified; but these projects undoubtedly carry them too far. The western system, from Cape Town, ought to stop at Worcester, 122 miles inland; and the 'Midland,' from Port Elizabeth should rest at Uitenhage, unless the 'North-Western,' also from the same port, were dropped, when the line might be carried to Graham's Town. Probably this extension would not pay directly any more than the Western to Worcester, but it would involve no serious loss such as will be sure to fall on the colony if lines are to be pushed inland beyond the limit of towns and paying trade. Natal has also her railway projects and is now borrowing a million and a quarter for the purpose of making three short lines of a total length of 105 miles. They will probably benefit the contractors much more than the colony for many a day, and so weak a colony acts very foolishly in thus hastily pledging its credit. Still more foolish will be any attempt to carry a line of railway into the Transvaal, a project already mooted however, and likely enough to be carried out if the glow over the annexation does not speedily die out. In such countries above all others, where the trade is of a very primitive kind, where the formation of roads offers no great difficulty, and where the coast is at no immense distance, railways ought to follow rather than precede population.

It must not be forgotten that there is not the least

likelihood of South Africa developing manufactures of its own. So far as has yet been discovered, there are no rich stores of coal or iron to form the basis of such manufactures. But we invariably find that when once a new country has got railways it betrays a craving for mills and looms and all the paraphernalia of production. It finds, of course, that these railways are expensive to maintain and wants to create traffic for them. If the Cape gets into this position, and has not the means to sustain it, it will be temporarily ruined; and the best way to keep out of it is to be modest, to encourage agricultural settlers, to be content with good roads and old-fashioned bullock-waggons, and to study to keep the taxes low.

For not only has the lack of population to be taken into account, but also the nature of the produce, which, in the case of South Africa, consists, and must consist, almost entirely of articles of food and raw materials of manufactures. These, in the present developed stage of many parts of the world whence competition comes, can afford little for land carriage. The herds of cattle or sheep, for example, which may be in the far interior of South Africa, are more cheaply driven towards the coast alive than they could be carried by railway, and their hides and fleeces do not require to be hurried to the coast in forty-eight hours to catch the mail boat at a given date. Conceive, also, the strange absurdity of running a train across a plain through ostrich farms, where there would be only bundles of feathers to transport sufficient in a year perhaps to furnish loads for a dozen or so of ordinary drays, and one can then realise what railways in the interior of Africa may mean. Her products are all of the crude kind, such as copper ore, feathers, hides, ivory, wool and hair, except a little prepared fruit and wine ; and her imports need be in no hurry to get inland, consisting as they do for the most part of articles of food and clothing, such as wheat and rice—for the Cape does not grow even enough corn for its own wants—cotton and woollen manufactures, and so on, all of which the people do not require express trains to take to their doors.

Again, our South African colonies have a magnificent coast-line, and the provinces already most occupied lie nearest the coast, so that, at the very most, all that can at present be wanted to open up the country is short lines of railway inland from the handiest port of shipment to the handiest up-country market depôt where roads would converge. I dwell on this because I think South Africa, but recently emancipated from Imperial control, has shown a rather dangerous tendency to go ahead in this direction. In 1869, its debt, including that of Natal, was under 1,500,000*l*., and now the total is nearly 6,500,000*l*., including the Cape and Natal Loans recently issued. This growth is due principally to the Public Works Department, and cannot be too carefully watched. South Africa **may** have a great future before it, if it only would abstain from mortgaging its chances.

At the same time it has to be admitted that of late years the trade and revenues of the Cape have shown quite an extraordinary expansion. Every year since 1871 there has been a surplus of revenue over expenditure, although the expenditure has been steadily growing. In 1875 this surplus reached 588,142*l.*, the total revenue being 1,602,918*l.*, and the expenditure 1,014,776*l.* A great part of this balance has been devoted to public works, as it fairly and legitimately might be. It must not be forgotten, however, that one considerable portion of the so-called revenue is not revenue at all, but capital, as I have already explained, and that the prosperity is so far only the result of an alienation of future State resources in the shape of land sold. The land sales and land rents produced together some 700,000*l.* of the total revenue of 1875, or nearly one-half. The rentals are, of course, most legitimate sources of income, but not so the proceeds of sales, which ought to be treated as capital; and I think no better argument in favour of a State's chariness in parting with rights over the land could well be adduced than the prices at which much of the soil of Cape Colony is alienated. Land can be bought often at a shilling an acre, and in the Transvaal has been sold as low as sixpence an acre, the Government surrendering all rights, except a small quit rent, which in a few years' time bears no adequate proportion whatever to the value of the soil, yet which cannot be increased. The prosperity of the Cape finances on this head ought not, therefore, to be made too much of; nor as immigrants flow in must her financiers be deluded by the show of wealth which this invariably produces. That they will alter their policy so as to secure to the State some portion of the increment of land value is, I fear, more than can be expected, but if they did so they might, after waiting a few years, build all the railways they require out of surplus revenue and rejoice in progress without State debt.

As to the indications which the customs receipts give of growing prosperity there is much more satisfaction to be expressed. No doubt, the loans which the Cape Government has raised of late years have swollen the imports till they exceed the exports in value, and the customs receipts have been thereby increased; but, that granted, the trade of the colony has on the whole made very satisfactory progress; and it is a trade which has benefited Great Britain almost exclusively. Our merchants have been the factors for Cape wool, and our ships have brought it to Europe. For the most part, also, the diamonds, gold, copper, ostrich feathers, wine, and other products which it is able to export have all gone to swell the totals of the trade which passes through English hands, and the bills representing which are finally settled in London.

So with the imports of the Cape and Natal ; they consist mostly of British manufactures and as the prosperity of these settlements increases, and their European population multiplies, the demand for these is sure to increase, for the reason I have already given—they cannot manufacture much for themselves. At present the Cape appears to be buying too much, and extending her credit rather deeply, but should she cease to borrow, and at the same time carefully limit the issues of paper currency by her banks, the trade account will very soon adjust itself. Her enormous exports of diamonds have, in recent years, no doubt helped the inflation too, and must be taken into account as a credit in her favour. It is said that the Great Kimberley Mine alone has furnished some 12,000,000*l.* worth of these stones, the sale of which in Europe added enormously to the buying power of the colony. Good while it lasted, this wealth is, however, only temporary, and should not be used to build a debt upon.

As the tariff is light both at the Cape and at Natal, there is practically little to hinder the natural development of trade with the mother-country, and now that two magnificent lines of steamers run regularly to most South African ports, we may reasonably hope to see a steady growth of the business between these and England. The Cape and Natal have not yet entered the competition either as sources of meat supply, or as corn or cotton growers, but there is no reason in the world why they should not do so in all three capacities. They are almost as favourably placed as America, and more so than the Australian colonies, and only want small capitalists as farmers and exporters to begin the work. Looking, indeed, at the natural advantages which these small African settlements possess —at their favourable climate, their rich tracts of soil, their immense plains capable of fertilisation if judiciously tilled and planted with trees; their mineral wealth in copper and possibly in coal, their splendid harbours, and their central position—I should say that they give infinitely more promise of future greatness than Canada.

But, I repeat, they must not be left empty. We cannot have a continual feud in progress between the inland Boers and the natives, nor the lives and property of settlers, Dutch and English, even occasionally at the mercy of these ruthless savages. The country must be fostered, emigration encouraged and stimulated, and the dream of universal federation and peace given up just for the present. If the Dutch settlers are all to be brought back within the range of British rule as those of the Transvaal have been, they must be made to understand that it is British rule and not the Government of the Parliament at Cape Town; that in return for protection they must submit, for example, to have certain privileges in their dealings with the natives curtailed for a time. This need imply no injustice, but it would hardly be fair, on many grounds, to the rest of the colonists to allow the suffrages of the Dutch, many of whom hate England cordially, to embarrass or even to thwart English intentions and an English policy in the development of the country and in the treatment of these troublesome natives. Fortunately, the English settler has penetrated in considerable numbers into both the Orange State and the Transvaal, and the process of assimilation is already on foot. Out of the mixed races which are thus fusing in Africa I think we may hope to see come a nation possessed of many high qualities. It will not, however, be just yet. For the present, I fear, South Africa, like other lands, may disappoint us. There will be no violent expansion, no great rush of prosperity. There may be rather an appearance of reaction and a time of dull business, should the present modes of opening up the country be persevered in, or should we have, one of these days, to encounter another native war on a larger scale than the petty squabbles which have sprung out of the Transvaal misgovernment and annexation.

CHAPTER XII.

AUSTRALIA AND NEW ZEALAND.

IF the newness of colonies like Canada and the Cape strikes a student of English migrations, that of the Australian and New Zealand colonies must do so still more. As colonies in the modern acceptation of the term, not one of these is two generations old, and even as a penal settlement New South Wales—the mother-colony, as it is fond of being styled—only dates from just ninety years ago. For a long time the magnificent continent now divided amongst five independent colonial establishments, as well as the neighbouring island of Tasmania, lay neglected in the fashion common with English Governments. Their only use in the estimation of these Governments was as a convenient place for the deportation of the home criminals, of whom our admirable civilisation furnished a substantial annual supply. Hence, for the first half-century of their existence the Australian settlements attracted few respectable inhabitants, and gave next to no sign of their future greatness and commercial activity. In 1825 fully one third of the population of New South Wales was composed of convicts; and at the time of the first gold discoveries, in 1851, the entire inhabitants of that colony, which then comprised both Victoria and Queensland, did not number 200,000. So with the other settlements which now exist as independent colonies. Tasmania, or Van Diemen's Land, said to have been originally discovered by a Dutch navigator named Tasman in 1642, and which was subsequently visited by both French and English ships before England fastened on it as a convict prison, ranks next in age to New South Wales. Yet it had not 10,000 inhabitants in 1825, at which date Queensland, Western and South Australia, and New Zealand had not, one may say, been heard of. In short, a generation ago, or hardly, the entire English settlers in Australasia did not probably number more than 300,000, if so many, and to-day they exceed 2,000,000.

This is newness and expansion united in a fashion which the world has never seen before, and, taken in conjunction with the migrations from the mother-country to America, Africa, and Asia, offers food for much speculation. By what extraordinary force was the English race suddenly stimulated into an expansiveness which made it found nations, and, as it were, overrun the world almost within the space of at most two generations? Here we have lived for many centuries cooped up in great measure within these islands, increasing in numbers but slowly, and seeing other races distance us in the task of subduing the savage and solitary places of the earth, till suddenly in these latter days we have overflowed in all directions, and, outstripping every competitor, have planted English-speaking communities east and west and south. We have done this, too, without betraying any signs of exhaustion at home, but, on the contrary, with every fresh offshoot have increased in prosperity, wealth, and numbers beyond all precedent. This is a very remarkable fact, which is perhaps yet too intimately connected with our new modern life to be easily explained; but it must make us at least cautious in coming to hasty conclusions as to the future of most of these offshoots. We dare not affirm positively either that the force which led to their upspringing is spent, or that it will continue. It is, however, unquestionably the fact that the peopling of Australia and New Zealand has had something in it akin to a spasmodic outburst. They were neglected, little visited, and barely delivered from their position as convict prisons, when the discoveries of gold in 1851, 1852, and 1865 brought a rush on one and another of the settlements which threatened to overwhelm their undeveloped and scanty resources. In the three years, 1853–55, about 180,000 persons were registered as having left the United Kingdom alone for Australasia, and up to 1876 they have flowed thither and to New Zealand in a diminished but still steady stream; the total emigration between 1853 and 1876 being set down at 804,272, or nearly one-third of the emigration to the United States during the same period, and 20 per cent. of the total exodus from the mother-country.[1] Each colony, as gold was found in it, drew a crowd also which was not English merely, but French and German and American, and by this means the raw material of future nations has been gathered together with extraordinary rapidity. Undoubtedly, but for this stimulus, the Australian colonies would not have yet been worth much to the mother-country, or very promising in themselves. But it is obvious that we must not regard this kind of thing as likely to recur. The novelty of gold-finding has died out for Australia and New Zealand, and the business of gold-mining has settled down into the humdrum affair of capitalists guiding organised labour and making what profit, or submitting to what loss, that labour yields. Gold-mining, in short, is in Australia much like lead-mining at home—a speculative affair, conducted on sober commercial principles. Not one-twentieth part of the crowds of people who raced to the 'diggings' five-and-twenty years ago, when gold was an all-potent allurement, made money or remained long at the work, but, once there, they had to find the means of living, and they became squatters, farmers, cattle-keepers, bushmen, or thieves, as their nature or chance determined,

[1] *Vide* Tables in Mr. Giffen's admirable Report on the papers relating to Emigration for 1876.

doing on the whole an incalculable amount of good to the new countries in ways which were never dreamt of by them when they set out. The total yield of gold in Australia and New Zealand from the time of the discovery of the metal in Victoria till last year is estimated at about 247,300,000*l.*, independently of what may have been carried off privately ; but that is a small sum compared with the wealth which has come of the flocks and herds and the corn which the soil of these colonies has been made to sustain and yield. At the present time Australia is richer in sheep, for example, than any other country in the world. The colony of New South Wales alone has within a third of the number of sheep possessed by the United States, and the wealth of all these colonies is in this respect prodigious.[1] Equally

[1] The handiest data for a comparison of the agricultural wealth of the colonies with European States and America are to be found in the *Agricultural Returns of Great Britain*. According to the tables appended to the number for 1876, the Australian colonies own altogether about 52,000,000 sheep, of which the New South Wales portion reaches about 25,000,000, or nearly half. New Zealand possesses nearly 12,000,000; so that altogether this group of English colonies has fully 64,000,000. This is a far larger number than any single European country possesses, Russia claiming to have only about 48,000,000, and France only 26,000,000, while Germany has only about 22,000,000. The United States, even, comes far behind with but 34,000,000. Of course, sheep are in a measure the peculiar objects of the Australian landowner's care, and a comparison made in other kinds of animals brings them out in a much less paramount position. Yet New South Wales, if taken by itself, bears the test in horses and cattle remarkably well, that colony having more than 3,000,000, or nearly as many as Italy, which has a fiftyfold larger population. Judged by population, indeed, it is astonishing that these colonies, taken altogether, raise so much 'meat,' for till within the last few years their cattle could be of little use to them except for sustaining an export trade in hides. Compared with other English colonies, the position of the Australian and

remarkable has been their progress in the cultivation of the land, which enables nearly all the colonies to be now large exporters of grain ; and I cannot, indeed, sum this matter up better than by quoting the glowing words of Mr. G. H. Reid, in his essay on New South Wales, published at Sydney last year. He says :—

If proofs of material progress are demanded, we can point to a population which rose in thirty years from 214,000 to 2,000,000 souls, or 834 per cent.; whilst during the same period the population of Canada and the United States increased by 660 and 126 per cent. We can point to a trade which rose in the same generation from less than 6,000,000*l.* to over 63,000,000*l.*, or 950 per cent.; whilst the increase in British trade was only 400 per cent., that of the United States 335 per cent., and that of Canada about 650 per cent.; and if told that Australian progress has seen its best days, we reply that the trade of Australasia rose from 63,000,000*l.* in 1871 to 87,000,000*l.* in 1874, an increase of 38 per cent. in three years. If we inquire further, we learn that upwards of 5,600,000 tons of shipping entered and cleared the ports of the colonies in 1874 ; that there are 70,000,000 head of live stock on our pastures, and nearly 5,000,000 acres of land under cultivation. There are 2,000 miles of railway open, and a far greater length in progress or projected. Upwards of 26,000,000 miles of telegraph, to which additions are being rapidly made, unite every part of the group with the rest of the world. The annual revenues of the several Governments approach 14,000,000*l.* sterling. The reader has only

New Zealand settlements is altogether paramount, Canada having fewer cattle and little more than a seventh of the number of sheep possessed by New South Wales alone, and the wealth of the Cape in this respect barely reaching that of New Zealand. Canada and the Cape excel most of the new colonies, however, in the extent of land under cultivation, as with their larger populations they ought to do.

to contrast these facts with our sparse population to get a true idea of Australian progress.

This is a very striking picture, and a true one, and it proves very abundantly that those who came to dig for gold stayed to perform labour more permanently valuable. The gold nevertheless lay, in other ways than as a bait to draw human beings, at the bottom of this extraordinary prosperity. It gave a handful of men an unprecedented command over every civilising agency for years, such as no people but the Spaniards of Mexico and Peru have ever had. When the Australians could export six, eight, or ten millions a year of the precious metals, it needs no argument to prove that they must be able to buy everything necessary for the development of the soil in a profusion no other people ever enjoyed. It is no wonder, with that fact in view, that the Victorians alone estimate the value of the machinery and improvements which they employ in tilling the land at over 10,000,000*l.*; and, of course, England reaped at first nearly the whole benefit of this prodigious export of gold, not only because it was brought to her shores for the purpose of being sold all over the world to the highest bidder, but because the Australians, by their very wants, made it a most potent stimulant of her trade. They had no time, while suffering from the gold fever, to produce anything on the spot—everything was imported, ready made, from 'home;' and thus, almost from the first, the gain to English manufacturing interests was very great. The gold worked on the interchange of traffic between the new lands and England with all the potency of huge loans—everything was prosperous, everything progressive and buoyant, and on the whole there could be no prosperity more soundly based, less liable to suffer collapse. There is, however, a side to this picture of prosperity which we must not forget, because, without noticing it, the position and prospects of these settlements could not be justly estimated. Australia has prospered beyond all precedent as a whole; but all the colonies have not prospered alike, nor have they all dealt in the same wisdom with their seemingly exhaustless wealth. They did not all, indeed, enjoy a gold rush, and some of those that did appear to have had their heads turned by the possession of it a good deal further than their safety warrants, and others have rather unwisely sought, without it, to imitate the extreme rapidity with which their gold-owning neighbours have advanced from raw settlements to rich colonies, and from rich colonies to ambitious embryo States. We find a general indication of this in the rather heavy debt that some of them have contrived to heap up—an item not included in Mr. Reid's glowing summary. For all the colonies its aggregate at the present time is about from 60,000,000$l.$ to 62,000,000$l.$ exclusive of the municipal and other local bonds which have been incurred. Even were this debt uniformly distributed, it would be a serious burden for a new region possessing only 2,000,000 inhabitants; but some colonies bear a lighter burden, some a heavier, and one or two of those that bear the heavier seem to me to be courting bankruptcy. New Zealand, for instance, has a debt of about 48*l*. per head of the population, and that of Queensland is about 40*l*.; and this in countries hardly yet capable of internal taxation is really enormous. No doubt, besides the gold vanity which acted on the former, and the emulative ardour spurring on the latter to rival its 'mother,' New South Wales— from whose apron-strings it parted so recently as 1859 —the possession of so much land has had a baneful influence, as I have already noticed, in inducing this extravagant mortgaging of the future. And that makes the case all the more serious, as we shall see.

But I must not pass an indiscriminate censure, nor, even in speaking of this debt, class it with those enormous piles of obligations which older countries have heaped together, either in wild extravagance or in wars, and for every conceivable iniquity. The very heaviest debt which any Australian colony bears has at least been incurred for a practical, useful purpose; and the 'per-head' test of a capacity to carry such debt ought not to be applied to them very rigidly. It may well be that communities composed almost exclusively of energetic members of the English race can afford to take on themselves burdens much heavier than the weak and nerveless French Canadians or the Kaffirs and Hottentots of the Cape and Natal. Soils differ too, and trade facilities, as well as mineral resources, so that, of necessity, one must examine the state of these colonies in some detail before endeavouring to form a judgment as to the prospects of their continued growth and prosperity. And I shall begin with New South Wales, not only because it is the oldest, and in some respects most prosperous of all the Australasian colonies, but because the lessons it affords are most valuable as helps towards an estimate of the position of the rest. Indeed I may say frankly, at once, that I am attracted to New South Wales because of its vigour, its wise fiscal economy, and its free trade.

For a long time after Victoria found its gold it distanced the mother-colony altogether, but of late years the latter has drawn to the front, and in many respects it is now the most promising of all the offshoots of England. It has a population of some 630,000, and an enormous wealth in cattle and sheep, besides mines of gold, iron, copper, and coal, which contribute not a little to the general prosperity. It imports from the United Kingdom alone more than 6,000,000*l*. worth a year, chiefly in articles of clothing, hardware, and machinery, and its total trade outward and inward reached 27,000,000*l*. in 1875. The gross revenue last year amounted to more than 5,000,000*l*., or fully 900,000*l*. in excess of that of 1875, and its public debt is only some 13,000,000*l*.—not three years' revenue. This dry enumeration might easily be filled up to great length, but the skeleton must suffice. It is enough to record that here we have a very thriving progressive community ; and in my opinion New South Wales is so to no small extent because she has been wise enough to let her resources have tolerably free play. Her customs duties—the taxes, that is, which almost alone are left for a young English colony to levy effectually—are, as a rule, remarkably light, except on some kinds of iron and some food grains ; and it is the intention of the present Government to lighten them still further by the transfer of some fifteen articles to the free list, substituting in their stead an Excise on tobacco, which will probably yield a good deal more than the 20,000*l*. or so lost by the transfer.

Next to the tariff, New South Wales is, no doubt, prosperous through its splendid mineral resources, which enable it to take advantage of that tariff, and to become, in a measure, the manufacturing colony of Australasia No better example of the value of free trade to the manufacturer could well be found than the progress which New South Wales is making in this direction.[1] Without doubt this progress tells upon our

[1] Mr. G. H. Reid gives a valuable table in his essay on New South Wales, showing the development of the manufacturing industries of that

intercourse with this colony. New South Wales is so self-dependent that she does not need to buy from us so heavily as she would do were her system protectionist. It is estimated, for example, by Mr. Reid that New South Wales provides herself out of her own resources with 10,500,000*l.* out of a total demand amounting to 22,162,000*l.* for the mean population of the colony in 1870-74. That is to say, calculating that in the years 1860 to 1864 the population required a certain quantity of imported goods, Mr. Reid estimates that as those requirements have in 1870-74 by so much fallen behind the increase in population, the home industries have therefore made the difference good. I doubt whether this reasoning will altogether hold water, because the state of the popula-

colony since 1855. I select one or two of the more important of these as an illustration of the text:

	1855	1864	1874
Agricultural implement works	—	—	45
Sugar works	—	1	67
Woollen cloth	5	5	8
Tanneries	60	94	114
Soap and candle	18	29	31
Distilleries and sugar refineries	3	16	55
Engineering works, foundries, &c.	15	108	158
Ship and boat builders	—	7	103
Shoe factories	—	—	50
Clothing factories	—	—	17
Coach and waggon factories	—	—	99

Besides these, there are of course many industries which are almost essentially local, and necessary wherever civilised populations gather, as well as those which arise directly out of the agricultural development of the colony, such as flour mills, saw mills, lime kilns, and wine presses, all of which show remarkable increase in numbers, and the wine presses especially, which have increased in ten years from one to 367.

tion is not now what it was ten years ago—there is probably a larger population of young in it now than then—but there is, no doubt, a certain amount of truth in the conclusion. We are not so much a necessity to New South Wales in many respects as we were ten or fifteen years ago, and her imports would be much less than they now are were she not compelled by the narrowness of her cultivated area to import nearly a million and a half's worth of flour and bread. In this respect also she is, according to Mr. Reid's tables, less dependent than she formerly has been; and it would probably be far more satisfactory for the trade of the mother-country with the colony were this dependence to disappear altogether. What New South Wales spends in bread must in her condition, to a certain extent, represent unthrift. As to her manufactures, however, we can well afford to witness the independence of this colony, seeing that her wealth is to a great extent still our wealth, and that it will probably continue to be so for many a day to come. The chief currents of her trade, as it were, will, through her banks, through English capital and shipping, and English dominance in Asia, continue in our hands, and we shall be partakers of her wealth however prosperous she may become—to the benefit of both countries, for it is meet that the hoardings of the old country should find fruitful employment in the new.

Distance must, moreover, check our supremacy as

manufacturers of many articles; but it does not yet fight against us as sea-carriers, nor as cotton-spinners or weavers, to any appreciable extent. And it is a very healthy sign for the colony and for England that New South Wales continues to sell us much more than she buys, and thus year by year, out of her own resources, increases her capacity for trading into all parts of Asia with profit. The mutual advantages which Australia as a whole and India and China ought to reap from an interchange of their commodities cannot be yet estimated, and ought to exceed the most sanguine dreams. Of these advantages, as of others connected with Asiatic trade, New South Wales is certainly preparing to draw the principal share. And we must look at this broader feature of her trade in judging whether it will continue to be as beneficial to us as it has been. Directly, I believe, we shall year by year do a smaller export trade to this colony proportionate to her population, and may hold our own only in special branches of manufacture and in miscellaneous articles, such as can be bought here cheaper than they can be made there; but the general intercourse between the two countries seems to me bound to grow, as well as the profits which the mother-country will draw from the entire trade of the colony. As a Free-trader, possessed of all the natural advantages which go to make a flourishing seat of manufactures, New South Wales must progress, not only in supplying her own wants, but as an exporter of industrial products, and with every step which she takes in advance some branch of our home manufactures will be touched; but the situation in its general features offers, to my mind, ample compensations.

There is only one heavy shadow which I can see to the picture, and that is the danger which New South Wales is in of rushing into a great railway expenditure, which may inflate her trade with us for a time to the ultimate hurt of both countries. On many sides her Government is pressed to do so, and there are projected extensions of her system, carrying the lines far inland beyond the limits of profitable traffic, which, if carried out too suddenly, might cause embarrassment. Although the stream of immigrants has not yet ceased to flow in Australia, as it has to the United States, the same causes would produce the same effects in the one case as in the other, and if taxation is made heavy and the finances become entangled, assuredly the stream will dry up. Yet population is the one great need of all these colonies, and not least of New South Wales, which has many millions of acres of splendid land lying desolate, or little better than desolate, and which has minerals of enormous value lying ready for the miner. At present the taxation of New South Wales is, one may say, next to nothing at all, because the land sales alone last year yielded nearly half the revenue, and in ordinary years land sales, land rents, and post-office and railway receipts yield about three-fourths of it.[1] Now, as I have already repeatedly ex-

[1] The following extract from a letter of the *Times* Sydney correspondent, dated January 22, 1877, gives a very clear idea of the position of New South Wales finance :—'Our Treasurer is to make his Budget Speech this week; but the publication of the Revenue Returns for the past year has anticipated to some extent the glowing statement it will be his privilege to make. These Revenue Returns are not only unique in the history of this colony, but have never been paralleled in the history of any British community. Our population is not estimated at more than 620,000, and the gross revenue for the year was not less than 5,037,661*l.*, or at the rate of more than 8*l.* per head. The previous year was a prosperous one; yet that which is just concluded yielded the Government a net increase of not less than 911,358*l.*, or not far short of an increase of 30*s.* a head. We owe this financial prosperity almost exclusively to the rapid rate at which we are alienating our public estate. The greater part of our territory is held on pastoral leases, the rental having been determined by an official assessment, subject to arbitration in case of dispute. The customary estimate of the proper rental has been based mostly on the state of the wool-market a few years ago. The rapid improvement in that market has enabled the lessees to make unexpectedly large profits, and they find it to their interest to spend these surplus profits in the purchase of land, so as to turn their leaseholds into freeholds. The consequence is that the revenue from land sales alone last year was not far short of one-half of the gross revenue, and amounted to 2,345,240*l*. Adding to this the amount received from rentals and other sources, the receipts from the national estate alone amounted to more than one-half of the year's revenue, being not less than 2,772,090*l*. Our revenue from taxation, properly so called, is small compared with what we thus derive from the Government being a large landlord. The Customs yielded 1,011,872*l.*, and beyond this there is no taxation proper, except about 100,000*l.* from licences. The balance not accounted for by the receipts from land and taxation is furnished for the most part by the income from Government services, such as railways, the telegraphs, and the post-offices. These services, however, are not intrinsically remunerative undertakings, and yield us no net revenue. On the contrary, they are carried on at present at a loss of about 250,000*l*. per annum—a loss which, of course, has to be made good from other sources of public income. Though the receipts from services appear in the general statement of gross revenue, they are more than counterbalanced by a set-off. The Government speculations in the department of internal communication do not really assist our revenue; on the contrary, they burden it. But the burden is one that is easily borne. So far from its provoking discontent, the

plained, the proceeds of sales of land ought not to be treated as revenue at all, but as capital, and if New South Wales will act sensibly, she will so treat it. Did the Legislature decide to spend on their public works every year only the amount netted by the land sales, it would afford ample means for extending railways and telegraphs as fast as they were wanted, and for improving harbours and making roads. Were this done, and the other expenditure all provided for out of revenue strictly so called—except the sinking funds on the existing loans—the position of the finances would be one of the soundest in the world, and in time the public works' revenues would yield the community some return for the enormous sacrifice it is making by parting with the soil in fee simple to squatters and farmers at a price which will probably look monstrously cheap ten years hence, as indeed it does in some districts already. The railways which New South Wales already possesses are yielding a respectable net return, and will by-and-by, no doubt, meet the charge on their capital debt; but there ought to be no capital to pay upon, except the savings of the community, and New

Government is incessantly besieged for still more railways, more telegraphs, and more post-offices. With such an overflowing revenue, it is not wonderful that the Government spent very freely and managed to run through 3¾ millions. It also extinguished the National Debt to the extent of three-quarters of a million, and advanced a quarter of a million to the Public Works account. Yet at the close of the year the Treasurer had a credit balance of not less than 2,720,807*l*.—a handsome sum with which to commence a year that is expected to be as prosperous as its predecessor.'

South Wales will need to take heed that the enormous sales of land do not lead her into spendthrift ways and many subsequent difficulties.

A very good example of what the wholesale alienation of the soil may lead her into is furnished by her ambitious neighbour, Victoria, which is at this very time in the throes of something like a political revolution upon the land question. Victoria has indeed been much more extravagant than her elder sister in several respects; but the land policy is essentially the same in both, only the bad fiscal system of Victoria, and its larger population, are bringing its evils sooner to the surface. In all the Australian colonies, in fact, the alienation of land has been most reckless, and the system of renting huge tracts to 'squatters,' while reserving to farmers, or 'free selectors,' the liberty to pick out and buy any portions they please from the land so rented, has led to purchases of large tracts at low rates by capitalists who can do nothing with them except feed sheep and cattle and prevent these farmers or selectors from finding a foothold. Thus it has come about that, in Victoria especially, whole counties are held by single proprietors in fee simple, to the detriment not only of the land revenue, but of the colonial prosperity generally, and already the Victorians feel hemmed in.[1] They cry

[1] Some interesting details about the lands of Victoria are given in a recent blue book on Colonial affairs (part i., 1876) by the Colonial

out that these huge estates must be broken up; and the party now in power, headed by Mr. Berry, came in on the express understanding that a heavy tax is to be imposed on holders of land above a certain average, in order to compel the squatters to disgorge for the benefit of smaller men. At bottom there are very strong grounds for the imposition of some such tax, but the proposal to graduate it according to holdings is a most unjust one. Probably enough, a sense of this injustice has induced hesitation on the part of Mr. Berry and his colleagues, and it will be well if they lay aside their project for a time until the colonists come to recognise more clearly what the true equities of land taxation may be. There is just as much reason to make a small farmer pay an acreage-tax on his 50

Government statist, Mr. H. H. Hayter. He says that the colony is estimated to contain 36,000 square miles of rich light loamy soil and 12,000 square miles of rich black and chocolate-coloured soils, besides sandy tracts and grassy downs of large extent. Of the total area of the colony, estimated at 56,447,000 acres, about 16,000,000 were alienated in the end of 1874, of which 12,205,000 acres were occupied in 1875. Of these little more than a million were under cultivation. More than half the land suitable for settlements is said to be already sold. Out of the entire population of about 800,000, of which the colony consisted in 1875, only 38,500 were holders of land. This is a dangerously small proportion, and the fact that such enormous tracts are held uncultivated suggests many ominous reflections. The recent purchasers of land appear to have been in a majority of cases squatters, whose interest it is to keep genuine farmers off the ground. The percentage of cultivated to occupied is hence less now than in 1872 and 1873. Besides the land which the squatters have bought, it would appear that some 864 of them leased in 1874 an area approximating 24,230,000 acres. It is their interest, or they think it their interest, to keep farmers off this land as long as they can.

acres as there is for compelling the squatter to pay on his 5,000. This land question need never have come on the colonies at all had they steadily refused to do more than lease the land on short-term leases, or had they even, as in the Cape, exacted the payment of a perpetual quit-rent sufficient to prevent vast accumulations. As it is, the combined policy of leasing large tracts and selling small, without regard to the lessee's interest, has already landed Victoria in trouble, and promises to bring Queensland, and perhaps New South Wales, into trouble too. At the same time a most dangerous incentive to extravagance has been furnished by the large revenues which these colonies appear to enjoy without the necessity of paying taxes. As wool-growing flourished, squatters made haste to buy up the land, and poured their money in every colony into the Treasury, just as they did last year in New South Wales, where a rising wool market enabled the squatters to pay over 2,300,000*l*., on account of the counties they had purchased. This, when spent as income and borrowed upon to boot, is a most dangerous kind of riches, and presently, when the land is all alienated and the squatter reigns supreme in his wilderness, the cry will rise everywhere, as in Victoria now, that the people have no room and that the Governments have no revenue. Land alienations may yet lead to revolutions in these colonies. Victoria, as I have said, has almost reached the revolutionary point now; partly because her area is smaller than her neighbours' and more widely absorbed by the squatters, partly, also, because she has wedded herself to a bad trade policy. It has seemed wise to the Victorians to become Protectionists, and Protectionists especially against the productions of their neighbours, and hence their trade is not so flourishing as it might be. While New South Wales goes on adding warehouse to warehouse and manufactory to manufactory, Victoria stands relatively stationary. Her cultivated area increases very slowly, and if the New South Wales trade which comes and goes at her ports be deducted, her export trade is also by no means abounding in expansiveness. With a population at least 150,000 in excess of New South Wales, her indigenous trade is not appreciably larger. The totals amount to several millions more, it is true; but about 2,000,000*l.* has to be deducted from each side of the statement on account of New South Wales wool, which, coming from the Riverine districts over the boundary, is first treated as imports to, and then, when shipped at Melbourne, as exports from Victoria. This helps to swell the apparent volume of the trade of the colony. Making this deduction, the total trade of Victoria is only about 28,500,000*l.*, which is substantially that of New South Wales. The imports, moreover, have latterly exceeded the exports, in spite of the high tariff, which is such a clog on the prosperity of the community. This excess is not due altogether to the borrowing propensities of the colony, though these are considerable. A certain amount of capital is flowing into this or into all colonies in indirect ways through loan companies and banks, in the pockets of private immigrants, and so forth; while, on the other hand, many small hoards of money pass out of the colony, of which no account is taken in the official records of exports. All these help to swell the buying capacity of the community, and no countries require more allowance to be made for them under these heads than the Australian colonies. From the money of immigrants alone, however, Victoria now gains perhaps less than any of her neighbours; and, unquestionably, the loans which she has raised, and is raising, for State and municipal purposes, had a strong influence on both her buying capacity and her revenue. These heavy imports, paying as they do large duties as a rule, make the inflow of large revenue apparently a thing to be counted upon. Should the imports fall off, therefore, as they will sooner or later be seen to do under the rigorous tariff, Victoria will be left to realise that she has yet to find a sure basis of national income; and this it will be most difficult for her to do with the land alienated and the country districts unpeopled. At the present time, the net income of Victoria from taxation —chiefly customs duties [1]—is only about 2,000,000*l*.,

[1] The customs duties of Victoria would no doubt be considered light

and the entire revenue of the colony (including land money) last year was fully half-a-million less than that of New South Wales. Should customs duties also fall off, therefore, the colony will have a sharp tussle before it readjusts its burdens, and may, amid internal convulsions, impose a land tax which will terrify emigrants from thinking of this colony as a home. How much depends on the customs will be obvious from the subjoined note of the Budget estimates of Victoria for the year ending July 31, 1877.[1] With a smaller

for many countries, and probably were felt at first to be so by the colonists themselves, who were flush of new wealth. As a rule, all articles of English manufacture, including clothing and tissues of most kinds, machinery and millworks, hardware and furniture, pay 20 per cent. *ad valorem*. A few kinds of woollen goods pay only 10 per cent., and some two or three articles are admitted free. When we consider the distance which English goods have to be carried by sea, however, as well as the fact that the colony is less superabundantly wealthy now than it was even six years ago, there can be no doubt that duties which rule at 20 per cent. *ad valorem* for most articles of utility are oppressively high. The Victorians clamour, however, that they are not high enough. By the latest accounts the Protectionists, who have come into power, are likely to act more vigorously in raising the customs tariff than in imposing a land tax, although there are considerable numbers of Free-traders in the colony.

[1] The estimates, as given in Gordon and Gotch's excellent Australian Handbook, were—Customs, 1,639,050*l.*; Excise, 166,600*l.*; land, including rents, 889,850*l.* (the proceeds of land sales alone appear to amount to about 600,000*l.* a year, all of which is properly chargeable to capital account); public works, i.e. roads, railways, and waterworks, 1,179,500*l.*, and various other small items, making a total of 4,385,716*l.* The expenditure is placed at 2,851,295*l.*, but that obviously does not include the 'working expenses' of railways and other public works. The expenditure for the year 1873-74 was 4,177,338*l.*, and since then the total has not decreased. Victoria has spent from first to last over 13,000,000*l.* on her railway system, some portion of which has cost more than 50,000*l.* per mile, a most extravagant sum; and the average for the Government lines is 32,863*l.*, which is also exceedingly high, and raises suspicion of con-

revenue, the debt is larger than that of New South Wales, and the railway and other improving schemes are by no means near an end. Altogether, Victoria ought to be a warning to the mother-colony to take care and not dissipate or alienate her resources, lest she also find herself in difficulties.

As regards the trade of Victoria with the United Kingdom, it is large and fairly satisfactory. Fully fifty per cent. of the total imports come from this country; both her jealousy of her neighbours and her incapacity for providing for her wants at home rendering such import a necessity. It is, indeed, a remarkable fact that, in spite of her tariff, Victoria is a much larger customer of the mother-country than New South Wales, and a much less promising manufacturer. Let her settle her land difficulty, check extravagance, and lower the tariff, and she may in some respects be a smaller buyer of our home manufactures, although probably a larger and more prosperous general trader, and capable, therefore, of affording a much wider field for the employment of English capital than she now has.[1] That is a long task, I fear, and we need be in

siderable jobbery. Nearly the whole of the capital thus absorbed has been borrowed.

[1] Some figures given in Messrs. Gordon and Gotch's Handbook enable us to measure the position of Victoria as a manufacturing centre. In all, the number of manufactories, large and small, was 1,684 last year, employing 25,647 hands, and with machinery, land, buildings, &c., estimated as worth 6,798,820*l*. Now, of these manufactories 16 were 'account book,' 47 'agricultural implement,' 9 'cutlery,' 107 'coach and waggon,' 93 'clothing and boot and shoe,' 124 'aerated water,' 87 'tannery,

no hurry to take alarm at the prospect of being ousted from the markets of the colony just yet. We are more likely to suffer by the temporary poverty into which Victoria seems to me to be drifting. Not that she will become absolutely poor ; but she tends to fall into the condition of the United States, and, with pampered industries languishing, with people out of work, and artificially kept from settling on the land, may in her very infancy put on the appearance of a worn-out nation, burdened as if with the sins and mistakes of centuries. No fate could be more deplorable ; but Victoria is at present courting it, and although I believe she will learn wisdom by her suffering, like other people, suffer she must. At present reaction has barely set in. The yield of the gold mines, is, however, steadily falling off year by year, and thus one strong direct purchasing power of the colony is lessened ; while all around her she has competitors running her hard in whatever she can produce. Her coal deposits are believed to be enormous, and she is rich in copper, possessing also iron, zinc, tin, and silver in more or less abundance ; but of none of these has she a monopoly, and the

---

52 ' fellmongery,' and 76 ' iron, brass, and copper,' with a host of lower numbers devoted to the production of either household requisites or of prepared foods for export. None of these compare for a moment with the substantial industries of New South Wales, if we except 'iron' and 'agricultural implement' shops, which are, we suspect, of an extremely insignificant kind for the most part. At all events, Victoria mines an almost infinitesimal quantity of iron ore and not much more copper. In fact, the production of the latter metal has no importance at all.

Newcastle collieries in New South Wales, to take an example, distance her mines altogether as a source of coal supply, while the mineral centres of that colony are also better located for ready development. In order to utilise her wealth in these directions Victoria must, in short, have a larger population, and deal more freely with her neighbours. All sound industries are built up upon a home market to begin with, and there can be no sound home market without a large population of varied wants and pursuits. I am by no means sure, however, that Victoria is going to get a large population speedily. The great exodus to her shores from Europe is over, and the stream which now flows towards Australasia is both small and much distributed. Victoria does not get the excessive share she did when gold was supreme. Nay, New South Wales, South Australia, and, above all, Queensland and New Zealand, entice, or, as it were, drive the emigrants towards their shores, and many colonists have lately passed from Victoria to her two nearest neighbours on either hand. If a shadow of dull trade or of internal fiscal dissensions overtake Victoria, her population may actually begin to dwindle.[1] New countries can never afford to trifle with economic laws and trust to their people enduring it. Colonists are not rooted to the soil like the bulk of the people n old countries, and are only

---

[1] The number of immigrants into Victoria, deducting re-emigration, is much smaller now than it was a few years ago. Thus, according to a

too ready to follow the nomadic instincts when in the least degree prompted by their discomforts to do so.

In many respects, then, the condition of these two leading colonies differs. Neither of them is free from dangers, but the danger of Victoria is the greater. New South Wales promises to be a great country in time, but she must move cautiously, and beware of the allurements of sudden wealth. As a country for emigrants there is, to my thinking, and in spite of rocks ahead, none to compare with her; and in proportion as population increases, her prosperity ought also to increase. Our trade with her, as I have said before, may not directly increase at the same ratio, except along certain lines of business, but our general prosperity cannot fail to be enhanced as she grows more prosperous, and while intimate relations with the mother-country continue.

It is time now to turn to the other colonies of the group. Some of them demand only brief treatment, but most of them have some qualities worth noticing.

table given in Mr. Hayter's report, the number of arrivals in the years 1865 to 1869 inclusive aggregated 30,738, and in the years 1870 to 1874, 28,134. In 1869 and 1870 the numbers were unusually large, amounting to over 22,000, but since then they have been extremely small, only 1,752 settling in the colony in 1872. Gold in New South Wales, and the attractions mentioned in the text, no doubt in part account for this falling off, which might therefore be esteemed temporary did no other causes crop up to frighten people away. The very unsatisfactory feature of the investigation into all the colonies, which I may note here, is the extreme paucity of women. In 1874 there were only 915 females to 2,452 males entering Victoria. This is not merely bad for the morals of the immigrants, but also very detrimental to the rapid increase of a native Australian population.

South Australia, for instance, which lies west and north of Victoria, resembles New South Wales in its general economic position. The colony has made considerable progress without at the same time endangering its future. The discovery and working of enormous deposits of copper at Burra-Burra in 1845 has contributed, like the gold elsewhere, to the wealth of the community, and helped to place it third in population and trade amongst the colonies of the Australian continent, without, at the same time, turning its head. At the date of the discovery of these valuable ore deposits, the population of the colony was barely 65,000, and its export trade under half-a-million sterling. By 1876 the population had increased to 213,000, and the export trade to about 5,000,000l. The mineral wealth had not succeeded in diverting the colony from agriculture either. On the contrary, the acreage under crops is larger, relatively to the population, than in any other Australian colony. South Australia possesses many natural advantages, and much valuable soil on which it can grow not food grain merely, but grapes of fine flavour and quality, and every description of semi-tropical or other fruit, as well as valuable timber; and these are not neglected. Attention is also paid to sericulture, and the attempts have been so far very successful. Of course, like its neighbours, South Australia has in some measure forestalled its resources; but its debt is comparatively very light, and it has, as yet, been under no necessity to depart from the almost free-trade policy on which its customs laws are based. English manufactured goods pay, as a rule, a duty merely of five per cent. *ad valorem*, and the taxes on luxuries and articles of food are, as a rule, light. It certainly seems strange to English eyes to see potatoes and prepared animal foods paying duty, and no doubt the sooner that all petty endeavours, such as these indicate, to be independent of sister colonies are abandoned the better ; but, as a whole, South Australia is to be commended for an enlightened mercantile policy, and has undoubtedly benefited by it. There is little chance of manufactures being established there on a large scale inimical to the products of England, were its population thrice what it is ; and so long as the colony continues to develop the soil, to introduce new objects of cultivation, and to spend spare energies on the mineral wealth within easy reach, it will continue to grow in prosperity and in importance as a customer of the mother-country. Its trade is as large with England now, and as healthy, taking its size into account, as that of any colony we have. There is a magnificent territory belonging to it, which only wants peopling, and the people will, no doubt, in time be found, although lately there has been some slackening in the arrivals and a corresponding falling away in the demand for land.

One great danger which the colony is subject to appears to be drought. This season's wheat crop, for instance, has been seriously imperilled for want of rain, and so scarce was fodder for the cattle, that in the early part of the season a considerable acreage of corn crop had to be cut down unripe to supply them with food. Owing to this, it is estimated that although nearly 970,000 acres were put under wheat originally, the yield of the present crop will not equal that of the two preceding years, although the latest accounts were much more favourable. As is to be expected in a new country where high farming is not pursued, the farmer preferring to draw on the natural resources of the soil, the ordinary yield of wheat per acre does not rank high at the best of times in South Australia, compared with the yield in England or France, being only about $11\frac{1}{2}$ bushels to the acre. This average will not be nearly reached by this season's crop, however, which is estimated at about 6 bushels to the acre only, or a decline of nearly one-half. Fluctuations of this sort may not be of frequent occurrence, but they happen now and then, and ought to increase the caution with which the colony commits itself to heavy outlays. After the population has spread, and the face of large regions has been changed by cultivation, by tree planting and irrigation, the climate and physical conditions may be so far changed as to make the country secure. In the meantime, cautious growth is the best. No doubt the bad harvest of 1877 will temporarily decrease the exporting power of the colony, and that may react on its imports from England and Asia; but on the whole we may expect its trade with us to grow, and it seems to be now on a very sound basis.

Very different, to my mind, is the position of Queensland, which, as a colony, has followed in the footsteps of Victoria rather than in those of New South Wales. Its population is considerably less than that of South Australia, being but 180,000 or so, and its export trade is lower by about a million. Yet the colony has continued to amass a public debt, which amounts to nearly three times that of South Australia; and it has made so little progress in solid agriculture that the total acreage under crop last year was only about 80,000 acres.[1] The natural fertility of the land is apparently higher in Queensland than in any of the

---

[1] Perhaps I could not do better than give here a sort of rough comparative estimate of the progress of agriculture, exclusive of mere sheep herding, in the various Australian colonies and New Zealand. The figures in detail are obtainable from the abstracts appended to our own agricultural returns, or more diffusely from the statistics scattered through Messrs. Gordon and Gotch's Handbook. According to Mr. Giffen's tables, South Australia is by far the largest wheat-grower, having had 898,820 acres under that species of grain in 1875-76, as against 322,000 acres in Victoria, 134,000 in New South Wales, 4,500 in Queensland, 91,000 in New Zealand, and 43,000 in Tasmania. These figures give a fair idea of the progress of corn-growing in the various colonies, although the areas under wheat crops were in several colonies less in 1876 than in the previous year. Some of them also devote larger acreages to other kinds of grain. Victoria, for example, had last year 124,000 acres under oats and 32,000 under barley, and New Zealand 168,000 and 28,000 acres respectively, or much more than all the rest of the colonies put together. If we include lands partially cultivated, such as lands under permanent artificial grasses and bare fallows, as well as the various experimental efforts at cotton and tobacco growing and the land under root crops, we get the following

other colonies except New Zealand, and that offers the greater and not the less reason for extending cultivation as rapidly as possible. Instead of doing so, however, Queensland has turned her attention to a large extent towards mines, seeking to develop gold, tin, and copper mining in particular, by every means in her power.

Queensland has, it is true, extended her sheep-farming more rapidly than even New South Wales, and

table as showing the progress which each colony has made according to its population in the reclamation of the land :—

Colony	Population in 1875	Acreage under all kinds of crops	Acreage cultivated per head
New South Wales	595,465	451,138	0·8
Victoria	815,034	1,126,831	1·4
South Australia	206,476	1,444,586	7·0
Western Australia	26,459	47,571	1·8
Queensland	172,402	77,347	0·5
Tasmania	103,920	332,824	3·2
New Zealand	375,721	2,377,402	6·3

New South Wales has a less total in 1876 by nearly 14,000 acres than in 1875, and would appear to be in some danger of neglecting the due extension of her agricultural pursuits in following after sheep-farming and mining and manufactures. According to the figures given in the last column of the table she has less than an acre per head under crops, and her imports show that she is not raising bread enough for her population. South Australia stands out most prominent of all, and New Zealand follows, Queensland lagging behind New South Wales without possessing the justification which New South Wales has either in the wealth of minerals or extent of flocks. New South Wales has such vast tracts which are not yet suitable for agriculture, being, compared with Victoria and Queensland, badly watered, that there may be some excuse for her slow progress in this direction, although I admit it involves danger; but there can be no excuse for some of these colonies. The true progress is that which goes neither too fast—outstripping population and foreign markets—nor too slow, making the community dependent on foreign supplies. The first thing which all colonies ought to study to do is to feed themselves with the products of their own soil.

cannot, therefore, be considered backward in all respects; but when all is said, sheep do not form a first-rate permanent source of national wealth, and ought hardly to be taken as a justification for heavy expenditure on public works. Yet Queensland has spent and is spending very freely. Her railway system is already much larger than that of South Australia.[1]

From this it follows, of course, that the taxation is very heavy, notwithstanding the efforts made to import immigrants, and get them settled in the land. According to a very useful table appended to Mr. Reid's essay already cited, the taxation of Queensland was higher per head in 1875 than that of any other colony in Australasia except New Zealand. It amounted to 3*l.* 5*s.* 3*d.* against 1*l.* 18*s.* 3*d.* in New South Wales, 1*l.* 12*s.* 10*d.* in South Australia, and 3*l.* 2*s.* 9*d.* in Victoria. This is, of course, exclusive of the proceeds of land sales and leases. In the financial year ended June 30, 1876, the revenue of the colony, including land revenue so called, amounted altogether to 1,288,377*l.*, and the expenditure to 1,314,932*l.* There was a deficit, therefore, as there had been the previous year, and the colony

---

[1] According to the accounts of the Treasurer of the colony for the half-year to December 1876, the amount spent on immigration during its course out of borrowed money was 55,000*l.*, and the railway outlay came to 226,600*l.* This kind of expenditure is constantly going on, and the colony has spent over 6,000,000*l.* on its railway system already, on which money it does not get a direct return of 2 per cent. Over a hundred thousand a year spent on immigrants, upwards of half-a-million on railways, form no slight outlay for so young a community.

has no means of making ends meet except by either increasing the taxes, by selling more land, or by borrowing as other spendthrift and impecunious states do. Taxation cannot be much increased, however. The import tariff is not indeed heavy, but it is pretty widely distributed, as is proved by the fact that it yielded nearly 500,000*l.* on a total import trade of less than 4,000,000*l.*, or say, roughly, 12½ per cent. over all *ad valorem*. Much of this is, of course, paid simply with the proceeds of the loans which the colony has raised in England, just as part of the income from land arises from the same source. Emigrants are settled on claims under Government guidance, and to some extent with Government money, so that the colony is not anywhere resting on the solid basis of its own resources. Nor with all these efforts at forcing is the land revenue increasing. There is rather a tendency to fall off shown by this source of apparent income. Possibly the enormous discoveries of tin said to have been made a year or two ago will help the colony out of its difficulties, but that is doubtful. I look rather for another financial and mercantile crisis there similar to that of 1866, only more disastrous, because now the credit of the whole community may be affected for years, while then it was mainly the credit of banks and private traders. Queensland is, in short, a country far too undeveloped for the pace at which it has gone, and with too few resources to fall back upon, therefore, when difficulties overtake it. There are no manufacturing industries of a solid character in the country, nor can there be any, so far as I can see, because Queensland is not favoured with the materials most essential to a country setting up in this way for itself. It cannot even take shelter in protection, and has no realisable wealth but its wool, hides, and tallow, its preserved meats, and its minerals, in the sale of every one of which it meets with the keenest possible competition from its neighbours. I can see no way out of the tangle for this colony, therefore, but through much financial disorganisation and long-continued struggles, for its debts and taxation are now direct hindrances to the rapid extension of land cultivation; and many of the immigrants who arrive at the colony's expense leave it and take refuge in New South Wales or Victoria from this very cause. For all that, Queensland nibbles at becoming a great manufacturing country, and has, amongst other ventures, recently established a joint stock woollen-weaving mill at Ipswich, from which much is hoped.

I am reminded by Sir Julius Vogel that I have sinned in omitting to mention the progress of sugar cultivation in this colony as a sign that it is not neglecting its opportunities, and also that an important gain has been secured by the works for storing water, which have rendered immense tracts of territory valuable. To the latter omission I plead guilty, though it does little to alter the real economic situation of the colony whose prosperity is reared on a basis of debt. But as regards the cultivation of sugar, I may at least plead in extenuation of my apparent remissness the fact that Queensland sugar has never reached England in noticeable quantities; not even last year, when the price of sugar was high enough to tempt supplies from the most distant quarters, did Queensland sugar find its way to this country in quantity sufficient to be noticed in our customs returns, if at all. No doubt the colony is making some progress in the production of sugar, for which it finds a market in neighbouring colonies, just as it is advancing in its wool-growing, although that progress is in a measure balanced by the comparative failure of cotton cultivation. What I complain of, however, is that much of this progress is, at best, progress under mortgage. Nay, it often means mortgage upon mortgage till there is no discovering the hard foundations of wealth beneath the pile.

But if the condition of Queensland be dangerous, that of New Zealand is much more so, although New Zealand is the most diligent of all the colonies in developing the soil. That colony has not been content with trying to rival Victoria ; it has sought to imitate Canada. Nay, it is almost unjust to hint that Canada has been as reckless as this, almost the youngest of all our great colonies. It is not yet forty years old, and it rejoices in a debt of nearly 20,000,000$l.$, which is obviously a heavy burden for a population which does not yet reach 450,000, Maoris included. Its taxation was 15s. per head higher than that of Queensland in 1875, and has since been increased, as has also the debt. Only the other day the Government of the colony had to borrow 500,000*l.* in Sydney, and the public works to which it is committed must entail a large expenditure for many years beyond the available income. By means of the huge borrowings in which it indulges, the colony is able to import far more than it exports, and is, next to Victoria, the largest customer to the mother-country of any in the group. All its railway materials, most of its clothing and its hardware and cutlery, come from England, and it has to go to New South Wales for some of its coal. The entire trade of the colony, out and in, was about 13,500,000*l.* in 1876, and the imports exceeded the exports by about 2,500,000*l.*; and this has been much the state of its account for at least three years. A large proportion of the apparent prosperity of the colony is, therefore, based on a quagmire of debt, and it is impossible to say what its real progress or prosperity may have been. A stimulant has been applied which has made its influence felt in every department of business; and whether the colony will be richer or poorer for the efforts it has made may almost be considered an open question. In the immediate future a disaster is not merely probable, but to my mind certain. The colony cannot go on spending, as it has done, without a severe recoil, and when that recoil comes a great part of the present show of prosperity will disappear. Instead of being able to import more than she exports, New Zealand will be reduced to buying only what the interest on her debt abroad leaves her money to pay for. And that interest will be by no means so easy to meet as it looks now, when the quickening effect of the foreign money is everywhere felt without any strong indication of the coming exhaustion and languor. But by-and-by, when this money is all spent, when it is no more to be had for paying the wages of thousands of men employed in carrying out a railway system far more ambitious and extended than that of Victoria, when the customs receipts are no longer swollen by duties paid on goods imported with this money, and the country sinks back on itself with a thousand miles of railway to maintain out of its own resources, besides interest to pay on its heavy debt, New Zealand must inevitably face bankruptcy and a trade demoralisation which it is appalling to contemplate. Her gold mines will not serve her then, nor her wealth in copper, silver, ironsand, and coal. She will be fortunate if she holds together and weathers the storm without the loss of half her population.

I speak strongly, because this subject is of vital importance. New Zealand has spoilt almost at the starting what might have been a career of prosperity such as few other countries could point to. The soil is rich and virgin, and no less than 12,000,000 acres are at present estimated to be adapted for cultivation, while 50,000,000 would be suited, when cleared, for pasturage.[1] There are many valuable minerals and some natural products of value, which by a judicious exploitation might all have contributed to increase the wealth of the colony. New Zealand, in short, had the properties within herself for becoming a comfortable self-contained colony, of a quiet, homely, and peaceful kind, such as the world does not readily furnish now-a-days; but it took the gold fever and the 'progress' fever, and presently will have to pay the penalty in exhaustion, and, I fear, considerable misery.

The only satisfactory feature that we can dwell upon is the fact that, so far, a certain success has attended the efforts of the Government at colonisation. New Zealand receives a larger proportion of the British emigration to Australasia than any other colony, and retains most of those it receives.[2] Land is being rapidly absorbed for purposes of cultivation, and the true wealth of the country is thus being developed. According to the returns up to March of last year,

[1] Gordon and Gotch's Handbook, article 'New Zealand.'
[2] The statement of the Registrar-General of New Zealand, Mr. W. R. Brown, for 1874, which is the latest available, gives the immigration of that year at 43,965, of whom 18,135 were females. The emigration was 5,859, so that the net increase in that year to the population of the colony was 38,106. Out of this total 29,025 persons were imported entirely at the colony's expense. The total emigration to Australasia from the United Kingdom in that year was, according to official returns, about 54,000. New Zealand had therefore a very large share.

about 2,400,000 acres were under cultivation, of which 91,000 acres were sown with wheat. This is a small proportion, and, of course, precludes the colony from being able to export this grain. Indeed, it has to import, which is always an extravagant position for a young colony to assume. Still the yield per acre—31 to 32 bushels—shows both good soil and remarkably good agriculture. Were new settlers to arrive spontaneously in large numbers, the colony might pass through its crisis without prolonged suffering. In the face of the enormous taxation, however, I do not see how these numbers are to be obtained except by a continuance of the present ruinous outlay. They will then cost the colony more than it can afford.

A certain amount of relief will also no doubt be given by the abolition of the provinces into which New Zealand was, till last year, divided. These provinces, with their separate councils and superintendents, were a source of expense to the country which was by no means necessary, and in a time of financial difficulty they would have almost certainly indulged in separatist views with the object of shirking their share in the national burdens. The agitation which preceded the abolition of these provinces gave indications of a party in Otago—the Scotch settlement—capable of raising the separatist cry even before the storm came on. There will now be no definite rallying point for such parties, and that will prove a very great advantage.

Otago, however, promises to be very restive under burdens which have been imposed upon it by the politicians to a considerable extent against its will; and, I fear, the cry for subdivision may again rise there to add to the general impotence when the colonists begin to reap the fruits of their rash lavishness.

In a short reply which Sir Julius Vogel made in 'Fraser's Magazine' to this essay as originally published, most of my conclusions regarding New Zealand are combated. Sir Julius denies, for instance, that this colony needs to import food grains; but my statement referred merely to wheat, the main food staple of the people. The chief object of his paper, however, is to prove that New Zealand is not over-burdened, and to prove this he first of all denies that the debt of New Zealand, all told, is 20,000,000*l.*, and then proceeds to show that the burden per head is less than that of England. His figures and reasoning on these points are, in my opinion, not quite fair, and in order to show their unfairness I will allow Sir Julius to speak for himself:—

There is no reference made to the native wars which in times past desolated that colony, whilst it is asserted that none of the colonies 'have tasted the bitterness of war taxes.' Nearly a third of the public debt of New Zealand might be attributed to native disturbance, instead of all being set down to voluntary expenditure on the part of the colonists. New Zealand, the writer says, rejoices in a debt of nearly 20,000,000*l.*, or something like 50*l.* per head of the population, which itself does not reach 400,000, Maories included. This statement exceeds the license which may be permitted to a statement in round figures. The population at the end of 1876 is officially estimated at 399,221 exclusive of Maories, or with Maories added over 444,000. The public debt, less the amount cancelled by sinking fund and the money unexpended in hand, could not have amounted at the end of 1876 to more than 18,500,000*l.* This gives a debt of less than 42*l.* 15*s.* a head, instead of the 50*l.* stated by the author. He is right in including the Maories, for they contribute largely to the taxation, and many of them are very rich. Supposing, however, they were excluded, the debt would be less than 46*l.* 10*s.* per head. I do not attach much importance to the excessive estimate which the author has made, for the debt per head of the population conveys no meaning if it is unassociated with the question of what the debt is for, and the capacity of the population to meet its annual charges out of their earnings. With the wages prevailing in New Zealand, the labouring classes, as well as the more wealthy, would not be distressed by double the amount per head of population payable for taxes in this country. The only true test of a country's burdens is the weight with which they fall on the earnings of the people. I might also ask the author to consider what Government expenditure in the colony means. In Great Britain the expenditure from the consolidated revenue does not mean interest on the cost of railways, nor does it mean much of the cost of education, police, gaols, and lunatic asylums. In the colony the revenue supplies all this, excepting some fees for education. When the capital burden per head of the public debt in this country has to be compared with that of New Zealand, the capital cost of the railways should be added, and the capitalised burden of the poor rates. In a paper recently read by Mr. Hamilton before the Statistical Society of London, the following passage occurred:—

In contrasting the indebtedness of New Zealand with that of the United Kingdom we must add to the National Debt the cost of railways, and capitalise the poor-law rates, which do not exist in the colony, thus:—

UNITED KINGDOM.

	£
National Debt, as it stood 1875-76	777,000,000
Expended on the poor, average for ten years ending Lady-Day, 1875, 9,216,053*l*. capitalised at 4 per cent.	230,000,000
Railways, 16,614 miles open December 1875	630,000,000
	1,637,000,000

Or, 40*l*. 12*s*. 1*d*. per head for United Kingdom.

I have already said that at the end of 1876 the public debt in New Zealand amounted to 42*l*. 15*s*. per head, including Maories, or 46*l*. 10*s*. without them. It has to be borne in mind that New Zealand has an immense landed estate. The railways have enormously added to its value. Its extent is about thirty-four millions of acres. For the last five years it has averaged for sales and leases an annual return of 820,000*l*. The population of the colony increases so fast that calculations based on the population to-day are fallacious to-morrow. It is evident, if population is to be a test, that a country whose population increased rapidly would be justified, nay, would be prudent, in more largely discounting the future than one whose population was nearly stationary. Again, railways in New Zealand may be regarded as substitutes for ordinary roads. These used to be made at the cost of the colony, and it was considered fortunate if the tolls yielded enough to maintain them. Now the railways are yielding a considerable part of the interest on their cost. The balance may fairly be set down against the cost of ordinary roads, only that balance will soon be bridged over. And, meanwhile, in place of ordinary roads they are equipped roads, including in their cost and net results the means for carriage and the motive power.

Now first of all I have to point out that it is an

indisputable fact that the population of New Zealand does not meet the debt charges out of its earnings. Not one-half the revenue comes from taxation, the larger proportion being made up of the proceeds of land sales and the gross earnings of the railways, whose net return does not pay more than half the interest on their capital. Judging by the tax-paying power of the community, therefore, New Zealand is enormously overburdened. I have again and again pointed out that the larger half of the revenue of all these colonies is not revenue but capital, and that to borrow on the security of capital is the height of folly. Further, the table of the debt of England given as a means of showing the relative burdens of the mother-country and her colony is inaccurate, inasmuch as it takes no account of local taxation other than poor rates, while it includes railway capital, which is not, strictly speaking, national debt at all; but it would be nothing to the purpose were it perfectly correct. The two countries cannot be compared, because the one pays out of its stored wealth and the other out of its borrowings. But in giving this as the English burdens Sir Julius should have been equally eager to include all the obligations of New Zealand. Has it no city debts, no local taxes, or needy people? He gives us the total of the State debt less sinking funds, but I have treated Christchurch, Dunedin, and Wellington as parts of the State, and hence my total of 20,000,000*l.*, a total that will soon be exceeded. He says further that railways in New Zealand may be regarded as substitutes for ordinary roads; and that is partly correct, partly nonsense. The greater part of the colony could have done for a generation yet with roads instead of railways, and the imposition of the costly burden of the latter on the raw and scattered communities has really no justification. The burden is not unlikely to become intolerable, since the lines will not pay and will have to be maintained.

I might go on to notice other portions of Sir Julius's paper—such as his glowing picture of the happy prosperity of this privileged colony, of the abundance of work, the eager buying of land and constant inflow of immigrants,—only that pictures of this kind have so little value against the broad plain facts of the situation. There are annual deficits in spite of the large expenditure of capital as revenue, enormous public works which do not return the interest on their capital, immigration and settlement stimulated by borrowed money, and every kind of industrial undertaking upheld by credits from English banks and loan societies. They are of little value, either, in the face of the gradual dying away of the outburst which Sir Julius himself was instrumental in producing. After another five years of the career which he mapped out for the colony before he left, we may feel more disposed to look at them closely.

Such being the general features of the economic position of this colony, it is hardly necessary to discuss the question of its tariff, or the minuter probabilities of the trade between it and the mother-country. Whether the tariff is high or low, that trade is sure to suffer a sharp recoil when the borrowed money is done. We cannot hope to sell to New Zealand the quantities that we have done of any of our manufactures except clothes, and even of these the demand must become less if the people get poorer, as the diminution in the average savings bank deposits would seem to indicate they are already doing. No doubt the tariff, which is as near as possible about 11 to 12 per cent. *ad valorem* on the invoice prices of the goods, will exercise a very strong effect against England in certain directions when the inflation passes away, although apparently it is not felt at present. Poverty will induce thrift, and thrift may stimulate the people to avoid the tariff charges by providing for their supreme civilised wants at home. To take one example: nearly all the Australian colonies had at first to import most of their boots and shoes, and manufacturers in England did a very fine business in consequence. But gradually, as they grew up, the colonies took to establishing manufactories of their own, and imported less and less of these primary articles. This has not yet been the case with New Zealand or Queensland to any large extent; but the tariff and pinching times may almost at once stop the home business in this line with these colonies. This is one of several domestic arts, as it were, which a new country is indeed justified in setting on foot as soon as it can, and New Zealand will certainly have every temptation to do so now. The hardware exports thence will also fall away for other reasons, and if we retain a business in cottons and woollens to any amount we may consider ourselves fortunate. The outlook for New Zealand is not bright, take it how we will. The colony has many mistakes to suffer for before it can emerge into greatness, and the old country must suffer along with it, were it for no other reason than that the colony has many millions of our money.

Of the minor colonies, Western Australia and Tasmania, it is hardly necessary that I should speak in detail. Both are at present too poor to be very extravagant, but the latter has contrived to get together a reasonable amount of debt, which appears to hinder its advancement to some extent. The island is a beautiful one, and full of natural riches, but its wealth is not yet developed by the presence of an enterprising population. Hardly yet free from the convict taint which stuck to it as Van Diemen's Land, it has not attracted the number of population which the country deserves to have, and, unaided by 'great gold discoveries' to dangle before the wealth seekers, it has been passed over. All the same, it has in it the elements of a very solid prosperity, and has displayed considerable energy in taking in and improving land. The colonists of Tasmania should become comfortable and even reasonably wealthy, although they will never take a great place amongst nations, or figure as large traders with this or any other country; and the pity is that so few colonists seek its shores—the population barely increased 4,000 in the five years 1870 to 1875. Should the recently reported gold discoveries in the western part of the island prove correct, this stagnation may pass away, to the ultimate great benefit of its business. Western Australia, again, is entirely a colony in embryo, about which little can be said, except that the territory is apparently a very attractive one, capable of sustaining a large population, and possessed of much timber, which ought to become a valuable article of export in time, were men found who could cut it and bring it to the coast. At present there are not 30,000 people in the entire colony, which, it is estimated, embraces an area eight times larger than the United Kingdom. Much of that vast amount of land is, however, as yet irreclaimable, like that of South Australia and Queensland; and indeed, speaking generally, all the Australian colonies are still more or less of the nature of coast settlements. Inland the population everywhere thins gradually off, so that the central territory, uninhabitable as it is said to be, for the most part effectually shuts off all chance of overland communication between one colony and another on opposite sides of the continent. Yet there is great room to spread, and to join hand to hand all round the magnificent coasts.

This isolation overland, to turn again to the general questions involved in the future of these settlements, must exercise, however, a most important bearing on the possibilities of a federative union of the mainland and Tasmanian colonies. There is no great central colony to form a rallying point for the rest, as it were; and the mere fact that all communication between east and west must be practically by sea for many a day to come, will make the colonies of New South Wales and Victoria strenuous rivals in the fight for leadership. Each will say that it is best placed for the seat of supreme government, and neither will give way until, as a refuge from conflict, some petty corner like Tasmania may possibly be chosen as a sort of neutral ground, just as the capital of the United States is planted in the insignificant 'District of Columbia.' That is, supposing the federation project carried out, which is, I confess, taking a great deal for granted. So far is it now from being so that I almost fear the past history of several of the colonies, brief as it has been, makes it impossible until many revolutions have occurred. Each colony has grown to have its own aims and ambitions, and its own burdens, to such a degree, that necessity alone will drive them towards union; although union is, more than any other conceivable thing, a necessity for them all, whether we look at them as requiring more population, as aspiring States, or as sitting defenceless and apart, ready to be a prey to almost the first sturdy marauder who penetrates to these southern seas—not by any means an impossible event.

I firmly believe that, were the Australian colonies to unite now under one federal government, the necessity which impels some of them to tout for emigrants would be at an end. People will grow used to have a great country in their eye over which they could wander at will, as in the United States, and the new greatness which would thus rest upon these colonies would draw many to their shores. Not only so, but the abolition of all customs barriers between the various States would materially aid the development of the peculiar resources of each, and might put an end, partially at least, to costly schemes of rivalry. The natural resources of New South Wales and Victoria would seem to fit them for becoming the industrial centres of the continent, while the others are adapted for every description of agriculture, and can furnish many raw materials, including cotton and silk of a most valuable kind. Break the artificial barriers away, and each district or province of the federation would attract to itself the kinds of labour most suited to its wants. We should have harmonious development rather than, as at present, rivalries which tend to hinder progress.

It is also necessary that these colonies should concert together and become one for purposes of self-defence. At present they lie open, and almost utterly without means of defence in the event of an outbreak of war between the mother-country and any ambitious European power, and their isolated efforts at self-protection are of necessity quite inadequate to their possible, or even probable danger. These colonies are, in short, only communities of miners, shepherds, and farmers; and, however admirable as such, they require to have at least the capacity for calling into existence the means of fighting for their possessions, should they be threatened. Great Britain has so many possessions, and such heavy stakes of another kind in India and China, that in all probability no European war involving her participation could occur now which would not tax her utmost spare energies in keeping the peace in Asia. There would likely be neither men nor means forthcoming to help the colonies, except so far as sparing them, perhaps, a few ships of war. In the main, therefore, they must look to their own resources, and federation would enable them, in a very short time, to do so effectually. By forming a Bund, or a single State, such as that of the American Union, they could introduce a military and naval organisation of sufficient strength to protect them against any but the strongest aggressive powers. I fear the world has hardly yet reached that state of civilisation which renders this unnecessary; but the colonists do not seriously occupy their thoughts with gloomy contingencies of this kind. Till they do there will be no serious movement towards federation, and without federation their settlements can never be strong and great. Union, in short, must at once lead to enormous changes in the government systems of several of them, and might also give them all an opportunity for revising the land laws, with a view to imposing taxation on the only kind of property capable of bearing it pretty heavily. A land tax and a light customs tariff should provide for nearly all wants, federal and provincial, as the country filled up with people, and the railways, if not feverishly extended, became re munerative. The obvious necessity which exists for providing for self-defence ought also to be a strong argument in favour of prudent spending with all the colonies, especially if they should have to make such provision separately. No cost that a community can bear at all weighs on it and cripples its resources like the cost of maintaining armed forces. But for the army and navy of England, we might at present have no national debt, and might almost enjoy the entire revenues of our railway systems as a relief to taxation. Armies and navies protect trade no doubt, but they cripple the competing force of the trader also ; and were the colonies in Australia to have to betake themselves to arms, they would find themselves in difficulties of a financial kind, however cheaply they organised their forces. At present only New South Wales and

Victoria possess any semblance of a force, and none of them have tasted the bitterness of war taxes. It will be well if they unite as one nation before they have to do so, and I wish the dread of that contingency would force them to cease their rivalries. At present they are weak because divided.

I must look on the Australian colonies, then, as at best a nation in a nebulous state, of which the fragments show here and there vigorous life, but whose coming greatness can only be guessed at. As regards the future course of British trade with them generally, there is little more to be said. Obviously it will be larger in some cases and smaller in others, and over all may perhaps be expected for years to come to show small augmentation, so far, at all events, as exports of British manufactures thither are concerned. As the more vigorous colonies develop their own resources, however, they will also do a wider foreign business, by which, as I have said, England will more or less benefit; but it by no means follows that they will then buy more English goods. Freights alone are against us, and must grow more so as money sinks in value in the colonies, and they become able to employ labour of the same quality as our own at something like an equivalent price. The wealth of England may then come to be increased, not so much by the sale of home-made goods to the Australians, as by the employment of her surplus capital in the sustenance of new industries there.

This has been the course, in fact, hitherto; and every industry which Australia has—just as almost every industry possessed by the United States—owes its origin, and no little of its prosperity, to English money. A new country has no saved money, strictly speaking, of its own; it has only the raw products of nature; and hence the price or value of saved money, or 'loanable capital,' in a new country is very high, by reason of its scarcity. On the other hand, labour is in most instances even more urgently needed than money; and frequently, in new countries, the purchasing power of money over labour is extremely low. This curious double scarcity tells, on the one hand, in favour of a strong flow of money from the mother-country, where it is cheap, to the colony, where it is dear, and, on the other, induces an equally steady flow of all kinds of home manufactures which the colony cannot afford to make for itself. Gradually this state of affairs should equalise itself, and industry after industry start into vigorous life, as the capital to start it and the hands to keep it going are found. The enormous amount of gold which the Australian colonies have found made their progress in this respect remarkably rapid; but home supplies of money have also had an immense influence. What that supply has amounted to no one can say, because the private importations of emigrants cannot be even guessed at; but we may gather some notion of its magnitude from the capital of the numerous banks and other companies with English capital engaged in the Australian trade.

The capital involved in the banks of Australia and New Zealand—which may be considered of English origin—amounts to about 9,000,000*l*., most of which has been found by this country; and besides this capital there are large deposits, and in some cases large reserves, portions of which may fairly be assumed to come from English pockets. The banks are not all, either. There are large numbers of mining adventures and agricultural companies, whose money, furnished by English investors, is employed either in lending upon mortgage or in developing property under direct English management. The finance companies, in particular, have not their capital merely, but also large deposits, all drawn from home, and employed in loans to squatters or farmers at higher rates of interest than could be got in the mother-country. By this means land is bought and, apparently, paid for; and by this means farms are stocked, produce raised, and the whole machinery of trade put in motion. The work done is most necessary and valuable; but the statistics of progress and wealth which the colonial budgets are founded on may well, under such a system, be most misleading. I am unable to give an exact statement of the amount of English money thus invested in the farming and mining of Australia and New Zealand; but the paid-up capital alone of the finance and loan companies amounts to over 3,000,000*l*., and it is a moderate estimate which places the deposits borrowed on the uncalled portion of many of these companies at another 5,000,000*l*. Add another 2,000,000*l*., which is within the mark, as investments in mines, and we have a very respectable total of more than 19,000,000*l*.— say, in round figures, 20,000,000*l*.—as the lent English money actively embarked in the internal development of the Australasian colonies. Were we to add private fortunes carried to the colonies, as well as English investments in strictly colonial companies, this total would be probably quite three times that amount, but I wish to avoid any appearance of exaggeration.[1] Even this total reveals a good deal regarding Australian pro-

[1] The following extract from a Melbourne paper, the *Insurance and Banking Record*, shows the total assets and liabilities of the Australian banks. From these figures it will be seen that the colonies now use enormous means of their own in maintaining the flow of their commerce, and that for their population they are perhaps the largest employers of banking credit in the world. 'At the end of 1876, in the six leading colonies, the banks' capital and reserves employed were 15,765,000*l*., the advances 52,288,000*l*., their liabilities were 48,133,000*l*., and their assets 63,898,000*l*.

'Looking at the figures from the stand-point of intercolonial comparison, it will be observed as between 1872 and 1876 how the largest increase of advances has been just in those colonies where general knowledge of their development would lead us to expect it. The contrast will be shown best thus:—

Advances	1872	1876
Victoria	£13,595,000	£19,138,000
New South Wales	8,726,000	13,627,000
New Zealand	4,060,000	10,017,000
South Australia	2,761,000	4,749,000
Queensland	1,487,000	3,400,000
Tasmania	892,000	1,357,000

gross, as well as of the source whence England draws so much of her wealth. Mere trade figures do not show nearly all her gains, and trade figures alone ought not, therefore, to be dwelt upon as an exclusive sign of the good which she reaps from her possessions. This huge capital engaged in banking has also another significance when we remember the peculiar dangers to which banking always subjects commerce ; dangers heightened in new countries in need of money by the constant borrowings on the security of land. Loans of all kinds are made by banks in their eager competition for business, and these loans often inflate prices like doses of paper-money. By-and-by a liquidation becomes necessary, and amid general loss and frequent ruin, values sink back to a point perhaps below their real level. It is to dangers like this that I refer when I speak of these colonies as buried under mortgages. The employment of capital in a new country is legitimately very profitable, but the tendency is always towards excess. Banks lend beyond their means, Government borrows, private individuals take great risks with no adequate means, and for a time all goes swimmingly ; but the reckoning day comes round, and then everyone finds that he has not means enough to meet his liabilities. Farmers cannot pay for their land or repay the banks ; the whole community has been trading beyond themselves, and treating as profits or revenue what should have been considered capital, and the consequence is a general smash. These liquidations have occurred in the colonies before, and they will occur again, involving when next they do some of the Governments in the ruin. In the meantime, however, the mother-country gains in all ways by their lusty march ahead. We get high usury on our money and good markets for our productions, and much of the saving of the colonists finds its way directly back to us. By a table published in the last emigration papers, I find that, between 1848 and 1876 inclusive, emigrants to the colonies and the United States are estimated to have remitted to their friends no less than about 19,800,000*l.* in money, all of which, in one shape or other, has added to our spending power. That again takes no account of the fortunes brought home by returned emigrants from all parts of the globe, or in part re-invested in the enterprises of the country in which they were originally won, in order that the interest thereon may be spent here. In all these ways England gains by the prosperity of her colonies, and, in one sense the more she lends them, the greater her tribute in return, whether their direct exchange of goods with her increases or not. All I deprecate is the lavish mortgaging of the resources of the State or community as such by heavy borrowings. Money is best risked on private account, and the states of Australia and New Zealand are too new to have laid on themselves the load which most of them carry. This I say, bearing in mind fully the wise provisions which they have all more or less made for the repayment of debt, because I deem these in themselves something of a snare, inducing more and more outlay in the faith that one day all will come round, and that the community will ultimately have, as it were, for nothing what it pays so dearly for now.

The outflow of capital from the mother-country to the colonies is thus, in several ways, at once a chief source of her gain and main danger of the future. Their lavishness will produce miserable reactions, the sufferings of which will recoil on this country as well as on the colonists. The position of the settlements we have briefly looked at is therefore rather a chequered one. We cannot say with surety what their future may be. All of them have difficulties before them, and though I think the Australian colonies, with one or two exceptions, much better off than Canada, and rather more prosperous than South Africa, I yet cannot say that any of them will make good in the future the startling advances which the generation passing away has witnessed. Yet the greatness of some amongst them seems secured, and so long as they are peopled by an English-speaking race, their union with the old country must be intimate in a mercantile sense, and the good they do her will in the main far exceed the evil. We shall in the next few years, perhaps, see our trade with Australasia both shrink considerably and shift in character; but it will still be in the aggregate a great trade; and if the colonies there would but unite in one, the field they would offer to the old country for emigration, for capital and enterprise of every kind, is such as North America alone could rival. This I say, bearing fully in mind the expectation that some at least amongst them must soon enter upon times of financial depression and shaken public and private credit.

CHAPTER XIII.

MEXICO AND BRAZIL.

THE condition of the South American Continent, taken as a whole, is not a satisfactory one, whatever way we view it. Politically it is split up into a number of separate States, few of which possess any real political vitality, and nearly all of which are too poor to obtain any stable position as traders amongst the nations of the world. The same dominance of the soldiery which has nearly destroyed Old Spain has helped to prevent hitherto the development of most of those offshoots from her which form the States of Central and South America. There is, to all appearance, an absence of the capacity for creating solidly based civil institutions in the Spanish race; and although these Spanish colonies have all thrown off the yoke of the mother-country, they have made next to no progress in the art of self-government. Not one of them all can show even an orderly, well-knit system of authority, such as Prescott, for instance, says—no doubt with exaggeration—the Incas of Peru or the Aztecs of Mexico possessed. The Spaniard of America is civilly a degraded being, by reason of his tyrannies and through the superstitions which have so long moulded the quality of his mind, and the mixed races and natives whom he has called into being or subdued, have never risen to the position of the peaceful, order-loving citizens of free States. Therefore we find continual wars going on, brigandage and murder rife, in even the most promising of these States, and an absence of any progress worthy of the name in every Spanish Republic save one. Public offices are filled through corruption, and integrity and fair dealing between man and man are qualities almost unknown. When contrasted with the United States, the utter backwardness of all South American States comes with startling force on the mind of the political student. The beginnings of life which society does evince there serve but to suggest, as it were, the corruption which makes one almost despair of these States ever developing into healthy political organisations. Chili alone amongst the Spanish States of South America has made real progress in the art of self-government, and has been blessed with internal peace for a generation. Amongst the rest the Argentine Confederation, Peru, and Mexico stand prominently forward as communities of whom much has been expected, but which have yet performed little. The Argentine Confederation had a war on the occasion of the election of the last President, and has had more than one civil disturbance since. The Government is too weak either to repress the soldiery or to prevent crime, and its outlying provinces are subjected to a terrorism from bands of ruffians which at times threatens to depopulate the country. What progress and enlightenment the Republic has is due mainly to the influence of people of other than Spanish nationality—English, German, Italian—and if these cannot get and maintain the upper hand, revolutions, bloodshed, possibly dismemberment, attend the future of this State. More disheartening still, perhaps, is the condition of Peru, where the Spaniard has more exclusive possession of the destinies of the country, and wastes its wealth to the top of his bent. To find another orderly government we have to leave Spanish possessions altogether, and betake ourselves to the vast Portuguese Empire of Brazil, which under the old reigning house of Portugal has attained to a certain importance and order. Poor as this may be, compared with the higher civilisations of the Old World, it nevertheless places Brazil first amongst the States of South America.

Of the petty States of the north lying between that Empire and Mexico I need hardly speak. They are all insignificant in every sense of the term. At the present time the United States of Colombia are enjoying one of their many civil wars, and the scattered communities of Ecuador, Guatemala, Costa Rica, Bolivia, and the like are both politically and commercially too insignificant to demand much notice here. Most of them have interest for the English reader only because they have contrived to get deeply into our debt. Having spent all that they could wring from the land or the natives in the countries to which as robbers they had gone, the Spanish settlers in these latter days took up the brilliant idea of plundering the English, and succeeded in a way that must have gone beyond their expectations. Hardly any of these small States do a steady trade with England, and their short flush of gold, with its accompanying burst of importation, has passed away, leaving them poorer and more wretched than before. Colombia has a considerable overland transit trade by the Isthmus of Panama, but it hardly benefits the Republic, and its own internal trade is extremely insignificant. More than one attempt has been made to establish an industry such as sugar growing and manufacture, but with the most indifferent success. Militarism and priestly superstition are the bane of all civil life, the malarious social exhalations which blight every enterprise. It would be waste of time to discuss at any length the fortunes and possible futures of these pettier States at present, even had we the materials. Possibly some day a brighter era may dawn on them, and the conflicts and jealousies give way to order and good fellowship, industry and peace; but that day's dawning is not yet visible. I shall, therefore, only give a few general figures regarding the trade of South and Central America, with a view to bring out more strikingly the contrast between these regions and the northern half of the Continent, and then pass on to the larger States indicated at the head of this chapter.

Exact statistics are not, of course, obtainable, but, putting together such as we have, the total export and import trade of all the Spanish States and Brazil together cannot have exceeded 115,000,000*l*. at the most inflated period of their trade, and last year did not probably exceed 106,000,000*l*., including the movements of bullion. This is just about the amount of the imports of merchandise alone into the United States in 1875, and the total trade of the States and Canada together last year exceeded that of Central and South America by from at least 150,000,000*l*. to 180,000,000*l*. I exclude, of course, British and Dutch Guiana from the estimate, as well as Cuba, and speak only of the Spanish and Portuguese States on the mainland. If we were to judge of this great difference between the trading capacity of the Anglo-Saxon and Iberian portions of the American Continent by the numbers of their respective populations, we should find little ground for altering the opinion which a mere contrast of the trade figures gives. In numbers alone Spanish and Portuguese America is almost as well off for inhabitants as the States and British America. In area and in quality of the soil, as well as riches of mineral resources, the former is even more favoured than the latter ; so that, by whatever standard we judge the position of the two, Spanish America lies far behind.

Generalities of this kind are, however, little satisfactory so far as our purposes are concerned, and we must look at several of the prominent States more closely if we are to form a sound opinion on their future. Population as between Saxon and Spaniard may be equal in numbers but of totally divergent qualities, and mere trade figures may give but little indication of the true nature of the progress or absence of progress which marks the history of any one State. I will, therefore, now take up the leading States one by one, beginning with Mexico and going southward so as to take Brazil by the way. The review shall be as brief as possible.

Mexico [1] is, perhaps, the finest territory in the whole world. Excluding the hot malarious lowlands by the gulf, the climate is generally exquisite, the soil surpassingly rich, and the mineral resources nearly inexhaustible and of the finest kind. This language seems like exaggeration, but it would be hard to exaggerate the excellences of Mexico in these respects. Had it been the fortune of Englishmen to possess that magnificent plateau, we should have prized it as the most precious of all our colonies. This favoured land has, however,

---

[1] Much of the information given in the text regarding Mexico has been communicated to me by my friend, Mr. J. W. Barclay, M.P., who visited the country in the autumn of 1876.

fallen to the Spaniard, and how he has used it takes not long to tell. The Spanish idea of wealth is summed up in three words—gold, silver, and gems. No matter how fertile a territory might be which they conquered, it had no temptations for them but as a store of these; therefore the Spaniards never developed the lands they settled on. They overran them, ravaged them, ground the indigenous population down to the very dust, hunted for silver and gold as wild beasts hunt for prey; and then built churches to show how pious they were withal. I speak of the mass of Spanish colonisers, and of the general characteristics. The results of such behaviour have been made abundantly manifest in Mexico, where the soil has been neglected for the mine, till the population of the present day—only a sparsely sown 8,000,000 to 9,000,000—does not find half enough work to do, and can often only relieve the monotony of idleness by forming bands of robbers, or indulging in 'pronunciamientos' against the Government. After half a century of so-called independence, Mexico is still a country almost without government, so far as the outlying provinces are concerned, without settled trade, and as uncultivated, speaking generally, as an Australian sheep-run. The present President of the country, if such he can be called, won his seat at the sword's point, and the 'ordeal of battle' has always been the chief test of fitness to rule in this 'Republic.' The Mexicans have theoretically one of the best forms of government in the world, and their laws are liberal and enlightened, but they get no good therefrom. Their constitution is like a giant's garments put upon a pigmy, who can move only by casting them off. Trade or industry, in such circumstances, Mexico can hardly have, and in spite of her magnificent soil and climate, almost her sole prominent article of export to this day is silver. The wealth of precious metals which she has displayed for centuries has, in short, been one of her greatest curses. Next in importance to her silver is timber, and in recent years England alone has taken from 300,000*l.* to 400,000*l.* worth of mahogany from her ports. Some progress is said to have been made in the cultivation of coffee, for which the soil and climate are admirably fitted, but none of the produce reaches England, and the quantity sent to the United States is very insignificant compared to what Mexico might easily produce. The clearing away of the old forests which is essential to the true development of a country, just as judicious replanting may be to its continued fertility, is but beginning, and betokens as yet little advance in the arts of peace. Were Mexico to devote herself to sugar growing or to coffee, cotton, indigo, or tobacco planting, or were she even to come down to the commonplace business of growing corn, after, say, the fashion of Chili—a by no means high standard, a few years might transform her territory into a land of peace and plenty; her patient Indian population, the bearers of the national burdens in every sense, would become happy and contented farmers, and a bulwark would rise up against revolutions and civil crimes, which not all the vile machinations of a stripped but still powerful and repulsive priesthood could throw down; ships would frequent her ports, and, instead of being known in the markets of the world almost exclusively by her 'dollars,' she would be as influential in international markets as the Southern States of the North American Union or California. What she is capable of, California, indeed, teaches us; and Texas, Colorado, and New Mexico, of old possessions of the Spaniard, will in due time give the world the same lesson. Take Mexico out of the hand of the priest-ridden Spaniard and it will grow rich. The country would, probably, be far better in the hands of the old Indian race, and the only earnest progressive reforming President it ever had was a 'full-blooded' Indian—Benito Juarez, who died in 1872. To him, more than to any other, is due the partial emancipation of the people from the gross tyranny of the corrupt Spanish priesthood. He disestablished and disendowed the Church, and through him it became possible in Mexico city for Protestant congregations to buy and worship in one of its principal Catholic churches. He it was, too, who stemmed the torrent of French invasion, when the clerical party, beaten at all points at home, got France and Spain, and, I am ashamed to say, England, to interfere, and who seized the opportunity which the withdrawal of French troops gave him of reasserting the right of the Mexicans to govern themselves free from foreign domination. To Juarez, more than to any other man, the Mexicans owe the secularisation of the enormous properties of the Church and the diversion of at least a portion of the enormous wealth thus released to purposes of education. He it was who decreed the abolition of nunneries and monasteries, and who forbade the priests to wear distinctive garbs in public; and a generation or two hence the fruits of his on the whole enlightened and vigorous reforming policy may perhaps become apparent in a higher enlightenment among the people. In all Spanish provinces priestcraft has played a part which it is no exaggeration to describe as diabolical; and if Juarez could but have abolished the priest in the minds of his ignorant fellow-countrymen as easily as he seized the Church property, we should say that Mexico was on the high road to a new grandeur. But that he could not do, and, like the civil constitution, the laws for the regulation of education are as yet nearly inoperative.

The most hopeful period of Mexican history has on the whole, however, been the last decade, and the outlook of the future is not entirely black. The default committed on her debt, in the beginning of 1867, effectually shut her out from the money markets of Europe when so many of her neighbours came to gather the gold they could no longer find at home, and to make shipwreck of their good name. Isolated from the sympathy of every foreign nation save the United States, after the death of Maximilian—whom, by the way, Juarez had a good right to shoot—delivered from the curse of French occupation, and left entirely face to face with her difficulties, Mexico may be said in a sense to have progressed. It would, however, be difficult to say the Mexicans have themselves improved or to show what Mexico has actually and in substance gained in these ten years. Property outside the capital is not much, if at all, more secure now than it has ever been. Bands of armed robbers haunt the country, and private feuds lead to murders now just as much as ever, and the old annoyances to the peaceable inhabitants on the Texan border from Mexican marauders have not a whit abated. The native Mexican, capable as he may be of great social improvement, if working under the guidance of apt masters of industry, has little or no opportunity of showing what is in him, and is content, apparently, to shed his blood in the cause of any blatant Spanish bravado who chooses to take the field against the lawful Government or to join the first robber-chief who gives him a chance of living in idleness and crime. The Spaniards in the country are indeed, to all appearance, incapable of doing any good as improvers of the soil, and all its best commerce is in the hands of Germans and Englishmen. Jealous, greedy of gold, cruel and arbitrary, the Spaniards can wield with effect only the slaver's lash in hounding the people on to dig for precious ores. Every solid improvement of which Mexico can boast, in short, she so far owes to the enterprise of Teutons or Saxons. Her railways have been built mostly by an English company with English money; her city improvements, where there are any, come from the same hands; and what manufactures she has flourish only when in foreign control. Nay, her very mines are passing away from the Spanish race, and becoming the property of Germans and Englishmen; and it is to the latter that she owes the economy and management of her mint as well as the best part of her banking.

It is our habit to speak of Mexico as a homogeneous Republic, over the whole of which a President who holds Mexico city has no difficulty in extending his sway; and here also we make a grievous mistake. The provinces of Mexico hang very loosely together, as those of any country must do where the means of intercommunication are few and difficult, where provincial antipathies run strong, and where corruption is so deeply ingrained in the official class. The very demands of the tax-gatherer are enough to place province at enmity with province, and so little cohesion is there amongst the component parts of the Republic that at present one province taxes the produce imported from another.[1] This provincial jealousy and want of co-operation is itself a strong retardant of trade; and to this we must add a most burdensome general import tariff. Allowing for the difference of wealth between the two countries, I believe I am not beyond the mark when I place the import tariff of Mexico at about twice the weight of that of the United States. So heavy is it that the Government gets little or no revenue. The customs officials at the various ports simply strike a bargain for themselves with importing merchants, and pocket what they please. But for some such arrangement, Mexico could scarcely import any European goods. The folly of such a tariff as this is all the more marked in that the erroneous but specious plea of 'protection' cannot even be set up in its behalf. Mexico has no industry worth mentioning to protect.

The picture which this Republic presents to us is altogether a very chequered one. Some things cause one to hope; but, on the whole, the reasons for despondency seem to me at present to predominate. We hear from time to time of the sincere desire of the warrior now in power, Porfirio Diaz, to do this and that for the good of the country; to build railways, to arrange for the payment of the debt, and so forth; but his tenure of office is as yet too precariously based for him to be able to carry his intentions out, however good. And as for

[1] Geiger's *Peep at Mexico*.

railways, Mexico has already about as many of them as she can manage. Bustle and a forced external trade along lines of railway are not what the country wants, but only a quiet or steady slow dispersion of the population over the land, and a gradual linking of all the parts of it together by local interests. The iron way can neither make a nation grow like plants in a hothouse nor ensure wealth and comfort to a people, and the evils of Mexico are certainly not such as a few public works and a little more debt would cure. The best thing that could ever happen to the country would be its deliverance from the Spaniard and Spanish bigotry and superstition; but the native Mexican is not yet capable of effecting that deliverance without extraneous aid. Therefore I am disposed to lean towards a gradual absorption of the country by the United States, and I am disposed to think that this is how Mexico will become civilised. The population, commerce, agriculture, and railways of the Union will gradually work their way southward until Mexico becomes in a manner absorbed. Those constant border robberies and Mexican raids also always help towards that end. It will be well for the poor Mexican, and not amiss for the Spaniard, when the order-loving Yankee takes hold of the magnificent land which the Spaniard has laid waste so long. In the hands of the North American Republic, Mexico would become a great province—perhaps, in time, a great independent

State—rich in many products really conducive to the wealth and well-being of the world. As it is now, the country is a burden to itself, and almost grows poorer by its increased trade, because its increase represents in too many instances not reproduction but waste. Not even its silver is utilised in developing the mercantile resources of the people.[1]

In marked outward contrast to this old Spanish settlement is the Empire of Brazil, which stretches over nearly half the South American continent. Ever since Brazil became an independent State, which it did

[1] The aggregate trade of Mexico with Great Britain appears in recent years to have averaged rather over a million and a half sterling, and Mexico has bought from us in some years twice as much as she has sold. Small as this trade is, it justifies the agitation now going on for a resumption of diplomatic relations with Mexico by England. That step ought not to have been delayed so long. It is not possible to get anything like accurate figures of the general trade of the country, but it would seem to amount to nearly 12,000,000*l*. a year including the silver exported, on which, in a coined form, a duty of 5 per cent. is levied, or little more than the trade of Ceylon. The greater part of the trade of Mexico is carried on with the United States. Mexico has a debt of the nominal amount of 64,000,000*l*.; of which, however, by far the larger portion was created by the French inroads and is repudiated utterly by the State, which in effect acknowledges only about 30,000,000*l*. altogether. It does not appear to matter much what is acknowledged, or what repudiated, for no interest is paid or has for many years been paid on any portion of the debt. In spite of this summary lightening of the burdens of the exchequer, there is very frequently a deficit on the budget. Jobbery, the difficulty of collecting taxes, and general maladministration in the provinces, help to produce this result; and while it remains the normal condition of Mexican finance, it is a purely fanciful proceeding to add year by year the over-due coupons to the foreign debt and say Mexico now owes so much. Her internal floating debt must have crept up since the French war to ten or twelve millions sterling, and that will have to be paid in some shape before the foreign creditor can come in for a share in the surplus of the future.

about the same time as Mexico, it has been, after certain fashions, a progressive one. A quiet trade has been carried on with Portugal and England; the Government has been, in a measure, good and secure; and population has slowly increased. Had the Empire been content to go quietly on, it might have been pointed to as one of the soundest in the world, and it is, in natural resources, probably one of the richest; but in these latter days it has caught the universal fever, and, by launching into all sorts of attempts to force on progress, has seriously endangered its financial stability and possibly its internal peace. Made up, as the Empire is, of a number of vast provinces, which hang rather loosely together, the heavy burdens which the Government of the present Emperor has assumed may not improbably lead to internecine conflicts of at least a civil kind at a not distant date.

But though that be a danger, it is impossible not to appreciate and commend the spirit in which much of the modern efforts at development have been undertaken. Enormous physical difficulties, for example, prevent free intercourse between the various parts of the Empire, and it has only one great navigable river at its command, the Amazon, which runs through boundless regions of tropical country difficult to reclaim by Europeans, and very thinly tenanted by any race. The eastern side of the Empire is, for the most part, mountainous broken country, and the fertile valleys which lie inland, or by the beds of the insignificant rivers, are devoid of roads that would enable them to convey their produce to the coast. Railways of some kind have, therefore, been a first necessity to the internal development of Brazil, and most of the expenditure which the Government has sanctioned or made, on its own responsibility, to procure them is most praiseworthy. At the present time, the country possesses some 1,300 miles of lines, but except the Don Pedro II. and the San Paulo lines, which are together about 750 miles in length, they form only the merest rudiments of a railway system, consisting of upwards of twenty short lines, which penetrate a short distance inland from the ports of Recife, Bahia, Rio, Natal, Santos, and others, or branch off from small towns on rivers in the interior valleys whence they go as yet nowhere in particular. They are all nearly a dead loss to Brazil. It will be a matter of great difficulty, however, to carry these lines far inland, or to connect them so as to establish land intercourse between maritime provinces or with the interior, not only because of the mountain passes which have to be crossed, and the swamps that must be filled up, but because of the extreme paucity of population and consequent insignificant chances of trade. At the present time, although two lines constructed with English capital pay good dividends, the fragmentary 'systems' cost the country a considerable sum annually to make good the guaranteed 7 per cent.

interest, and thus add to the embarrassments of a State whose debt charges amount to a full third of the entire revenue. Brazil is, in short, in this dilemma. Without railways of some sort, inland prosperity can never be assured, and railways cannot be built to pay without population. All the territory from a short distance inland to a few given points is at present shut out from commerce with the rest of the world; and the magnificent plain of Matto Grosso, which is drained by tributaries of the Amazon and by the great rivers of the Argentine Republic, is nearly tenantless for want of the means of reaching the markets of the civilised world. What has been done, though in its way to be praised, is hence but a mere first step. The Empire of Brazil is, therefore, only a great possibility, and all the attempts it has made to seize a permanent share of the trade of the world have been more or less failures. Along the shores of the Amazon a trade is being fostered by an English steamship company and a tug company, which may in time lead to important consequences, especially if the project for opening up the route to Bolivia by means of a railway past the Mamoré River rapids should ever be carried out; but even this promising field is difficult to cultivate for want of people.

In the main, therefore, Brazil must be considered a country beyond the reach of rapid improvements, and its physical configuration alone would demand much greater caution in making dashes at development than has hitherto been observed. Large sums of money have been spent in Brazil foolishly, both on public works and in attempts to supply the lack of population. It must, I fear, be said that the grossest jobbery has, for example, characterised the efforts made to import English and German settlers into Brazil; and the miseries which most of these colonists have had to undergo have certainly been of the most distressing kind.[1] Not only has it been found that the Teutonic element would not fuse with the Spanish and Indian, that there were religious and social differences preventing anything like free intercourse, but the mere possibilities of existence have often been absent. Rich as Brazilian soil may in places be, it could not support spontaneously crowds of people thrown at haphazard on particular spots. Emigrants from Europe have, therefore, often starved, rarely prospered, and usually were much more of a burden on the State than a benefit to it. They were sent out by enterprising emi-

[1] In the Blue Book (c. 777), 1873, a very harrowing account of the miseries endured by British emigrants to Brazil may be found, and the statements therein given have been fully confirmed by later reports. We read there of skilled artisans going out to starve, of settlements without food, colonies that have no market, land occupied and no means afforded for tilling it, and altogether get a picture of official neglect, and of the consequent misery of the settlers, which ought to be known to every household in the land. No greater mistake could be made than for an English or German workman to emigrate to Brazil. Only merchants or engineers have a chance of doing any good there. The whole condition of the country, its social economy, and its poverty are against progress, as we understand the word in our own colonies.

gration agents for the sake of the commission earned, and whether they starved or lived was matter of indifference to them, and every immigrant thus imported and neglected is calculated to have cost the State 100*l*.

Brazil has thus lost in all ways in the attempts to bring money-getting settlers to her soil, and I think many of her other efforts at wealth-getting have been nearly equally disastrous. Her population is peculiarly unfitted for competition with those of more civilised countries in the higher orders of industry, and even in skilled agriculture the common people do not by any means excel. Most of the ten or eleven millions of people who inhabit the country are cross-breeds, and inherit, as such usually do, the prominent vices rather than the virtues of both progenitors, or, at all events, are subjected to a social system which develops the worst features of their character. There are also numbers of so-called Indians, settled and nomad, whose labouring capacity is small ; and the best workers in the Empire are unquestionably the negroes. The pure Portuguese settler is, like his Spanish brother, mostly a lazy animal, who prefers to live by the labour of others rather than by his own. Had he been active and enterprising in any industrial sense, he would have cleared some portion of the immense Amazon forests ere now to give daylight and civilisation a chance. They do not possess the energy to be even decent lumberers, and prefer clearing the land for crops by burning—a wasteful and treacherous mode of obtaining a passing fertility. Slavery is, besides, not yet abolished within the Empire, the law passed for that purpose in 1871 being as yet wholly inoperative as a means of alleviating the abject condition of the masses and awakening them to work for self-interest. It is one of those compromise measures which, while declaring the slave free at a future date, leaves him for the present at the mercy of his owner. Labour is, therefore, highly inefficient, and owing to the stoppage of the slave traffic with Africa —or its extreme restriction—labour is also scarce. Slaves fetch high prices and do little work, the result being that Brazil is wholly unfitted to compete with British possessions or the United States, or even with distracted Cuba, in many walks of industry. Another result, of course, is that in Brazil, as in Russia, there is next to no middle class beyond a few merchants at the ports. There are the slaveowners, and the abject classes, Indians, negroes, and half-breeds, which make up the vast majority of the population of Brazil. The wealth of the Empire is, therefore, in comparatively few hands, and the Government has but a narrow basis on which to rely for its supply of taxes; and in consequence heavy import and export duties have to be levied, with a view, as is supposed, of making foreigners pay, and year by year, with these restrictions on trade and growing burdens, the power to make ends meet grows more difficult. Brazil wants to raise yearly about 25s. per head in imperial taxation alone, which is—the situation of the mass of the population considered—a far heavier taxation than that borne by our most heavily burdened Australasian colony; and yet it tries to raise this without taxing land. Although land is thus free, however, agriculture is not benefited. On the contrary, nowhere in America, perhaps, is the tillage of the soil pursued in a more slovenly manner. The soil is not cared for, but merely cropped till it becomes exhausted, and then new clearings are squatted on. The agriculturists of Brazil appear therefore to be as a class wretchedly poor, and in the hands of usurers who exact, it is said, as much as 75 per cent. interest on their advances in some provinces.

Out of a congeries of unpromising subjects, such as her ill-mixed and abject population and her disjointed provinces afford, Brazilian statesmen have, in short, sought to build up a great Empire, and it is no wonder if they have hitherto practically failed. Brazil does not grow, and never keeps hold even of any great branch of trade which accident may throw temporarily into her hands. The United States have long ago taken back their supremacy in cotton; and in all other leading articles of trade, except perhaps cocoa and caoutchouc, Brazil has to be content to come in for such share as her stronger rivals in all parts of the world leave her. The physical disabilities, so to say, already mentioned, may have something to do with this, but the poverty of the people and the dearth of labour have more. Brazil is, for example, a large exporter of sugar, which, one would imagine, might be refined most profitably on the spot; but it is not, and it is very doubtful whether it could be on a paying scale. Even in sugar, moreover, our own West Indian colonies, hampered as most of them have been, more than hold their own against her, and she is, of course, beaten by Cuba. Nay, her trade in diamonds even is in danger of being destroyed by South Africa. With immense tracts, suitable for sheep and cattle grazing, with fine corn-growing regions, and an enormous expanse of tropical and semi-tropical forests, Brazil exports very little wool or tallow and hides, and her timber exports do not deserve mention in the same day with those of Mexico. The commercial reports of our consuls at her principal seats of trade are nearly all gloomy. Nothing is stable, little thrives, and as to manufacturing industries the population are probably quite unable either to initiate or to maintain them. Brazil has had great sums spent on her by private as well as public energy, and yet she sees trade elude her grasp. The money is spent, and Brazil is no better than before. A chronic financial crisis has for years prevailed at her financial centres, and trade is as unstable as the morning breeze. Yet, utterly undeveloped and utterly unable to hold its own as the country is, it has contrived to get deeply into debt. About 50,000,000*l.* were spent by the Government on the insane and most disastrous Paraguayan war, and about 19,000,000*l.* has been raised in Europe, mostly in England, on Government account, for the purpose of making internal improvements, buying ironclads, and the like. At the present time, therefore, Brazil has a funded and floating debt amounting at the lowest computation to about 76,000,000*l.*,[1] if we include the paper currency and Treasury bills. Besides the national debt proper, the provinces of the Empire have each separate deficiencies of their own, being but little controlled in their spending by the central power. In the aggregate these debts amount to about 2,700,000*l.*, according to the table in Mr. O'Conor's last report on Brazilian finances. These debts are held in the country of course, and no doubt help to swell the totals of Brazilian banks; but, none the less for that, they embarrass the administration, and tend to push still further apart provinces whose loose political adhesion and divergent circumstances have already made them far more independent and jealous of each other than the well-being of the Empire should allow.

[1] I have reckoned the Brazilian milreis or dollar at 27*d.*, which is taking about our average par of exchange. If it were not for the depreciation which huge issues of inconvertible paper have caused, the milreis ought to be worth nearly as much as the United States dollar. I see, however, that Mr. O'Conor, in his report on *The General Condition, Finances, and Economic Progress of Brazil,* a report worth reading (*vide* Legation Reports, part III. 1877) habitually counts the milreis at 2*s.*

Besides this debt there is also, of course, the incidence of the railway capital, almost entirely foreign, which has been laid out upon the country. When the roads now projected and under construction are completed this debt will amount to fully 15,000,000*l.*, independent of what the Government has spent on the lines built out of its English loans. The system of raising money on guarantees is thus rapidly working the same mischief in Brazil that it wrought in India. The budget of the financial year 1876-7 showed a deficit amounting in reality to nearly 4,000,000*l.*, although disguised and wrapped up to appear much smaller. All the revenue obtainable from every source amounts but to about 11,000,000*l.* During the past financial year the internal funded debt has been increased by the amount of this estimated deficit, and the annual addition to the indebtedness of Brazil from deficiency of budgets has rarely been less than a million sterling for a number of years. There was an apparent, not a real, equilibrium in the inflated years 1871-2 and 1872-3 ; but ever since no expedient of issuing 'apolices' or internal bonds, no raising of the note circulation and treating of foreign loans as revenue, has been able to conceal the yawning gaps. Hence we may expect to see the estimated deficit for the year 1877-8, which is under a million, greatly exceeded, in spite of the anticipations of the finance minister from his short-sighted attempts to adjust the customs tariff by increasing its weight and extending its incidence. The revenue of 11,000,000*l*. or 102,000,000 milreis cannot be extended by such an expedient as raising the tax on imports of articles of luxury to 40 per cent. when the country is getting poorer every day, or by the imposition of a coasting duty, as it ought to be called, when foreign goods, which are already duty paid, are shipped from one part of the Empire to another. Still less likely to do good are the duties of 5 or it may be 10 per cent. imposed on goods imported for behoof of the foreign corporations whose money has been used for the development of the country These may indeed do more to turn away foreign capital from Brazil than any recent act of administrative folly—such as the decree ordering preference to be given to the railway iron of France over that of England—for they imply a direct breach of faith. Englishmen have made and worked railways in Brazil on the distinct pledge that they were to be allowed to import their materials duty free; and though this would have been an unjust distinction had there been any native capital or native companies capable of doing similar work, yet in the circumstances and seeing that the Government made such a stipulation in order to attract foreign capital and enterprise to a country devoid of both, the imposition of these taxes now is an unpleasant breach of faith and a piece of folly to boot.

The deficit, I think it may be safely predicted, will certainly next year exceed the estimate, for already an enormous pressure has been put on the country to bring the revenue up to its present level, a pressure borne by the interests most vital to the development of the State—those of its external commerce. Stronger proof of this pressure could not well be given than is to be found in the fact that the revenue has risen within the last ten years from about 6,000,000*l.* to its present amount. At the very time when the revenue of Brazil was thus only half what it is now, her trade was probably better than it has ever been since, for she was reaping her full share of the benefit which flowed to other countries from the civil discord in the United States. It is no exaggeration, therefore, to say that at the present time Brazil is labouring under an intolerable burden. Year by year the financial distress must increase as the Government forces more and more of its paper on the country in payment of debts for which it can find no cash, at the same time that it recklessly fosters unprofitable schemes for the improvement of the country. Every budget thus comes to be supplemented by ruinous 'extraordinary credits.' As the country is manifestly working up to and beyond the limit of its resources, the ever-recurring deficits are well calculated to excite the keenest alarm. Unless more money can be borrowed in the European market before long, or unless fortune brings a new wave of temporary prosperity, Brazil must soon pass through another crisis much more severe than that which has raged during the past few years like a low fever eating the vitals of the country away. Of course it is said that the heavy deficits are not real, being, like those of India, due to public works extraordinary ; but that is a mere delusion. A country which mortgages its future for the sake of works which are not now productive is guilty of the most dangerous of all extravagances. Brazil has not within her borders the raw materials for great national advancement.

The import duties now existing stifle the inward trade almost altogether, and prevent at the same time any healthy development of other sources of revenue. Brazil has a total trade amounting only to some 35,000,000*l.* on the average of recent years, and it must tend inevitably to grow less year by year, in the absence of artificial stimulants. At present the exports usually exceed the imports by some three or four millions sterling a year, and were that the result of cautious trading it would be a hopeful feature. As the result simply of poverty and a prohibitory tariff, it merely indicates that the absence of fresh loans must lead to a decrease in the demand for Brazilian products, and that from imports the diminution will pass in time to exports, till Brazil emerges from her troubles nearly stripped of her recent advantages. England, at all events, has little to hope for in the way of increased business from Brazil for some time to come, both the financial and the political influences being against her ;

and an embarrassed Government must, in any event, cause increasing disturbances in the trade balance. The progress which Brazil has made of late years is, in fact, as nothing to what she will require to make before her position is secure. Increased issue of paper to cover Government deficits means increased depreciation in the exchanges, increased difficulty in developing industry, and a greater risk to trade in all its branches. At present, the credit of Brazil stands high here in England, because people do not trouble to look at the situation of the country; but distress that cannot be hid is approaching with rapid strides, and Brazil, the most peaceable and in some respects the best-governed State in South America, will have to wade through deep waters before she can master the evils of her position. A better description cannot be given of the trade evils of that position than that of the Pernambuco Chamber of Commerce, quoted by Acting-Consul Corfield in his report for 1875.[1] 'The crisis,' says the Chamber, 'against which our unfortunate commerce has contended for upwards of four years still continues! From each year as it passes an appeal is made for the ensuing one, but the evil assumes each time more serious proportions! Failures continue, confidence disappears, credit is considerably restricted, trade is diminished. Well-established houses are ruined, and this tremendous concourse of alarming antecedents

[1] *Commercial Reports*, part v., 1876.

drags along with it the hope of seeing affairs take their former course, bearing in mind above all the guilty indifference with which these things are observed by the supreme authorities of the State.'

Pernambuco may possibly be at present suffering more extremely than some of the other provinces along the Atlantic coast. Labour is being drawn away from this and the other northern provinces to Rio and the south for public works and coffee planting; and both in sugar and cotton these northern provinces are beaten nearly out of the market. In the main, however, this description applies to the whole of Brazil. The country groans under the weight of its burdens, and little short of a miracle can prevent a disaster. At this very time famine stalks through the land, and the failure of the food crops will seriously add to the dangers of the financial situation. This is cold comfort to persons interested in Brazil; but it is a conclusion which might be supported by a volume of facts. I content myself with appealing to the general considerations I have here advanced.[1]

[1] The trade of Brazil with the United Kingdom has been nearly stationary for the last three years so far as our imports thence are concerned. So far as regards the exports of British produce to Brazil, the tendency is towards decline, and no doubt this decline will grow more clearly visible unless we will lend the Empire a few more millions to keep things going. In the aggregate, including the foreign and colonial produce sent through English agency, the trade of this country with Brazil represents about 21,000,000*l*., or more than one-half the entire business of the Empire. It is no insignificant item even in our trade, and its diminution cannot be viewed without concern. At present, however, there is

nothing in view to stop the decline, and we must be content to put up with it, trusting that a few years hence the Empire may master its difficulties and emerge a sounder and larger customer than ever. The value of the raw cotton imported from Brazil to this country was only 2,344,000*l.* in 1875, and in 1872 it was as much as 4,730,000*l.* Raw sugar yields a much more favourable comparison, but Brazil cannot hope to compete permanently with advantage in that article under her present labour arrangements. Coffee alone, amongst her important articles of export, shows a steady growth year by year, and may continue to be a large trade, though competition has lately prevented it from being a very profitable one. Next to ourselves Brazil's best customer is the United States, but its trade consists mostly of imports by the States. Brazil buys comparatively little in return. Brazilian coffee of course enters the Union free.

CHAPTER XIV.

THE RIVER PLATE, CHILI, AND PERU.

THE so-called republics of South America with which we must next deal possess more interest for the historical student than for the political economist. They are hardly so far consolidated or civilised—if we except Chili—as to make them full of any interesting lessons. Yet in some respects they are capable of affording warnings, not only to older communities, but to such recent settlements as our own colonies. Some of the River Plate republics, and Peru in particular, possess a record which, when closely studied, might make one despair almost of the possibility of fragments of old races being able to found new vigorous and prosperous States. The vices of the mother-countries seem to breed and develop in the new to an extent which makes them a curse to the earth rather than a blessing. I need not speak of Paraguay, which has been crushed nearly out of existence by its wars with Brazil and Buenos Ayres; but what shall be said of the Argentine Confederation, or above all of Uruguay? Except under a despot, neither the one nor the other has made substantial political or social progress since the yoke of the mother-country was cast off. At the present time the Confederation is said to be ripe for a new revolution, and Uruguay rejoices in the grasp of a dictator. 'Self-government' is in such communities a grotesque mockery, and respect for law and order a fair but unrealisable dream of the closet student. The little republic of Uruguay, which we may look at first, is endowed by nature with many advantages. As a pasture ground for sheep and cattle its uplands excel much of the 'bush' land in Australia, and its harbour of Monte Video at the mouth of the River Plate is one of the best located in all South America. Attached to Brazil, this port and the navigable rivers stretching away inland from it might prove the means of delivering that Empire from its torpor, and help to solidify its scattered and disjointed efforts at progress. Left to its own devices, however, Uruguay merely wastes all its chances and destroys the possibility of progress. For a few years it had a kind of feverish prosperity, owing to the loans it raised, and to the inconsiderate endeavours of English capitalists to develop industries in the country; but these have all ended, and Uruguay lurches towards a deeper anarchy than that from which it for a moment emerged. We here in England undertook, for example, to furnish Monte Video city with waterworks, and lost our money in the attempt; we built the republic a railway or two, and can get no interest for the money; and then, to crown all, we kindly handed several millions sterling to the shifty unstable government of the country, only to find ourselves laughed at when there was no more to be had out of us and pay-day came. The only terms on which we could get money out of Uruguay was by lending it more. The Uruguayans do not see the good of labouring to pay interest to the English merely for honour's sake, and prefer to spend the money at home and enjoy themselves. Of course this wealth, poured in from without, had the usual stimulating effect on the Uruguay trade, and in 1872 and 1873 its imports from this country reached a total of nearly 2,000,000l. annually, all kinds of produce included. Since then, however, the inevitable consequences have followed; and although we still buy nearly as much there as ever, or at least ship as much at Monte Video, we did not sell in 1875 much more than half what we did formerly. In 1876 our purchases from Uruguay were worth just about two-thirds of the entire value of the previous years, and the exports thither, though larger than in 1875, were little more than half those of 1872 and 1873. That they realised the figure they did was no doubt due in some degree to the fact that the Government and public works borrowed on have paid nobody. If the real consumption of Uruguay were alone taken, it would be found, I believe, that we do not in the best of times export to that country a million's worth of goods a year, but, as the returns from Monte Video include merchandise intended for Buenos Ayres and up-river provinces, it is not possible to give an exact estimate. Should, however, the English settlers be compelled to leave the country, and should the English companies and trade institutions established there collapse, as seems probable, our trade may almost die away altogether. Not but that there is a certain amount of private wealth in the country—every settlement containing civilised beings has some wealth—but the social disorganisation is so great, and the national and mercantile credit so utterly rotten, that active business is fast becoming almost an impossibility. Uruguay might compete successfully with our Australian colonies in the supply of wool of a superior kind, but, instead of that, gets hopelessly beaten. A great trade might be done in prepared meats and in raw or tanned hides, but nothing stable of the kind can, under the present order of life, be hoped for. A few years or months of peace, followed by a fresh struggle by the military brigands for the spoils of office, during which public works are destroyed and public credit ruined—this is, in brief, the ever-repeated history of this unhappy 'republic.' The best thing that could happen to it perhaps would be its seizure by English bondholders, who might forcibly 'attach' the land as security for their debts, and drive out the worthless Spanish half-breeds and adventurers, colonising it with sturdy Anglo-Saxon farmers. In the days of Elizabeth or of James I. that plan might have been tried, but in these times no one has pluck enough to make the attempt. In all fairness to Uruguay, however, it should be said that it has not been well dealt with either when under the mother-country or when in the grasp of Brazil, and to some extent its present degradation is, no doubt, due to the hardships and demoralising troubles of its youth. The question is, whether the present elements of which its population is composed bode a better manhood. I doubt it. The people have been trodden upon till they have degenerated into weeds of humanity.

The Argentine Confederation, which lies on the other side of the Uruguay River and the La Plata Estuary, and stretches northward by the side of Paraguay to the borders of Bolivia and Brazil, and westward to Chili, is in some respects in a worse plight than Uruguay, and in others much better. Highsounding as the name is, the republic itself is a very ill-hung-together group of so-called provinces, not one of which has any present good government, or, if we except that of Buenos Ayres, any substantial realised wealth. There are European settlers all over the Riverine Provinces it is true, and the territory between the Uruguay and the Parana is admirably suited for nearly every description of farming, so much so that it has attracted not a few Englishmen. There are also lands in the interior of a very high quality, which, although deprived of water communication with the east coast, might, if peopled and well governed, support comfortable and even wealthy communities. In short, nearly the whole of the eastern and central parts of the republic, as well as a great proportion of Buenos Ayres, and perhaps some of the land south in Entré Rios del Sur, are well suited for the European colonist, and might become the seat of a wealthy and highly civilised nation. The area of the republic is nearly six times that of the United Kingdom, and except in the centre, north, and north-west the country is by no means mountainous. On the contrary, it abounds in flat plains interspersed with grand forest regions that resemble the prairie lands of North America, and whose stock-feeding capacity probably excels that of much of the Australian bush. Nearly all these advantages have, however, been hitherto vitiated by bad government and internecine strife. The Confederation has almost always been more a name than a reality, mainly because the maritime province of Buenos Ayres, which, as lying at the throat of the country, so to say, and possessing much of the finest land in the temperate region, was best peopled and richest of all the settlements in the south, determined and still determines to be supreme and to legislate in effect for a'l the rest. Buenos Ayres was the seat of the old Spanish Viceroyalty, and that of itself gave the province a sort of traditional supremacy, which the people of the inland regions have always sought to overthrow. So lately as the last elections in 1874 there was an *émeute* in Buenos Ayres because it was said that the new President, Dr. Avellaneda, was not sufficiently a Buenos Ayres man, he being a native of Tucuman; and disaffection at the present moment slumbers, waiting only for the next favourable opportunity, while there are continually some disturbances occurring inland.

We may say that the provincial jealousy of Buenos Ayres is foolish; that as the inland districts in a measure depend on its port they should be content to let it rule; but common sense has unfortunately as yet little or no part in Spanish politics anywhere, least of all perhaps in these misnamed republics of the south. The Argentines are bent on aping the United States, and must have their provincial legislatures by the dozen whether they can afford them or not, each of which goes its own way and defies the Central Government when the whim takes it. Accepting the facts as they stand, we find that the Argentine Confederation at present practically makes no progress at all—in wealth or in anything else, but that lately it has to all appearance been going backward. The Supreme Government is too weak-kneed to be able to punish offences, political or other, done in the provinces or sometimes even at its own doors, and rebellion is, therefore, at times the most profitable trade a man can take to. The more successful he is the more certain is his pardon and probable his advent to power, and even if he fails he stands a fair chance of gaining much more respect than if he had kept quiet. This weakness and this rivalry between the sections of the Confederation have of course the effect of quickening the strenuous efforts at concentration made by the Buenos Ayres Government. A crying want of the inland country is railways, in order that they may share the markets of the more favoured provinces; and so railways have been built in all directions often quite without regard to the chances of their paying, chiefly to give the central power greater facilities of control. One line was opened in 1876 as far as Tucuman, a province lying close to the Indian territories of the north, and liable to be overrun by them, therefore a province little inhabited and incapable of furnishing trade to the line. The population is less than four to the square mile, and of that number more than half are of Indian origin. There are magnificent tracts of land in it, and it is well wooded and watered; but except the small sugar and distillery industries round Tucuman there is little basis of trade, and what there is stands liable to be destroyed in the next eruption. But it must have a railway for all that, though the rails should rust under one train a week. A railway would place it in communication with the capital and render control more easy.

If the Government can afford the expense, however, the railway may do good, and in time conduce to a more secure and peaceful state of affairs. But the 'if' is just the question. Altogether the republic possesses about 1,600 miles of railway, built for the most part by the National or Provincial Governments, and of this not more than one-sixth at the present time can be said to yield an approach to a satisfactory net return. The Central Government has got itself into difficulties by the lavishness with which it has set itself to 'improve' the country before there was anything in it to base improvements upon, and at the present time, as for nearly four years past, the whole community has been struggling in the throes of a national bankruptcy. Falling into arrears with its payments, the National Government has been compelled to adopt a number of questionable expedients with a view to make ends meet and provide for the service of the foreign debt, and under the pressure of these trade has been almost paralysed. I know of no more striking example of the effect of rash expenditure on a country than that afforded by this ambitious but ill-compacted State. So long as it could get the English people to lend it money, either in the shape of national and provincial loans or as private ventures, there was quite a brilliant outburst of seeming prosperity. Without any internal taxes to speak of being imposed, the revenue rose to an unprecedented figure, and everybody was, to all appearance, making money fast.

Directly the inflow of foreign money stopped, however, this process was reversed. Everybody began somehow to lose money, the national income dwindled, and with the growing impecuniosity of Government and people lawlessness and crime got a new lease of life. This temporary prosperity was found to be very costly, and it has brought the republic to the verge of an abyss over which I fear it must yet plunge. It is not very easy to give accurate figures regarding Argentine finance—there has been such an enormous amount of unblushing falsehood published about it—but the latest figures are of the most ominous kind. When this essay first appeared I appended a note here giving President Avellaneda's gloss of the situation; but I have since then received the public accounts of the republic for the last financial year, and they prove that Avellaneda did not tell the truth. He placed the debt of the Confederation at 12,000,000*l*. or so, and it is actually nearly 17,000,000*l*. exclusive of the excessive issues of paper made to keep up the national credit. At the present time the National Government appears to owe some 500,000*l*. of floating debt in London under various heads, and it is at its wits' end for money. I have therefore substituted for the original note an analysis of the budget given in the 'Times.'[1]

[1] The subjoined is from the *Times* of August 18, 1877 :—'We have before us the accounts of the Finance Minister for the past financial year, and they give more striking testimony than ever to the distressed condition into which a mad financial policy has brought the country. They also let us see something of the manner in which dividends, and, what

It must be remembered, too, that figures such as these by no means represent all the debt of the Con-
are still more onerous, sinking funds, on the loans are provided. As there are the usual attempts made by interested persons to mystify the public on these points, we shall take the opportunity to state a few of the facts. The basis of all is, of course, the revenue, and that for the past year was $13,583,633, neither more nor less; all beyond this was, in some shape or other, borrowing. The actual expenditure on administrative purposes was as follows:—Ministry of the Interior, $3,479,004; Foreign Affairs, $158,002; Justice and Instruction, $1,474,953; and War and Marine, $7,378,930—making altogether $12,492,080, or within little more than a million dollars of the entire revenue. But the Ministry of Finance required in addition $9,660,959, mostly for the service of the funded and floating debt; so there was a deficit of $8,569,415 on the accounts of the year, or more than the amount required for the entire debt service by about $2,000,000. These are plain figures which there is no getting over, and this deficit has to be added to one of $9,877,645 brought from the previous year; so that altogether the floating debt at the end of the last financial year was $18,447,060. This sum is juggled away by the manner in which the various fiduciary note circulations are brought in as sets-off to floating debt; but, apart from these fiduciary issues, these are the facts, and even with these the official figures show, contrary to the assertion of those who make it their business to uphold Argentine finance regardless of facts, that the debt has considerably increased during the year. According to the summary of the total debt of the Confederation for the year ended March 31, 1876, the net total debt, funded and floating, was $80,203,958; and at the end of last year, after deducting the amounts of two issues of notes, one of which was for $15,000,000 in provincial currency, estimated as worth $600,000 in silver, and the other for $10,000,000 nominally metallic, both of which sums went in part to meet Government obligations, the total debt was $84,013,129. But for the amount of these notes actually issued it would have been nearly $89,000,000—a tolerably large rise in one year, especially when it is remembered that heavy sinking funds are constantly in operation.

'Such being the simple official facts as to the position of the Argentine revenues and expenditure, we think it may be taken as proved that the dividends and drawings on the debt have not been provided from revenue, and the prospect of a further deficit is so decided this year that what has been true in the past is plainly true now. But how, then, have the dividends been met? Partly by borrowing in London on pledged stock, and partly by these note issues in Buenos Ayres. We will take the dividend paid last September as an example, because the accounts relating to it are given in the official report, all save one, which has been federation. One source of confusion in estimating its total has been the separation of the Buenos Ayres debt from that of the Confederation, because it is in the nature of things only a fictitious separation. Since Buenos Ayres reasserted its supremacy in General Mitre's war in 1868, it has practically been the republic. All the revenues worth mentioning are collected by it, and it may be said to have complete control of the Customs; for although the two great rivers are navigable far inland, there is really little river trade independent of the capital, and the Customs House of Buenos Ayres is therefore the main prop of the national

sent in too late for insertion. Of the money then due $600,000 was provided by the above-mentioned issue of $15,000,000 notes of the Province of Buenos Ayres, the currency of which is so depreciated by successive issues of this kind that the dollar note is worth now only some three halfpence or twopence. The rest of the money was provided by Messrs. Baring Brothers and Co. on the night before the dividend became payable, apparently on the security of 1,000,000*l*. unplaced stock of the 1871 loan which had been handed over to them some time before by the loan contractors, Messrs. Murrieta. Many people remember to their cost the anxiety, misery, and distress which the probable failure to meet this dividend caused, and the accounts show both how it was provided and how narrowly the republic escaped default. The last dividend paid was met by the issue of metallic notes—i.e., notes supposed to be convertible —by the Provincial Bank. An issue of 2,000,000*l*. nominal was authorised, but it was not all required at that time. Should the deficit on the current year prove to be anything like $7,000,000, however, all the balance and more will be required to enable the Government to pay its way; and there can be no doubt that it is now compelled to have recourse to credit, as usual, and that the present dividend and drawing is no more paid from revenue than the last, whether the Government paid the needful money into the Provincial Bank or not. Last year the Minister tells us that he had recourse to temporary borrowings to the amount of $14,017,782, which cost him $1,307,822, or nearly 10 per cent., and with a dwindling revenue and an increased floating debt he can scarcely be in less necessity now.'

finances. Apart from that, Buenos Ayres is the sole substantial part of the republic, and contains more than a fourth of the entire population—by far the most industrious and wealthy fourth. In Buenos Ayres city and province there have been large numbers of English settlers and merchants, and many of them remain still, with the Germans, quite the most solid part of the population. There are also Italians and French, in greater or less number, all contributing to make Buenos Ayres more important than the whole of the rest of the republic put together. The provinces of Santa Fé, Entré Rios, Tucuman, and Corrientes, whose joint population nearly equals that of Buenos Ayres, have no revenue to speak of, and perhaps would not pay it to the National Government if they had. Two of these have also their own foreign debts, and these ought to be added to the Confederation debt and included in the total. Now including the blown-out obligations of the poverty-stricken Buenos Ayres city itself, the debt of these provinces in Europe alone at present amounts to about 5,500,000*l.*, bringing the total direct interest-bearing debt of the republic up to over 22,000,000*l.* The average rate paid on this debt is probably not less than 12 per cent., perhaps more including the sinking fund charges, which are in themselves now of monstrous amount compared with the results which the country gets from the money. By means of the cumulative system which makes all these loans merely terminable annuities for the holder, the capital coming back in an ever-increasing ratio as the amount needed for interest dwindles, the sinking fund charges on these loans now almost equal the charge for interest. Time was when the suspension of this foolish drain of capital might have saved the republic from default, but I fear that time has gone by. The houses involved in these loan operations have preferred to keep up a show of complete solvency when the reality was not, and the rickety fabric they have laboured to build will now probably tumble altogether about their ears. For the funded debt of republic and provinces is by no means the entire financial burden; as will be seen from the extract from the 'Times,' the currency paper is swollen most recklessly, and the Buenos Ayres paper dollar is now not worth twopence. The so-called hard dollar currency is fast following in its wake, and it is no exaggeration to say that under the accumulated weight the republic staggers towards financial ruin.

Treating the debt of the republic as a whole, whether called national, provincial, or guaranteed, we find that there is a total interest-bearing debt of about 25,000,000*l.* borne by less than 2,000,000 of people, of whom a large portion are either Indians or half-breeds. This includes the railway guarantees the exact amount of which I have not been able to ascertain, but which I have taken to represent about 2,000,000*l.* of capital. The borrowing of this money in one shape or other has led the whole country astray ; and were it not so rich, so highly favoured by nature, one would say at once that there must come, on the heels of the recoil, collapse and national disruption. Since 1873 trade has, indeed, fallen off, especially import trade, to an enormous extent. The Government has had to borrow secretly in London to sustain its credit and to issue paper-money at home, till trade has become a gamble, and at the same time lawlessness has spread in the interior till the settlers are fleeing for their lives. Nothing could well betoken more obviously decay and dissolution than the accounts which fill even the Government papers of the crimes of robbery, murder, and rapine committed, apparently, with impunity in the inland regions, where with so much assiduity the authorities have laboured to plant ' colonies ' after the manner of Brazil. These colonies were in themselves good, and had, probably, a much better chance of success in many parts of the Confederation than in Brazil, owing to the two magnificent navigable rivers ; but in some regions they are almost threatened with dissolution, if they be not altogether broken up.[1] With this, the

[1] I had collected a number of extracts from the Argentine papers illustrating the dangerous condition of the rural settlements, but find that they would be both too horrible in detail and too long for embodiment in this chapter. Instead of the details, I confine myself to the following extracts from the Buenos Ayres *Standard*, a paper which cannot be accused of painting the affairs of the republic in lights unfavourable for the Government :—' The state of the camp is now such that it is unsafe to go alone in broad daylight. Armed gangs of ruffians, well known to the public, hover about the environs of the small towns, to follow the single

normal state of affairs, revenues are of course ruinously affected, and every year shows a yawning deficit, which the Government has no means of making up except by the printing press. Dependent for gold on the customs receipts, and unable to pay the foreign debt charges without gold, a heavy tariff has been imposed on both imports and exports, part of which is exacted in coin, with the result that the imports have dwindled to half their amount in the years of inflation, and the total revenue of the Confederation is not now much more than half what is required. Confusion and embarrassment haunt all departments of the administration and of trade for want of means, and by reason of the absurd restrictions imposed. The Government now actually levies a 10 per cent. export duty on several staples of export, with which it has to compete closely with several other countries in the markets of the world. In the midst of these most severe financial pressures the deputies of the Argentine congress vote themselves increased salaries.

At the same time it would be unfair to hide the fact that the Confederation has made some progress in material resources during the past generation, or to

traveller. They are splendidly mounted, and laugh at the authorities; it is therefore as much as a man's life is worth to travel alone.' 'On all sides we hear people complaining of the awful increase of crime, both in town and camp, which is causing such alarm among peaceable Europeans that many are thinking seriously of leaving the country. It seems a similar plague of blood afflicted Buenos Ayres from 1823 to 1833, until checked by a strong hand.'

deny that this progress gives ground for hope that the future may yet see something of the dreamed-of prosperity. Discarding the illusory inferences to be drawn from revenue and imports in the past few years, both bolstered by borrowed money, a very brief statement of the growth of its export trade and its character will prove that all has not been waste labour or money. The export trade rose from 4,240,000*l.* in 1860 to 8,200,000*l.* in 1870, and to over 9,000,000*l.* in 1873. In 1875 the figures were still higher, reaching about 11,000,000*l.*, in spite of the stagnant condition of trade nearly all over the world. In 1876 there was, it is true, a considerable falling off; but there can be no doubt that, in spite of such backwardness, very substantial progress has been made, proving the great capacity of the country. Its flocks and herds bear witness in the same direction. The numbers of sheep in the republic must be greatly exaggerated at 80,000,000,[1] and they are, whatever their number, of very inferior quality; but that the farmers and cattle graziers of Buenos Ayres possess enormous wealth in this direction is beyond question. The Confederation is hence a rival to Australia in the supply of wool, and competes with our colonies with some success for the Continental demand. The ox hides of the Confederation are also very valuable staples of trade, for which it finds a growing demand; and it is not improbable

[1] Mulhall's *Handbook of the River Plate Republics.*

that the present war in the East may temporarily divert still more of that trade to the River Plate. Efforts are also being made to utilise the meat supply for the European markets ; and should they be successful, the Confederation will have every ground to hope for an accession of wealth in that direction. At present almost the sole use that can be made of its superabundant meat supply—the republic is said to have within it from fourteen to fifteen million horned cattle of a kind —is to convert it into jerked beef, or to reduce it to the substance known as 'Liebig's Extract.' As yet, however, the export trade of the country rests on a very narrow basis, and the swollen figures of the last few years may represent exhaustion as much as progress. The country has had to strain and to sell all it could get together to meet the calls of the usurers into whose grasp it has let itself fall. With all this growth, therefore, the republic can hardly be said to have any land under cultivation, as we understand the term ; though, undeniably, progress has been made by the farmers of Buenos Ayres, and all that is wanted is good, economical, and secure government to enable it, after the storm, to surmount all difficulties. These wants are, however, very large indeed when a Spanish colony is in consideration, and at the present we can only hope doubtfully. The National Government is affected with the weakness of impecuniosity, and knows not which way to turn in order to repair the gaps in a crumbling revenue. We might say that the high customs tariff ought to be reduced, and that a land tax should be imposed, seeing that the provinces now reap what benefit there is derivable from its rule ; but these remedies are hardly possible in the United States, and in the Argentine Confederation may not be dreamt of. The customs revenue is about the only thing on which the national executive can depend, just because it is the only kind of revenue which it has strength enough to collect with reasonable completeness, and the country is now so mortgaged that it may be doubted whether a reduced tariff would for some time add much to the revenue from this source. Be that as it may, Argentines are not in the mood to be convinced that it would be good to reduce the tariff now. On the contrary, the present high tariff is triumphantly cited as a means of reducing the imports, which have in 1876, ' for the first time this century ' a newspaper says, been brought lower than the exports. As there is next to no gold in the country, this reduction must continue, and go further, if means are to be found to pay the foreign debt charges, towards which the proceeds of the larger exports must go. Hence the high tariff, both import and export, but especially import, finds much favour. It is like cutting a man's throat to prevent him from choking, perhaps ; but desperate diseases need desperate remedies, and the Confederation must be allowed to muddle its affairs as it best can. In the meantime, whether national bankruptcy supervenes immediately or not, it is certainly not a place to which Englishmen should emigrate. They stand a good chance of losing their money if they do, and perhaps their lives also. Every mail brings accounts of outrages perpetrated on the peaceful settlers ; and the zone of anarchy is, it would seem, a widening one, as is to be expected when the Government is weak-kneed, childishly extravagant, and incapable.

Nor can we expect to do a larger trade with the Confederation in the immediate future than in the past. Not only are the anarchy, the poverty, and the tariff against us, but the trade connections of the republic appear in any case to be drifting partially away from us to the Continent. France, Italy, Belgium, and Germany are all coming forward ; and this competition, combined with the other causes I have named, reduced our exports to the River Plate in 1875 to little more than half what they were in 1872, and reduced those of 1876 to only some two thirds of 1875. Our imports thence have only once exceeded 2,000,000*l.*, and appear to stagnate at about 1,500,000*l.*[1] This is, of

[1] Our principal trade with the Confederation consists in the import of hides, wool, skins, and tallow, and the export of cotton and woollen goods, and metal-works, hardwares, &c. As regards our imports, the values of the tallow shipped to British ports fluctuate considerably, but on the whole are pretty well maintained, affording rather an evidence of the extreme variability of the trade capacity of raw undeveloped countries than a sign that we buy less from the republic. The same may be said of skins and furs, which ran from 750,000*l.* worth in 1873 down to 399,000*l.* worth in 1874, and up again to 523,000*l.* worth last year. Hides, bones,

course, matter for regret, but until Englishmen can venture to settle in that country as they would in the United States, we can hardly expect it to be otherwise. This I doubt whether they will ever do; race antagonisms, creed antagonisms, and a climate only in parts favourable to the propagation of northern Europeans, all tell against wide-spread settlement by people from this country. We must therefore be content to do but a limited part of the trade of the Confederation, and may for some years see that trade dwindle to figures much within even those now ruling. The Argentines will, indeed, buy as much from us as we please, if we will lend them the money to pay their purchases with; but since we have ceased doing that, they are either not buying at all, or inclining to carry their custom elsewhere; our possessing the bulk of the carrying power alone giving us any great foothold in the country.

and so forth, show the same movements. As regards exports, however, the tendency of values is steadily downwards. Cotton goods have sunk in value from 1,300,000*l.* in 1872 to 556,000*l.* in 1876; hardwares have dwindled from 202,000*l.* to 54,000*l.*; linen and jute manufactures almost as much; and metals, wrought and unwrought iron, were much less last year than in 1874, the highest year, the figures being for 1874, 883,000*l.*, for last year, 325,000*l.*, the lowest figures since the inflation began. It is just the same with woollen goods, which have sunk without intermission in five years from 474,000*l.* to 150,000*l.* These serious diminutions are of course reflected in the smaller articles of trade, such as leather goods, machinery, glass, and earthenware, haberdashery, and the like, and must be attributed more to the growing poverty of the republic and the bad tariff than to the success of other nations in competition with us. It is in buying and carrying the exports of the republic that these are beating the English importer and shipowner, rather than in supplanting us as sellers. With the further advance in the tariff made in the end of 1877 we may look for a still greater contraction in the trade.

Altogether the picture which this republic presents is a curiously chequered one, and we can only say that in its government it is unfortunately as yet thoroughly Spanish, while the best elements in its material prosperity are not Spanish. The struggle between the elements of corruption and decay, and those of progress and order, is not yet half over ; and what the end will be no one can predict. For myself, I look for further strife and attempts at disruption, or at the very least for a financial overturn sure to come when some of the banks and financial houses now neck and ears involved in Argentine affairs give way, if not before ; and that being so, I say, ' Avoid the land.'

Passing westward to Chili, we at once enter a territory where this struggle of opposing forces may be said to have ended on the whole in the triumph of the best elements, which at the time of its hard battles for freedom helped to form the interesting and singularly-placed little community. As everyone knows, Chili is a long narrow strip of territory cooped up between the Andes and the Pacific Ocean. It has a coast-line of about 2,000 miles, and its greatest breadth does not much exceed 120. Much of this long fringe is quite unfit for cultivation, owing to the manner in which it is cut up and intersected by spurs of the mountains, which run down to the shore ; but there is also a deal of it very fertile, and the warmer northern and midland parts abound in minerals. Everywhere, moreover, there is easy access to the coast, so that water communication is extremely abundant, and the Chilians suffer little serious inconvenience either from the extreme length of their country or from its being cut in two by the little semi-independent Indian State of Araucania—the only aboriginal community left on all the American continent that has any pretensions to be a State. Though thus shut in to itself and the trackless ocean, as it were, Chili has been a fairly prosperous country, as well as a singularly peaceful one, and to-day unquestionably enjoys the most settled Government of any offshoot of Spain. This may be due in part to the neglect with which Spain treated it while she had it, but more perhaps to the mixed character of the inhabitants, and the facility with which any part of the country can be reached by sea from the seat of Government. This in itself makes successful insurrection nearly an impossibility.

The trade relations of Chili have always since her independence been very intimate with England, and her population contains a large admixture of English or English-descended people. The gallant efforts which Lord Cochrane made to free the country from Spain, and the heroism he displayed, have given the English name a prestige in Chili which it has never yet lost. That being so, her trade prospects and capacities have a peculiar interest for us, and I am happy in being able to direct the reader to a recent official publication, which contains an elaborate and most valuable account of the country.[1] I can do little more here than summarise the conclusions of this report, if indeed I have space left efficiently to do that.

Chili being a country at peace with itself, we need not concern ourselves with its Government, except when the acts and policy of that Government touch the springs of trade. And on this head there is on the whole not much ground for complaint. The debt of the republic is only about 10,300,000*l.*, involving an annual charge of some 8*s.* per head, and the Government is not very extravagant in its pursuit of development projects. More than three-fourths of the debt is due to railways, of which the State has about 400 miles in operation, and most of the rest is due to the last struggle with Spain, so that the country is not overdriven. It does not indeed require to be in this particular direction, having such easy communication with the coast. What difficulties Chili has, therefore, are not due in the first instance to its debt. Yet the country can never be said to have established a sound and permanent trade in any staple, except its copper, and in that also it is now experiencing and has for years experienced a keen competition from Spain and Australia, which has seriously impaired its supremacy,

---

[1] Report by Mr. Rumbold on the 'Progress and General Condition of Chili' (*Embassy Reports*, part iii. 1876).

and is in these dull times so reducing prices as to make the entire trade unprofitable. The rise of the American settlement in California and of the English colonies in Australasia, gave misleading spurts to the trade of Chili in another direction which have not been maintained. Its old customers have become its successful rivals in corn-growing, and Chili is finding itself almost beaten in the supply of an article which many of its fertile valleys are peculiarly fitted to produce. The same instability which has marked the course of Brazilian trade also marks that of Chili, which requires a large population in its own neighbourhood to become in reality, what some have named it, the England of the Pacific. We find, however, that there is a certain progress, although marked by many severe fluctuations and return waves, and, as a rule, the exports of the country have exceeded the imports in a wholesome degree. Chili has succeeded in widening the range of her trade in the midst of her very defeats, and can now export, not merely corn and coffee, but also cattle, horses, timber, wool, and hides in moderate amount. According to a table given by Mr. Rumbold,[1] the proportion of the total exports which now falls to agricultural products is 43·60 per cent., that of mines 45·17. There could be no more satisfactory sign than this advance in the agricultural prosperity of the country. Mr. Rumbold indeed points out that the

[1] Report already cited, p. 373.

balance of trade has been against Chili of late years, and this is no doubt a danger which must not be lost sight of; but, should no fresh stimulus be given to the import trade by fresh borrowings abroad, it is a danger that must soon right itself. The difficulty of obtaining a market for the produce of the country for a year or two should itself tend to check the over-luxurious habits of the Chilian upper classes and compel a wholesome retrenchment. This, of course, means a diminished import of foreign goods, and that is a consequence which we shall have probably to look for during the next few years. The Franco-German war gave the last brief period of feverish activity to the Chilian trade in cereals, the effects of which on the spendthrift luxurious class have hardly yet passed away. That Chili will altogether lose by the present stagnation what she has gained as an agricultural nation I do not for a moment believe. She has the task of supplying Peru, at all events, on her hands, and partially furnishes Bolivia and the Argentine Confederation with bread; for in what I consider real agricultural development she is ahead, not of these only but of every other State in South America. The commonplace business of growing corn is, after all, a higher occupation than driving cattle over boundless plains; and an unsettled country, which grazes cattle but does not till the soil, is a far way from solid comfort and established wealth. Owing partly to their increased poverty, however, the Argentines are not such free buyers of Chilian corn now as they were a few years ago, and were peace assured within their borders they might soon themselves turn exporters. Overpowered in the markets of Europe, Australia, and South America though Chili may be, she is still able, however, to send her corn to all markets, and to sell it in all at a price, and that of itself is an immense gain.

The least satisfactory feature which I find in the country is the peculiar manner in which the farmer is hampered. Land is apparently held on a tenure quite as bad as our own, and the country is affected with the absenteeism inseparable from the possession of huge estates. Leases where they prevail are short also, and little incentive is therefore given to improvement, so that the tendency is rather to exhaust the soil. There have been many improvements made in the Civil Code of late, however, and perhaps the day of a revised tenure of land is not far off.[1]

---

[1] The condition of the Chilian peasantry would appear to be very abject. A portion of them are settled on the land attached to the large farms, and may, in some cases, enjoy a 'rudimentary state of comfort and civilisation,' but large numbers are miserable proletaires, who have no fixed abode or regular family ties. These wander from place to place where work may be had, or, like the Irish peasantry, leave their native land altogether, and find work elsewhere. Many have gone to Peru to work on the railways. Clearly a class of people such as this affords no basis on which to build up a soundly prosperous State, and before Chili can attain to substantial greatness, commercial and political, the numbers of the settled small cultivators must be greatly increased. The state of the rural economy of the country at present will be best seen from the following table, which has been compiled by Mr. Rumbold from official

Considerable results may not unlikely flow from the extensive silver mines lately discovered in the north. Till the mines of La Florida were opened up Chili was almost without precious metals; but the annual output of silver is now considerable, and will at least help to make good the probable decrease, not to say absolute cessation, in the out-put from the copper mines of Atacama and elsewhere. The trade of Chili must, however, be dependent in the future on its agriculture more than on its mineral wealth, even supposing it possessed large deposits of gold; and every-

statistics, and from whose report the above particulars are taken. The figures relate to five of the most productive provinces:—

Name of Province	Total Number of Properties	Total Area of Province	Number of Haciendas[1]	Aggregate Area of Haciendas
		Cuadras[2]		Cuadras[2]
Concepcion	587	217,740	69	136,362
Linares	205	232.831	46	134,370
Nuble	3,869	252.667	216	169,978
Curicó	498	197,154	158	127,899
Department of Talca (The returns for the whole province of the same name are incomplete.)	656	258,448	101	131,730
Aconcagua	1,462	562,854	68	The area of the haciendas is not given; but some of the largest and finest estates in Chili are situated in this province.

[1] Large estates. [2] A little over three acres.

This is a most unhealthy state of affairs in a young country, and accounts for the fact that, although a new country, Chili enjoys the privilege of sending no small proportion of her scanty population to help to people other lands. Mr. Rumbold says that 75,000, out of a total population of about 2,400,000, are at present supposed to be away from their native land.

thing which tends to stimulate the people to efforts at higher cultivation, and that induces a widening in the range of crops produced, must be regarded as of the utmost importance to the country. There should be no restriction on exports in the shape of either customs' duties or vexatious port dues, and every encouragement ought to be given to the peasantry to settle down to the cultivation of the soil. Government expenditure ought to be reduced as far as possible within limits easily bearable, and every encouragement given to the breaking up of swollen estates or to the granting of long leases.

At present there is a tax on all leases of more than ten years, amounting to 4 per cent. on the rental, and this acts as a practical prohibition of any but short-term holdings. Nine years and eleven months is therefore the common term, and that does not induce capitalists to occupy or to spend money upon the land. This tax should be removed, and free opportunity given to those who have means either to lease the land or buy it. The latter step would be the preferable, and it seems that a certain pressure is now being put on the enormous estates, through the operation of the agricultural tax, which falls heavily on large properties while exempting small, and by the law which compels an equal subdivision of property between children. The Government, on the other hand, cannot be altogether exonerated from the charge of extravagance and the recent annual deficits which threaten to become chronic ought not to be allowed to exist, if the nation is to maintain its pre-eminent position in South America.

The deficit in the budget for 1874 was as much as 1,369,000*l.*—a very large sum on a total expenditure, ordinary and extraordinary, of 4,502,000*l.* For 1875 the estimates were nearly as unfavourable; the budget showing again a deficit of more than 1,000,000*l.* No doubt this is, like our Indian deficits, a result to be chiefly ascribed to the prosecution of public works, and may so far be justified; but it is not all so, and Chili ought not to indulge in heavy outlays on such works while her ordinary budget cannot show a favourable balance. Moreover these estimates and amounts, as well as those for 1876, are to all appearance the most favourable that can be made. In Chili, as in Spain, finance ministers like, it seems, to make a fair show in their anticipatory statements, which the stern facts at the year's end belie. Accordingly all recent years have shown an actual deficit beyond the estimates in the ordinary revenue, while the expenditure has always been swollen by supplementary credits. That this should be so is a grave circumstance, and the country cannot be considered free from financial danger till these overdrafts and irregularities are at an end. If they cannot be put an end to, the country will in time go the way of its neighbours

One significant fact may be pointed out in this connection as throwing light on the public capacities of the Argentine Confederation to bear its burdens. Chili has a larger population than the Confederation and a much smaller debt, it has rich mines and splendid agricultural resources, peace has ruled within its borders for a generation, and it has had special windfalls of trade, yet apparently it cannot make ends meet. How much less its neighbour and rival, whose country is untilled, whose inhabitants are preyed on by Indians and escaped thieves, and whose ambition is beyond measure more costly!

The trade of England with Chili may not increase much in the next few years, it may even decrease; but what of it there is may be looked upon as sound, and we have little cause to fear home-grown competition there. As in other parts of the world, there is a high tariff against the English merchant, some 25 per cent. *ad valorem* on the average, and that will no doubt tell very severely should prosperity cease to shine upon Chilian efforts at development; but it is not unlikely that the worst force of this has been spent already, and at all events the tariff does not bolster rickety industries at home. The trade of the last three years has been contracting, and we may hope that, tariff or no tariff, the limits of this contraction have been nearly reached. If they have not, Chili will suffer by the decline much more than England, for the aggregate trade between the countries, though only 8,000,000*l*. or so at the best and reduced last year to but 5,500,000*l*., is all-important to Chili. I cannot do better than quote Mr. Rumbold on this point :—

The trade between Great Britain and this country is on a sound basis. The imports and exports nearly exactly balanced themselves up to the year 1855. The exports then took the lead by one-third, and in 1861 rose to double the imports. They have not ceased since then to exceed the imports, and last year did so to the amount of 1,000,000*l*. sterling. But not only is the Chilian trade with England on a sound basis, it may be said to exhibit peculiarly healthy features. Chili sends us seven-eighths of her bar copper (in 1874 7,063,710 dollars' worth of copper bars out of a small total value of 8,143,661 dollars), and almost all the rest of her mineral produce. She further ships to the United Kingdom nearly three-quarters of her surplus agricultural produce. On the other hand she takes from us over fifty kinds of raw and manufactured articles, most of which are of first necessity, and, whether worked up or consumed in the country, largely contribute to its general wealth and well-being.

The only remark I would make as to this pleasing summary is about copper. The price of that article has fallen in the last four years 40 to 50 per cent., and I doubt whether it can be now mined and exported by Chili save at a loss. At all events the stocks of Chilian copper in both England and France have been accumulating lately for want of a market, and a crisis in the copper trade generally appears to be approaching. Perhaps the loss on this head which Chili will have to suffer may be made up for the time being by a larger demand for her cereals—wheat, maize, and oats. Our exports to Chili have, of course, fallen off like those of other countries, compared with the inflated years, especially woollen exports.

Mr. Rumbold's summing up of the general position of Chili seems to me also so exceedingly good that I willingly substitute his words for mine in taking leave of this part of my subject :—

The blessings which Chili enjoys she owes to the pure traditions implanted in her administration by the founders of the republic; to the preponderating share taken in public affairs by the higher and wealthier class; to the happy eradication of militarism; to the sedulous cultivation of innate conservative instincts; to the nearly entire absence of those accidental sources of wealth so lavishly bestowed by Providence on some of her neighbours; to the consequent necessity of strenuous labour rapidly repaid by a bountiful soil; to the patient endurance and capacity for toil of her hardy population—above all, perhaps, to the neglect of her former masters, which, when she had cast off the yoke, drove her to create everything for herself, and called forth exceptional energies in the nation. Most of these may be summed up in two words : work and shrewd sense (*trabajo i cordura*). It must, of course, not be forgotten that she is indebted for much to a climate as nearly perfect as any to be met with on the globe; to a smiling sky, beneath which everything thrives; to the grand mountains which not only have contributed to her wealth by an abundant supply of the baser but more useful metals, but in the critical period of her infancy guarded and isolated her from too immediate a contact with the troublous communities around her. Not a little, finally, she owes—and should not forget that she owes

—to foreign, mostly English, energy and assistance; to the strangers who have fought for her, taught her children, built her railways, and traded to her ports, and to the not inconsiderable admixture of foreign blood that leavens her population. The Chilian people have now attained a remarkable degree of prosperity; but, if friendly criticism may be permitted to one who sincerely wishes them well, they have lately shown some signs of the intoxicating effects of good fortune. Though partly at present under the sobering influence of a commercial crisis, which is likely to be protracted longer than is now apprehended, they are still inclined to go somewhat too fast. They have certainly withdrawn very much from excessive speculation, but they are still bent (the Government and upper classes in this giving the example) rather on decorating and beautifying their house than on setting it in more perfect order. A first visit to the City of Santiago cannot but be matter of agreeable surprise to an intelligent European, but after a more lengthened stay the ambitious growth and luxury of the town will probably seem to him out of due proportion with the power and resources of the country of which it is the capital. One is, indeed, scarcely prepared to find ninety miles inland, at the foot of the Andes, a city of some 160,000 inhabitants, with such handsome public buildings, stately dwelling-houses, and exceptionally fine promenades. What, perhaps, strikes the stranger most —next to the marvellously beautiful situation of the town —is the atmosphere of aristocratic ease and exclusiveness pervading it. Unfortunately it is an absorbing place, drawing to itself too much of the wealth of the country. The dream of the provincial Chileno is to make enough money to build or buy a house in Santiago, and there live at ease. It has thus become an idle, expensive, and, so to express it, an artificial capital of a busy, thrifty country. It is also a place of ugly contrasts, for cheek-by-jowl with palatial structures the most dismal hovels are to be seen there, poverty flaunting its rags at every step in the broad sunshine, instead of being relegated to remoter suburbs as in European great cities. It is termed by its inhabitants 'the Paris of South America,' but is more like slices of Paris dropped down here and there in the midst of a huge, straggling Indian village.

Only two republics now remain to be dealt with—Bolivia and Peru. Regarding the former there is little to be added to the general observations made in the previous chapter, for Bolivia is a country till recently nearly shut out from the rest of the world—a country, as one of its friends has assured me, that has been 'fearfully wronged.' Its outlet towards the sea is a sandy waste, and its chances of foreign trade, though much improved by a railway to the coast, are still small unless it can get the free use of the Amazon and the La Plata rivers, or find better accommodation through Peru. Containing within its area a population perhaps as large as that of the Argentine Republic, and endowed with enormous mineral deposits, amongst the rest its famous silver mines of Potosi, and large regions of magnificent agricultural land, Bolivia is yet one of the most insignificant States in South America—a country governed by the priests and the swash-buckler adventurers who are accustomed to carve a way to the Presidential chair with their swords. Although material improvements have been made lately therefore—roads built to many parts of the republic, and a certain degree of order maintained—we cannot speak with great condence of the future of this State. However inexhaustible the mineral wealth of the country may be, its gain therefrom is and has been small, because this wealth passes into the possession of the few who have been too ready always to retire to Europe to spend it, while the mass of the population grovel in abject poverty. The revenues of the State are under 600,000*l*., and there are the usual deficits which weak and extravagant Governments cannot exist without creating. The total direct trade of Bolivia with this country is a little more than half a million a year, of which our exports thither did not, up to 1875, represent as much as 100,000*l*. In the last two years the figures show some improvement, reaching nearly 223,000*l*. in 1876, and so far this may be taken as a good sign. Yet, and granting that a certain amount of merchandise finds its way into the republic by way of Peru or Chili, of which we cannot give an estimate, the trade of Bolivia with England is at the best small. So insignificant a result, even supposing these totals in fact doubled, with a wealth of natural resources so excellent and varied, tells its own story. There is little to hope for from Bolivia for some time to come. The day may come, however, when Bolivia will emerge from its darkness, and when by way of the Amazon or through Chili or Peru, if not by its own solitary port at Cubija, intercourse with England will be greatly extended ; for the possibilities of the country are very great. At present the people are too acutely poor to be good customers ;

but this may change in time, although the possibility is too remote to be much dwelt upon. All we can do is to aid the advent of the better day by all the means in our power short of abetting the Government in extravagance.

We must now direct our attention to Peru—the land of Pizarro, the country of the Incas, those wise despots whose empire seems a fabulous dream when placed side by side with the picture which the unhappy country presents to-day. There is indeed no portion of the Spanish possessions in America which presents so miserable a spectacle as this fragment of the ancient dominion of the 'children of the sun.' From being a fertile, thickly-peopled region stored with all riches, it has become 'a howling desert.' Instead of good orderly government we have often the most lawless brigandage—at best brigandage organised—and the only developments to which this brigandage has treated the much-abused country have been debt and jobbery. No longer able to work the valuable silver deposits which Peru contains, the enterprising officials worked guano instead, and borrowed on it, and so got credit at home and abroad to the fabulous extent of nearly 40,000,000*l*. nominal.[1] From first to last this

[1] The go-ahead recklessness of the rulers of Peru cannot be better illustrated than by comparing its financial position with that of the Argentine Confederation. The interest-bearing debt of the latter is roughly little more than half the amount per head of Peru; yet Peru, with a population of at least a million more than the Confederation, has a total foreign trade which barely equals the Argentine exports. Nearly

new source of gain has probably poured from 70,000,000*l.* to 80,000,000*l.* into Peru in one shape or other, enriching the adventurers who ruled it, and the innumerable satellites of the contractors—loan-mongers and the multifarious financial leeches who delight in such countries. All this money has gone in two ways: to enrich the governing classes and enable them to despise honest labour or anything honest or honourable on the face of the earth, and to fill the pockets of financial schemers. If there be a third use to which it has been put, we find it as a corollary to the first— the ruling cliques being able to buy useless ironclads and to surround themselves with soldiers out of the foreign money. Here, in short, we have a country which by a little wise handling might have been one of the richest in South America, which at one time mined large amounts of silver and gold, which latterly quarried millions of tons of precious manure, yielding vast sums of money; whose slopes, valleys, and mountain plateaux needed but irrigation and the husbandman's care to yield rich harvests of nearly every tropical and semi-tropical product that could be named; and what does it exhibit to us? Sloth,

four-fifths of the Peruvian exports, moreover, are made up of substances which are, as it were, forced out of the country in order to provide means for the enjoyment of the rapacious drones who eat up the country. With so little trade, with a population that the Government cannot tax as it would, and with revolutions a matter of nearly annual occurrence, it is easy to understand that the condition of this wretched country must be low indeed. If the Argentine Confederation has a doubtful future, who shall dare hope for Peru?

barrenness, corruption, anarchy, misery, debt, railways
'to the moon;' ironclads, for wild spirits to rebel with;
and nearly every conceivable social scandal and political
abortion. The advantages of Peru have originally been
greater than those of any other Spanish American
State, except Mexico, and all we can now say of her
is, that her disgrace and ruin have also been greater.

To-day Peru is a spectacle among the nations. At
this very time, after having become miserably bankrupt,
instead of directing her attention to the true sources of
her wealth—irrigation and the tillage of the soil—her
head is turned with the new project of the Yankee
railway contractor, who has engaged to build the
remainder of one of the maddest, and in some respects,
I believe, one of the worst constructed railways in the
world—the line which he boasted was carried to an
elevation of '16,000 feet above the level of the sea.'
This railway, called the Oroya, cost, it is said, about
4,500,000*l.*; it has been an absolute loss in every
respect—a worse loss than the many similar projects
that have cursed Peru. But it is to be completed to a
point further inland, because the contractor has held
out the prospect of being able to reopen the flooded
and abandoned silver mines of Cerro de Pasco. A
company has been formed, and its paper is now pour-
ing out on an already paper-swamped population at
home, or is finding its way in the shape of bills to
London. Peru has built over 2,000 miles of railway

altogether already, and not one line out of the whole twenty odd making up the total is at present a paying concern; hardly any yield 1 per cent. on their capital. Even the little Lima to Callao line, owned and worked by an English company, which formerly paid pretty well, has been brought almost to the verge of ruin by a competing line, built by the Government as a means of plunder in reckless disregard of private rights. The bulk of these railways must, to all appearance, go to ruin, if the character of the administration of the country does not change. The devastating sloth-loving Turk has not done more harm to the old Roman Empire of the East than the Spaniard has done in Peru.

It may indeed be said that calamities such as that terrific series of earthquakes and the tidal waves induced thereby, which lately wrought such havoc in the country, could not fail to demoralise the hardiest spirits and induce a disregard of everything solid and progressive. This might, no doubt, be the case were these calamities of frequent occurrence, but they are so rare that their effect on the minds of the people should not be greater than that of Vesuvius on Southern Italy. Not only so, but the uplands and vast plains which stretch from the inner flanks of the Andes far across the continent are nearly exempt, if not altogether exempt, from the evil effects of these earth-storms. They affect the coast and the lands by the coast, not of Peru merely, but of Bolivia and Chili. Peru has, indeed, no more excuse for her disgraceful condition on the score of these visitations than Chili has, and we cannot avoid laying all the blame of her misery on the race that nearly three centuries and a half ago got a foothold in the land. Three centuries ago! South Australia, a creature only of yesterday, with a handful of people, has as large a trade as Peru. All the Australasian colonies together have not got her population, and yet they carry on a trade greater almost than all Spanish America ever knew, except in the palmiest days of the robbery of the races whom the Spanish marauders overthrew.

At the present time the trade of this magnificent country is mostly composed of substances, every shipload of which, in present circumstances, means a step nearer the ultimate utter impoverishment of the land. These substances are guano and nitrate of soda (cubic nitre), both powerful fertilisers, which it does not seem to strike the Peruvians to utilise to any appreciable extent at home. They are simply good things to sell, and to borrow or cheat upon. No doubt Peru could afford to export a large portion of these valuable deposits in any case; but it seems bent upon exporting all as fast as possible for the sake of gold, the thief's only wealth, and certainly no regard whatever is paid to the true interests of the land. What might not Peru do in sheep-farming alone, were agricultural pursuits to be as industrially cultivated there as in the Argentine Confederation even! Probably no wool in the world would find so ready a market or be so widely prized as the soft silken coat of the Peruvian llama or alpaca sheep. So also Peru could produce excellent qualities of cotton in almost limitless quantities, and, instead of being dependent on Chili for food-grains, ought to be herself a large exporter. Owning the rich plains of the Montana, irrigated and fertilised as they are said to have been when the Spaniards descended on the country, Peru is capable of becoming almost the Mexico of South America. Alas! that we should speak of all these capacities only to realise the more forcibly the impossibility of anything worth mentioning being made of them in the present condition of the country. The Peruvians want gold and silver, and will build railways, will flood the world with their promises to pay in order to gratify this lust; but they will not work. With few exceptions Spaniard and Indian are alike in this respect, only that the Spaniard idles of an evil nature, and the Indian from the hopelessness of a life that long oppression has made a blank.

At the present time Peru has no important exports except raw sugar and wool, and these are insignificant beside the figures of guano and nitre. The sugar cultivation is chiefly in the hands of foreigners—not Spaniards—and is the only cultivation of any promise in Peru. But it is carried on under considerable difficulties; and the probabilities are, that once Cuba is free, and with South Australia successful, Peruvian growers would, like Brazilian, find themselves at a disadvantage. Her production of cotton appears to be on the decline, and India is sweeping out of her hands the once profitable trade in Peruvian bark, while no sensible increase is visible in her exports of llama and alpaca wool. Her exports to England alone were, indeed, larger in value last year than in previous years, solely because of heavier shipments of guano. They reached a total of over 5,500,000*l.*; but, on the other hand, her imports from England have dwindled steadily till they are now little more than 1,000,000*l.* The financial condition of the country is, indeed, such that it is hardly possible for it to either continue a good customer to any country or to establish any industry with the hope of success. Owing to the fraudulent manner in which the Government has taken advantage of the banks, either in borrowing from them and not paying back, or in emitting inconvertible paper, all business has suffered most ruinously on exchange operations, and credit within the country is nearly destroyed. In spite of this, the extravagance of the governing class continues, apparently, as great to-day as ever. Political opponents are pensioned off by the parties in power, and a herd of loafers is thus gathered to eat up the resources of the country. After the flush of wealth which elated these people from 1868 to 1873, they have no nerve left in them for self-denial, had they ever possessed it; and although there are no more foreign loans to be had, although the import trade on which the customs revenue mainly depended has been largely reduced, and although the population of three millions odd—more than half Indian—is either unable or unwilling to pay taxes, the 'civil establishments' crave for their usual mess of pottage. Only the other day the Government wanted to borrow from the banks of Lima half a million *soles* (dollars) in gold, and it made no scruple to break its most emphatic obligations, when making the new guano contract last year, in order that 700,000*l*. a year might be secured out of the proceeds of the guano exports for the benefit of the loafers aforesaid. For the same reason, every effort is made to push the nitre trade in opposition to the guano. The Government is not, it is true, inhumanly selfish in this, because it must pay its backers to be allowed to exist. It does not, therefore, itself pocket all the proceeds of this large traffic : part of the money goes to soothe its political opponents, and to keep the permanent wire-pullers of corrupt political cliques in good humour. This very diversion of the proceeds of the large exports is itself, however, a barrier to any sound import trade in the country. The money released by the default on the debt does not enlarge the spending power of the general community. What of it is not absorbed by usurers in London and Paris enriches rogues in Peru.

This is a most distressing spectacle, the details of which might be multiplied almost indefinitely; but I forbear. All that need be said is, that when compared with Peru, the Argentine Confederation seems a land of plenty, and even Mexico a country of promise. There is at present little to hope for in that quarter, then, and the trade of England cannot develop there for many years, if ever. More probably it will sink into greater insignificance, as it has been steadily doing since 1873, or even 1872, unless we are prepared to tempt the Peruvians with another supply of money, either to help heirs of that 'Messiah of Railways,'[1] the late Mr. Henry Meiggs, to develop the neglected silver mines of the interior, or to enable them to clear out with greater expedition the nitrate deposits that nearly cover the province of Tarapaca.

I have now done with Spanish America. The review has been rather summary perhaps, for the subject is in some aspects supremely interesting; but, judged by the present or proximate value of the commerce of that region with England, it has been full enough. I only regret that it has not been favourable. Perhaps the necessary brevity of these observations

[1] Such was the blasphemous epithet applied to this Yankee contractor by some of the venal press in Lima—*vide* Duffield's *Peru in the Guano Age*, a graphic little book; also the recent effusions published on Meiggs's new project.

may have heightened the depressing effect of the picture as a whole, because I have been compelled to leave out of sight all those minute details which serve to relieve even the shadows. In the main, however, I fear my observations have been too mild rather than too harsh and gloomy. Dismembered, ill-governed, mostly priest-ridden, Spanish America will, to all appearance, grovel through its history till races capable of higher destinies take possession of the land.

Although for more than three centuries in Spanish and Portuguese hands, a large part of South America is still an undiscovered country. There are gleams of light, however, in some regions of it. We may venture to hope doubtfully for Mexico, for the Argentine Republic, for Brazil, and more surely for Chili, partly because they are not exclusively Iberian. Nay, there is even a chance for the distracted republic of Columbia and for Venezuela; and slowly, but possibly with good prospect of ultimately gaining a position amongst civilised nations, Bolivia, thanks to foreign enterprise, has lately been emerging from her darkness.

Some of these countries will, we may hope, always give England a certain share of their trade, whatever its volume; but on the whole I fancy the destiny of their foreign trade, be it great or small, lies more with the United States and with our Australian colonies than with us, and that the regenerating forces which they nearly all need will come mostly from the former.

Already the enterprising North Americans are pushing their wares into all the markets of the South Pacific and Atlantic, and the trade between Chili and Australia, at all events, though dipping very low, has never been altogether submerged. As one looks at the map one sees that such trade currents, north and south, east and west, would be the natural ones, and it is by no means an extravagant notion to entertain that at some future day the busiest marts of the world may lie on that continent and between it and the Anglo-Saxon settlements in the Southern Ocean. The North, with its enormous stores of coal and iron, its fine energy, and order-loving communities, may dominate in time over Central and South America, and command the heavy manufacturing trade and the machinery supply of the whole continent: while an equally energetic race in Australia and New Zealand may find outlets there for special products and command at least a fair share of custom in the South, as well as give an important impetus to local development along the South Pacific coast. In this contest England will in time be worsted, just as in the far East her children, working from their vantage grounds in Australia and Western North America, may in time be greater merchants and rulers of labour than she is now. This is a far-off dream, perhaps; yet it is impossible not to see that foundations for its realisation are being laid, and that the commercial future of South America, when its yet distant better day comes, at all events, does not lie with us. We hold much the largest share of the trade at present, partly because of our splendid steam mercantile marine, but we are being elbowed now and may by-and-by be beaten. Be that as it may, in the meantime trade is dull and the prospect by no means bright in South America, wherever we turn, for the English manufacturers. In the most prosperous States there extravagance has been rife within the last decade, and a burst of extravagance means always an after-fit of parsimony, forced or voluntary. If we ourselves are now suffering from the effects of long-continued extravagances, how much more must those still half-organised communities be whose populations have little or no realised wealth? I fear that the worst point is not yet reached by some of them, and that business in most parts of South America will be slow and nearly profitless for the English exporter for several years to come. When it revives again he may find himself partially forestalled by Germans and Americans. That, however, is not a matter in itself to create alarm, for were the trade worth fighting for now we could perhaps beat both in the supply of most staples; yet that probable conflict, as well as the present depression, must be taken into account in any casts ahead, and the very lowness of the stream of business just now conduces to make us give up the conflict. German houses are forcing their way into strong positions in Brazil and the River Plate, as well as in Mexico, and draw the business out of our hands even for the supply of our own goods.

CHAPTER XV.

THE WEST INDIES, AND OTHER MINOR BRITISH POSSESSIONS.

MUCH that would be interesting might be written about the minor foreign possessions of England—those which are not colonies strictly speaking, but merely estates to be worked for the benefit of their alien masters. Their trade is not, however, of sufficient importance to warrant any extended inquiry into their condition, and I shall content myself therefore with a very brief indication of the more salient features therein. As everyone knows, the small properties of England abroad are very numerous, ranging from the minute Heligoland, Gibraltar, and Hong-Kong to the Gold Coast, the West India Islands, and Ceylon. Most of the smallest in the long list are quite without the range of my subject; but the West Indies, in the widest sense of the word, and the Gold Coast and Ceylon, deserve a moment's attention. I shall begin with the West Indies as the oldest and in some respects still the most important of these minor territories. Commercially the most important portions of the British West Indies are Jamaica, Trinidad, and the strip of mainland known as British Guiana.

Jamaica and Demerara have been for long—the former especially—a source of sugar and rum supply for this country, and in recent years these countries and Trinidad have rather risen in importance, owing to the disorganised state of Cuba. Not only has part of the trade of Cuba passed over to the comparatively insignificant island of Jamaica, but a minute part of its population also, with results very favourable to its industries. Others of our West Indian possessions have, of course, benefited in a like degree, and in, at all events, the two articles, sugar and rum, trade has of late been reasonably flourishing throughout the British West Indies and Guiana, while in some fair promise has been afforded by the efforts to cultivate coffee and tobacco, although in others the former industry has almost died out, owing for the most part to the competition of Ceylon and Brazil and to the lack of labour which has weakened all these colonies for generations. The supplies of cocoa make up, however, in some degree, for this falling off in coffee.

The possible subjugation of Cuba, however, may do a good deal to upset this promise of prosperity, especially if pacified Cuba be able to retain her slave labour as heretofore. Cuba has always been the favourite source whence the North Americans have drawn their foreign supply of sugar, and none of the British possessions have been able securely to divert the course of that trade towards themselves. The cotton cultivation experiments in Jamaica have, moreover, been complete failures, and the progress made in the production of sago is quite insignificant. In Guiana and Trinidad there seems further to be a difficulty in maintaining the population at its present level except by constant coolie immigration ; while in Barbadoes the blacks tend to swarm too thickly. Trinidad is better off than Demerara, and flourishes ; but is rather isolated, and does not escape feeling the want of labourers. Throughout the West Indies there is, in short, nearly everywhere some special drawback to complete prosperity either in the competition of neighbours, or the rivalry of cheaper producing regions, or in the climate, the disorganised state of the population, and the fluctuating demands of foreign markets. There has been a great deal of mistaken legislation and much wasted money in these regions since the emancipation of the slaves in 1834 ; and there can be no doubt that the sudden liberation of these poor creatures in a state utterly unfit to enjoy freedom was nearly entirely ruinous to the British West Indies as English trade tributaries, whatever the ultimate good to the blacks may be. The only justification of the measure was the practical impossibility of making emancipation gradual. The hope of some of them has therefore come to be fixed on coolies brought from East India, and in others it is just possible that a race of native negroes may grow up capable of working and willing to extend by small farming the productiveness of their regions. In these circumstances the future of these islands and territories is a matter which calls for much more attention than the English public is likely to give it. Putting the Spanish colonies out of the reckoning, there are enough elements of difficulty in all of them, except perhaps in Trinidad, to make the Government somewhat anxious. The effects of the labour revolutions are not nearly at an end in any one of them. Considerable accumulations of debt affect almost all, and there is great difficulty in making ends meet in some, even in prosperous years, owing in the main to the excessive cost of the imported labour. Should trade reverses overtake them, the home Government may possibly have to lighten their burdens more than it has yet done, and it has had to do a good deal. In Jamaica itself, the Government debt has been, in one sense, considerably reduced within the last ten years, if we deduct the invested sinking funds; but considerable local obligations have been, on the other hand, contracted, which help to make the total uncovered debts of the colony still about three-quarters of a million. British Guiana, again, has been put to the expense of nearly 250,000*l.* for immigrant coolies, and owes altogether, under various heads, about 340,000*l.* Trinidad has also a debt of 200,000*l.*, and most of the smaller colonies have either already incurred a certain amount of debt, or are an annual charge upon the Imperial Treasury, and some of them are unquestionably, for all that, ill-developed and indifferently looked after. Others, such as the Bahamas, seem to be gradually losing their trade, and to be in a measure dying of inanition. Other parts of the world more favoured than they beat them out of the market, and the money spent on them yields no adequate return. Yet nearly all of these possessions are, or ought to be, of high value to this country for their trade alone. The West India Islands send us on an average nearly 5,000,000*l.* worth of raw produce every year, and buy more than half as much from us exclusive of their direct trade with other countries. Jamaica, as it fills with the younger race of thrifty, industrious, negro small cultivators, will, it is to be hoped, in time get over its troubles, and become a very valuable possession in a commercial sense. Every step which the thrifty class of negroes takes towards comfort and affluence will increase the importing power of the island. Its exports are now steadily rising in value and amount to more than 1,500,000*l.*, but this is a small figure to what Jamaica may yet reach if judiciously governed and nursed.

There are other ways, however, in which these possessions have a high value—those on the mainland particularly—and it is a surprising thing that more has not been done with them. Guiana forms an admirable *point d'appui* for trade with the inland region of the Northern Amazon valleys and with Southern Venezuela, were these countries opened up as trade intercourse with Europe might open them. Trinidad is, in this respect, also admirably placed for intercourse with Northern Venezuela and the valley of the Orinoco, and does now have a limited business in that direction. The island is at present perhaps about the most prosperous of all our possessions in that quarter, and has (for its size) a large trade, partly of a transit character, with the United States, as well as with Canada and several countries in Europe. As the States of that part and South America get settled, a new life will come to some of our territories, and we shall find that their possession enables us to command at least a fair proportion of the trade of that region—a trade which is growing even now. But for the foothold which these islands and our possessions on the mainland give us, I am inclined, at all events, to think that our chances would in no long time be small as against the United States, should these become wise enough to throw off the hampering manacles of protection. Their ingenuity and perseverance are threatening to beat us in certain departments of engineering trade in spite of the fetters.

In the home aspects of this West Indian trade the chief factor is sugar. Had the West Indies not been able to supply us with very cheap raw sugar during the last few years, the French must, I think, have beaten our merchants and refiners almost entirely out of the market. Many West Indian growers have been put to great straits by the competition as it is; but so far they have on the whole enabled us to hold our own in the main departments of the trade, and the comparative failure of the French beet crops for the last two years compelled French refiners actually to resort to our possessions for part of their supply, to the injury of their best monopoly. The high prices which ruled in sugar during the autumn and winter of 1876-7 have brought direct benefit to the West Indies; and were labour cheaper or more plentiful, there is little doubt that our planters could hold their own in the now less buoyant markets against all comers. While they can plant with even tolerable success in dull times, there is no danger of England being driven permanently out of the sugar markets of Europe, although for certain qualities of refined sugar she may not be so good or so cheap a source of supply as countries like France or Holland, whose people are taxed to keep up the profits of the manufacturer and secure a monopoly to a knot of rich people.

These are but one or two of the interesting points connected with the trade capacities of our West Indian and Central American possessions, but they will suffice to show that England should not lose sight of them amid her many greater ones. Once on a time they, no doubt, were dreamt of as forming the beginning of a great empire in that quarter—a counterpoise to the Spaniard, a means of wrenching trade from the Dutch—but that dream has gone and has given place to an unmerited neglect. We cannot colonise Central America, it is true, with Englishmen; but with care and attention, with some of the vigilant self-seeking mastership which is so diligently carried out in India, more might be made of what lands we have there than is now the case—possibly also much good might be done to the wretched communities which surround us. The labour difficulty is, next to English apathy, the most serious drawback on the prosperity of some of these colonies. Much more care is no doubt taken now of the coolies imported from India than was formerly the case, but there must always be a certain amount of callousness and cruelty connected with this method of importing hands. It is slavery more or less disguised, and may seriously impede the development of these settlements if great vigilance be not exercised, both over the expense which the import system causes, and over the condition of the indigenous population who are in some cases injuriously competed against by this State-subsidised labour.[1] In time, perhaps, the mischief

---

[1] Mr. J. L. Ohlson, the secretary to the West India Planters and Merchants Committee, wrote to *Fraser's Magazine* (*vide* the No. for October, 1877), to call in question my remark that the coolie immigration is disguised slavery. He points out that these people are well treated on the whole, and return to their native land generally with a considerable

may be got over by the spread of the negro population
—already overcrowded in Barbadoes—and every encouragement should be given to the free negroes to become small farmers in Trinidad and Jamaica, and also
perhaps on the mainland. The old system of immense
plantations cannot be successfully carried on without
slavery of some kind, call it by what name you please,
and the subsidised labour immigration of the West
Indies may yet bring some of them to ruin. In all of
them it induces a most illusory kind of prosperity, inasmuch as no real prosperity can spring from any source
outside the people who live and die on the land.

amount of saved money. Their engagements are entered upon volun-
tarily, and there is no kind of fraud or chicanery practised upon them.
I am very glad to hear this, and I have allowed the observation originally
made to stand in the text partly in order that I might give publicity to
Mr. Ohlson's statement. I may be permitted, however, to say that I did
not refer so much to the methods of importation—which I indeed knew
and stated to be much improved—as to the condition of the coolies in the
West India Islands. It will not, I take it, be denied that during the
term of their indenture they are not their own masters, that they are
herded together without any ties of home, and that few women are ever
to be found amongst their number; nor will it be asserted that in this condition of dependence they are not subject in a large measure to the caprices
of individual overseers and owners. Now, what I meant was, that in
elements of existence like these there is hardly room for much human
kindness. The coolie gets his wages and his food, and after a certain time
he is free; but otherwise I do not see how he differs much from the old
slaves. His going home again with money in his pocket is not to my
mind the happiest feature of the case either. If he is so well off in the
islands, why not let him bring his wife with him and settle there if he
chooses? Why the perpetual renewal of immigrations which is sapping
the resources and mortgaging the future of some of the most promising
of these possessions? The whole system is economically false, whether
it be directly cruel or not, and I fear it is not without traces of 'callousness and cruelty.'

Perhaps the most important minor possession of England, after the West Indies and adjacent tracts of mainland, is Ceylon. Its trade now reaches a total of nearly 11,000,000*l.* a year all told, and with England alone a total of from four to five millions. The profit of a good deal of the balance is, no doubt, absorbed by English merchants, manufacturers, and planters, and the island is altogether a considerable source of wealth to this country. The character of its trade is, however, such as we might expect from the position of the country. Its subject races are almost throughout made to work for the benefit of their masters, and for that alone. Hence the prosperity of Ceylon is for the most part the prosperity of the English coffee planter who has taken possession of its uplands and absorbed the labour of the population in the one industry which he has found profitable. There has, indeed, been some improvement in the condition of the natives of late years, and there have been several public works executed of a kind that may in time prove highly valuable to the people, but as yet these changes cannot be said to have reached the nation at large. It is the European who benefits almost exclusively by the railways, by the harbour works at Colombo, and by the roads and irrigation works. Here, as in India, the labours of the European in making his own fortune have borne hardly on the masses whose wages are not raised though their living may be dearer, whose industrial area is narrowed, and to whom the emoluments of higher official life are perforce almost entirely denied. The greater portion of the import trade of the island consists in food for these people, who, were their energies not devoted to growing coffee for the benefit of Europeans, could well raise more grain than they require within their own island. I am, therefore, inclined to doubt whether Ceylon is really more prosperous than her big neighbour, and whether the process now going on be not a process of decadence and exhaustion. There is no native middle class extending throughout the island, no fusion of races going on; and all enterprise is in the control of the European, or at the very most of the European and the mixed white races descended from the European races—Portuguese, Dutch, and English—who have successively held the island. Should by any chance the artificial state of prosperity now subsisting be swept away, either by the competition of cheaper-grown coffee from other countries, such as Mexico, or by some change in the circumstances of the ruling power, it would probably be found that Ceylon has been in considerable measure impoverished under English dominion, and its condition, in short, is not very different from that of the Dutch East Indies.

It must always be remembered that prosperity is a treacherous term to use in speaking of the dependencies of any country which are not in the modern sense colonies—dependencies, in other words, whose dominant classes grow rich in great measure at the expense of their subjects. Still it would be unfair to deny that according to our lights we have lately striven to do something for Ceylon. We are bestowing education on such of the natives as will take it; we are restoring some of the gigantic irrigation works of the island's ancient kings; and the extended attempts which are being made to introduce the cultivation of tea, as well as the mining and other efforts engaged in for bringing out the resources of the country, may all perhaps tell in time in some degree for the benefit of the people. They will tell very slowly, however, and in the meantime it must not be forgotten that with all the increased trade of Ceylon the bulk of the population hang now as much as ever on the verge of want all their lives long. The more one thinks of it, the more one sees that there is no tyranny on the whole so oppressive, no exactions so severe, as those of the modern trader and modern English appropriator of the lands of the weak. He does not mean to be unkind, probably enough never suspects that he is so; but his object is gain, and it is an object which compels him to give his servitors no peace. In the keen race after wealth he has to grind the faces of the poor, he learns to regard the people he has made subject from the one point of view of profit and loss, and in all his efforts at improving the land this profit and loss is almost the sole regulator of his calculations. The man who has once embarked on this course becomes blind to the simpler and nobler dictates of humanity, his ideas of justice are warped by his worldly interests, and his rule becomes a degradation to himself and to his subjects.

Making all allowance for exceptions honourable to the English race, I fear it cannot be denied that such is broadly the effect of our rule in Ceylon. The island is prosperous only in a diseased, feverish fashion, not naturally and by reason of improvement in the condition of the people. And as to the mere trade, its prosperity is, even in this narrow sense, by no means at present a growing one—at all events with England. Some portion of our export trade thither has been diverted to the mainland of India by the competition of English manufacturers established there, and aided in some slight measure by the tariff. Its total, therefore, stagnates at about a million, and our imports from Ceylon, which fluctuate more decidedly according as the yield and prices of coffee are good or bad, do not show much real progression. The trade of the island, so far as it grows, grows therefore with our colonies and with the mainland of India. Fortunately the island has little debt, and its taxation is not perhaps excessive, so that there does not appear to be the discontent in it which exists in India, nor the extended misery. It does not progress much, however, nor has it so many hopeful elements in its position as one might expect.

We are not able to interest its native races in our rule, or to make them take on English habits and absorb English ideas as the negroes do, nor can we assimilate them the one with the other. What another century of our rule there might do, with our efforts at educating the people, it would be hard to say. Perhaps the land would be cultivated more thoroughly and the exports and imports would be much greater, but I doubt whether the people would be substantially the richer or the more European in their ideas. Ceylon would almost have had more chance of becoming again a happy prosperous island had we been possessed of slaves there whom a British philanthropy could have emancipated to the discomfiture of their masters and the ruin of the island—from their point of view—for some generations. In the meantime we cannot calculate that Ceylon, with its two millions of people and upwards, will do much more than it has done to extend British trade. Our coffee planters there may continue to keep it in a foremost place amongst European markets, and it may export a little tea and Peruvian bark or a few pearls and a little plumbago, but its trade will not be much more than it is now for some time to come, if at all. The Singhalese and Tamuls and Malays are now what they were under the Dutch and Portuguese in nature and habits, with only the difference that we do not treat them with the hard cruelty of their former masters. They get wages for what they do—low wages, it is true, but still wages, and they get a certain measure of justice as between man and man. For all that, it appears to me that our hold over the people is essentially weak, and that we cannot really spur them up to take part with us in the renovation of the island even if we would. Our trade in Ceylon will therefore remain what we ourselves make it, and that alone.

There is little to be said about any other possession of England except perhaps West Africa, about which it would be easy to indulge in much speculation. I must refrain, however, were it for no other reason than that our trade in that region is yet too insignificant to deserve analysis. The possibilities of the future are also, to my thinking, vague and not over-promising. Should we be drawn into expeditions and tentative appropriations in the Congo valleys—a course which the discoveries of Stanley may perhaps render possible, as they certainly may make it tempting—I believe we may incur serious troubles in that region. As it is, with the king of Dahomey on our hands and the unsubdued Ashantees still threatening us on the Gold Coast, the game of ruling them is hardly worth the candle. Our total trade with this region is not more than a million and a half a year—surely not enough to justify expensive wars and demonstrations and a heavy annual waste of life. We have, in my opinion, subdued quite enough of the world without tackling the bloodthirsty African tribes who infest the Gulf of Guinea. I should be sorry therefore to see energies wasted in this quarter which might be much more profitably spent in our colonies proper. Let the Portuguese expend their energies there, where their possessions are both larger and older than our own.

Perhaps it may be interesting to say, in conclusion, that the aggregate trade of England with all her minor possessions, exclusive of those particularised here and in other parts of this book, amounted in 1876 to about 9,000,000*l*. This does not of course include the trade of Hong-Kong, which must be considered part of the trade of China, but it includes that of Gibraltar, which consists almost entirely of the export of stores for the use of the fortress. The exports to these possessions exceeded the imports by nearly a million, owing for the most part to the demands of the military stations, and the excess may therefore in some sort be taken as a measure of the money cost which these stations are to the country. It is not, of course, a true measure of that cost any more than the total figures are a true index of the total trade of these minor possessions, but roughly it shows us that we have to pay away at least the major portion of the profits of our trade with the small possessions in the mere daily expenses of our Imperial outposts on the Mediterranean and East Atlantic. Compared with our total trade, such a cost is a mere bagatelle, however, and, so long as the trade of our minor possessions suffices to meet it, we may have good reason to be satisfied. When we find, however, that some of them grow little or no richer under our rule, that many of them get into debt and trade considerably on credits, Government and other, we may have some doubts whether the position is so very sound as it looks. As a whole the smaller spots which we own all over the world have not quite so bright a record or so hopeful an outlook as we could wish, and I doubt whether some of them, such as the Mauritius, the West Coast settlements and Ceylon, will have much to thank us for when our day of supremacy in them is over.

CONCLUSION.

THE end of this prolonged investigation has now been reached. Necessarily brief and imperfect as the data are, enough has been, I trust, advanced in regard to most of the countries under review to enable us to form a judgment on the questions raised at the outset. We can tell what has in a general way affected British trade, and also what is likely to affect it in the near future. Although the details of the position may be continually shifting, there is enough fixed and lasting in the tendencies of events to enable us to say, with a certain approximation to dogmatism, what England has to expect. When I first began to write on this subject in 'Fraser's Magazine' nearly eighteen months ago, I dwelt on the general stagnation of business which was affecting everyone with gloomy forebodings as to the future of our trade. To-day, as I write, that stagnation is in some respects greater than it was then. It touches all departments of business almost alike, and extends, more or less, to all quarters of the world. The hoped-for revival could not fail to be put off in Europe by the long agitation over the Eastern question, and the ultimate outbreak of war between Turkey and Russia; but in quarters where that dispute could exercise only a very remote effect, trade has gone from bad to worse month by month. In the United States and Canada the hope was all the winter of 1876 in the coming of spring, and when spring came and passed it was transferred to the outbreak of hostilities, which the Americans eagerly hoped would throw business in their way. A momentary spurt of activity in the corn trade seemed to justify this hope, but when it passed off everything settled down again to the dreary level of hand-to-mouth business. Not even the exportation of dead meat, so successful during the winter, could reanimate the drooping energies of the trade speculator or pioneer. Nor did the demand for instruments of destruction do more than stir for a brief period that section of trade. And now the hope of the United States lies once more in their last year's overflowing harvest. Should it prove in the end as profitable as men have eagerly hoped it might be, activity will spring up again in all directions, we are told, and the great Republic, with the weaker British colony dangling at its heels, will rush ahead in a new career of progress. I venture to disbelieve in this revival almost as much as in those that have gone before. Nothing affecting the permanent economic condition of the country has in the least been changed; and until its industries are delivered from the oppression of bad laws, let alone overgrown capitalists, America must continue to go through depths of suffering and spells of idleness to an extent of which she has not dreamed.

As in the States and Canada, so in most parts of South America, and in all the leading countries of Europe. Everywhere there is a stagnation and a negation of hope. Only the Empire of Russia, India, and some of our Australian possessions can be said to keep up the export level of the few inflation years, and in some instances to excel them. Yet India has again been groaning beneath the burden of grievous famine, and China is devastated in parts by both famine and pestilence, so that her trade prospects also grow darker and darker; while Russia is in the position of a man in a desperate financial situation who parts with all he has at any sacrifice, in order to try and save himself from bankruptcy. I am not exaggerating, then, in describing the low condition of business enterprise and possibilities as at present nearly universal. It is fully more universal now than it was twelve months ago, and England, from her far-ramified trade, feels it more now than she did then. Month by month her exports have been declining, and month by month producers are content to take lower prices in order to get rid of their wares, till the country feels the strain with something like acute pain. Our only consolation is that none of our near neighbours are better off than ourselves. Germany is feeling the miseries of checked enterprise, and the recoil of wild gambling, more acutely than we do, because so immeasurably poorer; and even rich, self-sustaining, and industrious France finds that the ways of the world are not all smoothness to her, for her exports also are falling off this year as well as every other country's, and her general foreign and domestic business is sensibly weaker now than it was a year ago. Should her harvest be so poor as to necessitate considerable imports of grain next year, her financial troubles may develop themselves in a manner not hitherto looked for. Everywhere, of course, a quiet business of a kind is going on, because everywhere people have to live, but that also sinks more and more in all countries to the level of necessities.

There is, further, a certain amount of work and a certain expense which has to be incurred for the maintenance of much of modern improvements in the means of intercourse established nearly everywhere; and as countries have, on the whole, become greatly more wealthy in recent years than they used to be, the level of necessity is in this and other respects a higher one now than at any previous time in all civilised countries. What may be called the potential credit of most trading countries is also more developed now than ever it was before, through banks, financial companies, and the consequent utilisation of the savings of communities. Trade does not in any country, therefore, sink down to a point which it stood at, say, twenty years ago. It only goes back a few points, in the case of English export trade not more than a million or two a month at worst, and in other countries in proportion to their staying power. Thus, also, home trade, pure and simple, may be even greater than ever, especially if, as with us, a country has given large credits abroad. This relative retrogression causes in itself, however, a great amount of misery, loss, and disorganisation, and I wish I could hold out hopes of its coming to an end, but I cannot. A vast medley of causes are at work tending to prolong the present stagnation, and perhaps to aggravate it, until it trenches on what I have called necessary business. Some of these only have I been able to indicate. Nothing has, I hope, been made more clear in the preceding chapters than the startling extent to which nearly every country with any pretension to civilisation, and some with none, have rushed over head and ears in debt, often without rhyme or reason, and nearly always with an utter disregard for the consequences. Many of these countries cannot hope to master the effects of this conduct within this generation; some of them have yet to taste the bitterest of its fruits; and while this is the case it is impossible to say when trade prosperity, advancement in scientific development, in the arts of peace or in social industry, can again be their lot. Any estimate of the amount of this debt, taking all countries together, is almost an impossibility; but I am sure that the estimate of Mr. David A. Wells, in the paper already cited, is much within the mark. He says roughly that since 1860 the debts of the world have been increased by about 6,000,000,000*l*., of which nearly one-third has been wasted in wars, one-third in unproductive enterprises, and one-third in private industrial enterprises now yielding no revenue. I think that this last third should be probably half as much again, and that the sheer waste or almost sheer waste of the world during the last seventeen years has not been less than 8,000,000,000*l*. From the time of the Crimean War till now it cannot be less than 10,000,000,000*l*. The mind is unable to conceive what such a sum means, and in one way it is an utter mistake to treat it as dead loss to the world. This money and more may have been lost to individuals and communities, some considerable portion of it may have been used to blow tens of thousands of the working population of the earth out of existence, and in all lands whole classes of people may be poorer in consequence; but it does not follow that the work done by means of much of this money has not been good, any more than that the money is now all out of existence. Just as much of the money has found its way into the pockets of those who grow inordinately wealthy at the expense or by the folly of their fellow-men, so does much of the work endure which the money was sunk in accomplishing. The industrial capacities of most countries have been increased by their capital expenditure, and the area of human employment probably permanently extended. But the burdens of nations have also been at the same time extended, and for not a few of them it is still a question whether the burdens or the advantages will win the day. The debt problem is hence a most serious one in every country, and in some it is more than serious. It contains within it the elements of greater disaster to nations than any that the world has witnessed, and may yet destroy the fair prospect in more than one community. A community of nations can always afford to risk and lose outright a considerable portion of its savings without serious injury, but what no community may be able in the long run to withstand is the after-burden of this lost money. France, England, America, Russia, and other prominent dealers in credit, may find a day come when their separate and national debts choke up the very springs of national life, embitter the existence of their people, and serve to stir up within them uncontrollable social ferment. Clearly debt is a momentous agency in modern progress, of which but some of the tendencies have yet been recognised. The enormous masses of capital which are still productive— probably at least three times the sum lost—are themselves elements of danger, for none can say how soon they may become unproductive; and the manner in which debt is made to beget debt, credit to uphold credit, and in which cosmopolitan money-lenders dexterously manipulate the very dangers of a community for the purpose of deepening their hold on its life-springs, cannot be looked at without misgiving. Suppose a reckoning day to come, and real value to be demanded for the thousands of millions which figure as the 'assets' of credit institutions all over the world, what would they fetch? This may seem an absurd question to those who treat the credits which swell the totals of banks, say, as realised or realisable wealth, but I am by no means sure that we may not have to ask it some day with anxiety. How much of the so-called wealth of the world is realised wealth, in short, and how much mere credit notes and IOU's for wealth dissipated?

Questions like these would lead us to rummage among the very foundations of modern civilisation, and I cannot linger over them. There are others of nearly equal present importance to the subject in hand, and, amongst these, the first place should, I think, be given to the political and social questions still unsolved in nearly every civilised country. As we turn them over one by one it is hardly possible to resist the impression that the world is standing on the threshold of strange evolutions, and perhaps a new era. We have but to look across the Channel to France to see society quivering to its utmost verge in the throes of a momentous civil contest; one of hundreds it has already gone through, and to all appearance by no means the last. The time has not yet come for victory to be decisive in either camp, nor will it come while Ultramontanism is treated by National Governments as a product of civilisation to be paid for with money from the national treasury, and the Papacy as the visible embodiment of Deity. The possibilities of prolonged conflict almost make one despair that a worthy and satisfactory decision can ever be reached. The priest and the soldier band together in France to keep men in slavery. Turning to Germany, can we say that the signs there are much more hopeful? Undoubtedly there is calm—hardly ruffled—strength apparently defying assault, but what is beneath? Possible social upheavals, a great groaning under the intolerable load of a military rule; hordes of armed men kept from their honest toil for the glory of a power-grasping family, which brooks no rival even in those preteuntios, sham deities of the Vatican. We see creed hatreds kept under only by this iron heel; and beneath all, mutterings of anarchy—dreams of ideal States and a world all at peace to be reached by a great blood baptism, wherein all these producers of human misery—emperors, soldiers, priests, and placemen—shall be cleansed away for ever. I do not for a moment say that German energy, German love of order, and German patience may not in time overcome all these elements of discord; but, in the meantime, they exist, and the very poverty of the land aggravates the danger which they threaten. The land is full of pinching and misery, stagnant industries, and a sense of weariness and pain, which give more force to the doctrines of communism than if they were preached by a voice from heaven. The German Empire will have to justify itself by new conquests, as all empires have had to do, or by-and-by perish.

And as to Austria, the broken-limbed, race-divided Empire-kingdom which limps along in perplexity and fear, have we need to say anything of it, except to point to the unfusible fragments of old enemies found within its ragged borders? Can it advance to the position of a great trading power while trembling for its existence? Or if we turn to the north and east, to Russia and Turkey, now wearing each other out in a struggle that seems likely to seal the doom of both as despotic empires, do we not find abundant food for thought but little for hope? Is the future bodeful of anything but change, of upheavals which may usher in orders of government and of life all over these regions of which we can now shape no distinct outline? All the world, in truth, is shaking itself as if out of a long uneasy slumber, and, from far-off China to the new settlements in the United States of America, men's minds stir with problems religious, social, political, and ethnological, which bode the world little rest till a great settling of accounts has taken place. What the future shall be none can tell, but on many points of the horizon the glare is lurid enough to please the Prince of Darkness himself; on all there are dark clouds which show that the new age of science and so-called development has yet to justify itself.

Within a narrower range the same disorder, the same signs of change, are abundantly visible. Look, for example, how unsettled are the relations between master and servant, how unsatisfactory the position of labour as against capital : the open discontent, the frequent mutinies, and never-ceasing discord which goes on between employers and employed. This is a branch of my subject which I have forborne to dwell much upon when treating of individual countries, because it would have led me into discussions for which I could not possibly have found room; but it is an all-important element in determining the future prosperity of every country. As far as I can judge, England is probably fully the furthest advanced towards a peaceful and just solution of this most difficult question; but that is not saying much. The boards of arbitration which have lately become prominent in the North are already exercising a beneficent influence, on the whole, in preventing strikes and in adjusting with an approach to fairness the reward of labour. But these are only in embryo, and do not as yet work without strain, as the strike in Northumberland and the dispute recently submitted to Mr. David Dale proves. It is, therefore, difficult to say whether they do more than hint at what the ultimate basis of peace must be. One thing alone is certain, that in all countries, as men grow in intelligence, as education does its work, those arrangements of business and industry which conduce to the enriching of the few and relative impoverishment of the mass of men will have to be largely modified; and in England that truth is hardly admitted yet by even the most earnest advocates of the arbitration panacea. Abroad, the position of the working classes seems to me a very backward one. Their means of influencing employers of labour are perhaps as strong in France as anywhere, because of the hold which the people have upon the land; but in the case of the few large industries which France possesses—the silk and linen weaving, the sugar refining, the iron works, and the woollen manufactures—the workpeople are, as a rule, quite unable to effect any change in their condition, except by resort to the ruinous expedient of strikes; and these are so liable to be stopped by the soldiery, or are so feeble from lack of cohesion and funds, that they cannot be called efficacious. French artisans and mill hands still work, therefore, on the average quite twelve hours a week longer than those of England. In the United States, again, the working man appears to me to be in a far more hopeless condition than with us, in proof of which I may cite the remarkable case with which the leading railway companies of the Union lately decreed autocratically a 10 per cent. reduction in their employés' wages. These wages had been already reduced nearly to the bare existence level. The temporary success of the servants of several of the leading companies in stopping or disorganising all traffic in revenge for this reduction was no real sign of strength. It was rather the fleeting triumph of despair, and was, moreover, due, more than to railway men, to the riotous aid of the hungry artisans and miners who crowd the centres of industry, enjoying the blessings of protection and the privilege of earning starvation wages in order that a few capitalists or speculators may be able to boast that they are establishing the competitive capacities of the Union on a sound basis. These railway riots—when taken in connection with the hunger and discontent of the general working population—are, indeed, a ghastly commentary on the progress of the Union, and their suppression, which was certain from the first, proves not merely the helplessness and mad folly of the workpeople in seeking to fight protection, but rivets their chains anew. The sympathy of order-loving citizens has left them, and they seem now likely to remain subject to the tyranny of prohibitive laws and selfish corporations till rich and poor threaten to plunge headlong together into the same whirlpool of ruin. The despotism of the four or five railway autocrats has at all events been made secure till bankruptcy threatens or overtakes their overgrown debt-consumed roads. And as to the general working population, it is enough to say that the community in America offers no wide variety of small employments to which men can turn. There are few

VOL. II.

separate and independent centres of manufacture, either, some of which might be flourishing while others are dull. The whole body politic languishes together, and a time of languishing is a bad time for the working man in any country. In the States it probably means death by hunger to many, before a better day dawns. At present it indubitably means low wages, half work or no work to hundreds of thousands.

This question of the future of labour is indeed a most interesting and tempting subject, but I must not pursue it. I referred to it only to show the chaotic and unsettled state into which the new wealth of this generation has hurled society, in its larger sense, everywhere. That a new order will come out of the chaos in time I doubt not, but it has hardly yet begun to appear; and until the position of the servant is elevated till he becomes a sharer in some well-defined and governable shape of the profits which come from his labour, we cannot be said to have approached peace. Where, as in America, democracy has hitherto played into the hands of the capitalist exclusively and in the most barefaced fashion, the war which must precede a lasting peace can hardly be said to have begun. Nowhere in the world is the capitalist so merciless and so much a law unto himself as in the 'free' Union, and the railway despots afford but the most prominent example of what pervades all branches of industry, and must pervade them till the people make the laws for the benefit of all instead of for that of a very selfish and rather contemptible though very rich handful.

It has often surprised me that some of our great English railway companies have never tried the partnership experiment with their servants. They are in a better position to do it than almost any other large employers of labour, not only because of the numbers they employ, but because they serve a very imperious master—the public. This would itself put upon the bulk of their servants the necessity of complete subordination, and they would only at most occupy the position of small shareholders, whose stake in the welfare of the company would suffice to hold them interested in doing their work well. The most enlightened of all our railway companies—the Midland— gives, I believe, a sort of gratuity to its well-behaved servants every Christmas, but its manager might carry his sympathies with democratic thoroughness farther, and institute, say, 1*l*. preference shares, convertible in time into ordinary stock, and open for investment by servants of the company only. The effect would, I believe, be almost magical, and the risk of insubordination just nothing at all. The 'captains of industry' everywhere must in time admit their servants to a partnership of this kind; and I am inclined to think that, other things being equal, the corporation or country which does this first and most thoroughly will command the strongest hold on its markets, because the best power over its workmen. Co-operation in the sense in which the word is now used is a pleasing delusion, but partnership in the sense of all sharing, according to a degree determined by their thrift, in the profits of labour, partnership which would not interfere with the management and controlling interests of the large capitalist, but which would yet check his tyranny and order his greed, is a practicable enough end to aim at. At present the effects of much of the labour which men have to undergo are debasing and even brutalising. Modern science is, indeed, making us pay a fearful price for what it has given us, and we cannot contemplate the changes which are everywhere being introduced by the adaptation of forces of nature, by skilful machinery invented for doing what without it would have been beyond the reach of human powers and endurance, without almost a dread. These mighty forces and ingenious engines are fast becoming in their turn men's tyrants. More and more the labour which is wanted from us is brute labour—the work of trained animals. No wonder that men thus reduced feel a deep misery in their lives, and occasionally break out in revolt. No wonder that they need the strongest inducement to work steadily and well.

At present, however, there are more obviously pressing questions affecting the trade of England and of the world than this one of labour and capitalist. Apart even from the political aspect of the immediate future, there lie many questions which have been partially raised in the preceding chapters and directly touching our own trade, which therefore possess for us a deep interest. It is obvious that whatever upheavals, social or other, may occur, people must, as I have said, live, and in living they create trade. The teeming millions of China and India, of our colonies and America, require some clothing and food. Population is nearly everywhere more or less on the increase too, and that in itself enlarges the range of human wants, while wealth is accumulating still, and in spite of waste and folly, in many centres of industry and amongst thrifty peoples. Almost every rush of speculative adventure leaves behind it also certain permanent results, a modicum of gain, and, therefore, the aggregate trade of civilised nations can never altogether die away, or often recede to a point which would imply return to the level of a generation ago. In our own case the dulness which now exists by no means yet implies that our trade has sunk to what it was even ten years ago. On the contrary, it is in more respects than one as great as it has ever been. Last year, for example, our imports reached the largest total ever known. This is a signal proof of the wealth of the country, and still more, perhaps, of the enormous grasp which the distribution of that wealth over the world has given us upon the products and trade of every other country. So far our investments, at all events, have not proved generally unproductive. Whether last year's large import totals were due to the fact that, as some think, we were calling part of our invested capital home because it had become unproductive abroad, or whether we accept them simply as a proof of our abounding riches and a widespread foreign trade, they are nearly equally significant. We have possessed, and so far do still possess, almost immeasurable hold over the producing capacities of other countries. But in laying out our money to develop them we must, in many instances, have been adding to their intrinsic wealth also. By-and-by, in the natural order of events, some of them ought to be able to do without us as money-lenders, at least, and perhaps may be able to establish as against us a competing power in other directions where our wealth may now be supreme. Setting aside political and social considerations, this is one of the most urgent questions which we have to determine, and it is this which gives such deep significance to the steady retrogression of our export trade at the present time. In all that I have written on this subject, it has been my object to point out not merely the extent to which English money may have benefited or hurt other countries, but to examine into the growth of their competing power.

Now it has, I hope, been demonstrated that whatever the investment of English capital may have done for the investor it has not as yet, except in a modified.

way in one or two cases, led to the actual establishment of a solid competing power against ourselves. The competing power, where it does exist, is with countries to which we have not lent heavily, and with whom it ought to be noted our business rather improves than otherwise when the competition is strong. To some borrowers, public and private, English gold has hitherto proved almost a pure curse, increasing the burdens of the people, corrupting the Government, leaving behind it hardly a trace of good. Of these Turkey, Egypt, Peru, Paraguay, and other South American petty States form the most prominent, if not the only, examples. To others, such as the Argentine Confederation, Brazil, Russia, Spain, and Portugal, the borrowed money, English and French, has been but a doubtful blessing. Amongst our own colonies also a certain diversity is visible, some of them, such as Canada, having become steeped in debt to little good purpose, and others, such as New South Wales, showing signs of wonderful progressive vigour. In all cases the outpour of gold, chiefly English, the spoils of the commerce of the world, has had, to a certain extent, an inflating influence more or less injurious according to the energy or lack of energy displayed by the borrowers, and to this inflation has been due in part the extraordinary expansiveness of British trade in the last quarter of a century. Hitherto we chiefly have reaped the advantages of this inflation, but when the weak communities have gone to the wall, or when the sound nations have recovered, have as it were assimilated the over-doses of progress to which they have been treated and again start forward, will this supremacy be continued?

This question is to me, after all that has been said, still most difficult to answer. I have spoken of two classes of countries which have come under our power as traders and money-lenders—the weak and wasteful, and the strong and enterprising; but there are others. We have India to deal with, which is ours and not ours, whose poverty and whose competing power, so far as relates to internal commerce, are both unquestionably developing to some extent by the very efforts we are making to extract the most from a possession which we inwardly feel convinced we shall one day have to give up. Then there is China, a mighty nation of deft toilers, with a destiny, uncontrolled by any external force, as yet hardly to be guessed at; and there are various nations of Europe which, possessed like ourselves of an old civilisation and great industry, much intelligence and enterprise, and a large amount of wealth, can assume the position of rivals without having first to adopt the burden of being our debtors; while, finally, we have the United States, the largest receptacle of our surplus population and our surplus wealth in the world, and which, though by no means independent of us, is yet hardly in our power. What shall we say of these? Has the wave of change and development, which has stirred the world, done nothing to lift them nearer our own level? Will the supremacy, which we have so signally maintained at the start, continue ours even in the near future against the forces which have been awakened in most of them in part by our own instrumentality?

Those who have read the preceding essays will remember that I have generally come to the conclusion that *as yet* our supremacy has not been substantially interfered with. The backward wave which has swept the trade of the whole world downwards has been due to causes too universal to lead us to suppose that any special decrease in the producing and monopolising capacities of England has occurred. This age has been an age of eager development and of equally eager borrowing, outside as well as within the range of our influence, and a period has come to these correlative manifestations of its spirit. Exhaustion has shown itself in many quarters, and in all soberness has supervened on the previous mad haste. Hence dull trade, hence retrenchment everywhere. We can safely say, therefore, that the dominance which free trade and an admirable natural position, as well as very abundant national resources, have given us has not so far been lost. Let the conditions be the same as they are now when business enterprise again revives, and we shall on the whole be able to retain the position we now hold. We shall be the largest carriers in the world, the largest manufacturers, and the most extensive employers of both labour and money. The resources and advantages of this country in ships, in machinery, in mines, in skilled labour, in teeming population, in unopened stores of coal and iron, and in geographical position, are such as no other country can at present lay claim to, and with these we have nothing to fear. Not only so, but year by year the growth of our own colonies in wealth and certain kinds of producing capacities must tend to strengthen our hands, and to make the trade supremacy of England more assured. No other country that the world has ever seen has had so extended an influence, and run over the length and breadth of it as ours has done, and as yet there are almost no signs of the decay of this vast empire. Judging by the length of time that previous communities and nations have held a similar dominance when once attained, we ought to see none of these signs for generations to come; and the vigour of some, at all events, of our most prominent offshoots is emphatically still the vigour of youth.

This is the assuring side of the picture; but it has its darker side as well, and to this we must not foolishly close our eyes. To begin with, wherever we turn almost we find among civilised people a disposition to combat our supremacy growing more and more keen. Others as well as ourselves have treasures of coal and iron, flocks and herds, and the means of organising labour; others have magnificent harbours, and an ambition to share in the industrial movements of the time. In Europe alone there are not wanting signs that our manufacturing and maritime supremacy is disliked and being fought against with steady persistence. During the past year or so an agitation has, for example, been going on in both France and Germany for the imposition of higher protective duties as a means of keeping out English competition; and the protectionist party in Germany hopes yet to win the day. In France the battle is not yet fought out, and it would be impossible in the still by no means fixed state of French politics, to say how it will turn, but the signs that crop to the surface indicate that a strong and possibly prevailing party intend to erect a ring fence round the commerce of France if they can, and the triumph of democracy would, as we know by sad experience, by no means ensure the adoption of a liberal trade policy. Even Spain is putting up the import duty on coal, on English manufactures, and otherwise endeavouring to mend her tariff in the direction of self-containedness—especially as against English goods; and Austria, if politics leave her time, will not fail to follow in the same course. The very dulness of trade which has succeeded the burst of prosperity tends to aggravate these symptoms. While the world was going ahead, while anybody could borrow to the top of his bent, and above all, while Englishmen opened their purses to every adventure from every clime which promised them business, there was a sufficient stir and show of prosperity to prevent people from feeling pinched. But that is now all changed. The money is done, or all in the hands of those who can exact hard usury; the dreams are over, and nations are left with huge public works on their hands—railways, mines, shops, machinery of all kinds —that they do not know what to do with, so they raise the cry, 'England is ruining us by underselling; we must be protected.'

Most prominent of all in taking this attitude have been the United States of America. That country has received more of our money in one shape or another than almost all other countries put together; and being enterprising, it has gone ahead as no other has done, anticipating the future with a fury of activity which threatens to embarrass its progress for at least another decade, perhaps for a generation. It has not, however, been money borrowed for public works, reckless speculation, and the envy of ambitious traders, which alone have caused the determinedly protectionist attitude of the States. They have a huge war bill still to pay, and this has itself given a force to the protectionist arguments which a less needy treasury would never have suffered them to have. During all the so-called prosperous years a high tariff was therefore maintained, which, now that poverty has come on the people, is clung to, by those who benefited by it most and who are the last to suffer, with more energy and feverish anxiety than ever.

The more stagnant trade becomes the more persistently indeed do the Americans cling to their pet notions. At the present time the whole country is suffering more or less severely from over-trading and over-speculation in railways and mines, and the suffering is greatly aggravated by protection. Yet the free traders can hardly get a hearing. As the adventitious props of large railway loans are removed, therefore, the commerce between England and the Union grows narrower and narrower; certain departments of English manufactures are shut out from the American markets altogether, and others barely keep a foothold. At the same time internal competition is diminishing profits within the Union itself, and reducing wages, until the nation, which ought to be full of vigorous life, busy in expanding over the unoccupied interior the benefits of civilisation, and absorbing surplus population from all parts of the Old World, is filled with men in forced idleness, and actually sending emigrants from its shores to free-trading New South Wales or back to England.

We cannot expect that this protectionist delusion will be over soon in the States, which must suffer until they learn wisdom. They may maintain their barrier against our merchandise as high as it is at present for some time to come; and being at the same time much less likely to obtain the large sums of English money which poured into the country before the panic of 1873, there is little chance that our trade in that quarter can revive. The Americans will not have the means of paying for imported goods at tariff prices, however willing to do so, and as we repay to them the bonds we hold in exchange for bread our purchasing power will decrease also. Other markets must soon in part take the place of that of the United States for both our buying and selling. And as in the States so in other wealthy countries. We shall have to face, therefore, not only a greater preparedness for competition in some of our best customers when trade does again revive, but also a barrier put up against us more or less high, and in not a few instances may find our natural and acquired advantages unable to overcome the opposition. Our enormous wealth and the extent of our investments in many countries will of course, to a certain extent, give us a mastery; but it cannot do all, and if nations see fit to shut us partially out of their markets, we must, for a time at least, submit. I do not believe that the trade of the world can be long carried on upon the one-sided principle that each country is willing to sell as much as it can, but none willing to buy; but it is so now in some quarters and may be so in more before truer ideas prevail.

Necessity gives the excuse for it, and it is not apparent to the average Frenchman, the Austrian, the

Italian, the American, or to the Spaniard, that taxes on international commerce are of all taxes the most onerous and far-reaching in their disastrous consequences—the cruellest to the labouring man, and favourable only in modified degree to the capitalist. To one class almost alone in the world would protective duties now be of any real value, and that class is the English landowner. He is a monopolist of a very ancient but by no means satisfactory type, and free trade seems to me to threaten his monopoly more and more every year, just as his monopoly at present threatens to prove a serious check on the return of prosperity. We have now come to the real ordinary level of a humdrum plodding existence, and on that level, with all foreign nations free to send us their spare bread and meat, with the great extension which production has attained in countries where land is cheap and unincumbered, English landlordism, in the old sense, is rapidly becoming an impossibility. The land monopoly is doomed under free trade just as utterly as any other monopoly, and the sooner our landowners wake up to the fact the better. Not only so, but the sooner the people take cognisance of the dangers which may soon threaten us by reason of our land being but half tilled and determine to find a cure, the sooner may our trade depression pass away. We are accustomed to think that the buying powers of the country make us perfectly secure, and that we can go on neglecting our home agricultural resources—worth from 300,000,000*l.* to 400,000,000*l.* a year even now—because it pays to spin yarn and weave cloth. But supposing the market for that yarn and this cloth grows less, what then? What but a decrease of our buying capacity under which unthrift of any kind becomes a serious danger. We can easily see this by the course which our trade is taking now. With much diminished exports our food imports are larger than they have ever been, and in order to pay for them we are parting with some of our savings—with the bonds of other countries, which we bought in the days of our prosperity; we are, in other words, exchanging our available capital to a certain extent for food, and in proportion as we do so our power to regain dominance over the world's commerce when it revives is lessened. The extent to which our population is crowded together in towns, the badness of our agriculture, the expanse of our baronial parks, of our waste lands, common lands, and game preserves may therefore become the sources of enormous danger to the country. In order to maintain our position we must utilise all our resources to the best advantage, and we have not done this with the land at any time, least of all since we became world caterers. English land-laws and landlordism will therefore have to be modified so as to permit us to increase the producing capacity of the soil, and I am disposed to think that the manner in which new countries like

America, where the soil is but little encumbered, can beat down the price of agricultural produce in our markets will materially help to work the necessary revolution. Bad harvests in former times often crushed the agriculturist and land owner at the expense of the community, but they now impoverish them, and the English landowner has, above all men, cause to curse free trade.

In all respects except this, free trade has been an immense boon to nearly all classes of the nation, and what it is to us it cannot fail to be to other nations. In the meantime, however, these nations do not see this; and in addition to the natural dulness which comes of reaction, we shall have to feel more and more the effects of an artificial one. At the present time it may be said that none but some of our own foreign possessions are in a position to carry on an increasing trade with us in the near future. The export trade from England to the United States is not now half what it was in 1872. With Germany, Spain, and Italy we may possibly do a greater business in the immediate future, but generally the European outlook is not, any more than the American, very hopeful. We have but the negative consolation that none of the nations whose business is now less with us show a decided capacity for becoming our successful rivals as manufacturers and traders.

The complications in Eastern Europe, which have resulted in the present huge and ghastly war, must of course disarrange our trade with that quarter of the world; and, as I have already pointed out, the triumph of Russia means our partial, if not complete, exclusion from a large and very profitable market. By-and-by we shall discover, and mourn over, the unspeakable blunder we committed in siding with the Turks, not alone in this momentous quarrel, but over the quarrel of a generation ago. In the event of Russian victory the traders of Russia are certain to supplant us, with the aid of the German perhaps, all over Turkey in Europe. Not all our ironclads ten times over, nor all our fleet of trading steamers, nor our huge factories and boundless wealth, will turn the heart of the liberated populations of European traders towards us, or prevent a high tariff from shutting us out then, as we are already shut out in Central Asia. English supremacy has received a moral shock which will be felt in India and the Eastern seas, and which may touch our profitable position even there. Nor would it be much better for us were Russia beaten, for then the devastating capacities of the brutal Turkish horde would most likely leave little basis for trade with any body in the country.

The lesson of all this is not hard to learn. What is done cannot be altered, and we must strengthen ourselves while and where we still have the power. Our colonies, on the whole, continue our steadfast friends, and we cannot too assiduously cultivate their friendship and trade, whatever form it takes. Some of them may be embarrassed and needy, some have deep waters to pass through ere they grow to manhood, but they offer a great field which we cannot now safely neglect for other dreams. In order to maintain their prosperity and our own, we ought first of all to encourage emigration to them without ceasing; and it would be well if some of the energies which we are, I fear, wasting in the popular endeavour to Europeanise and 'develop' India, were spent in reclaiming the lands of Australia, or of New Zealand, or of British Africa, whose plains might yet rival America as a source of cotton supply cheaper than the American. One day this country may bitterly regret the millions of Englishmen whom India has swallowed up for nothing but the seeming gain which the sacrifice of their lives has brought to the traders and the leisure classes in England, for whom we are working that empire to the death. Emigration is, moreover, absolutely necessary at the present time to extricate some of our colonies from their most dangerous position in other respects. I will not dwell on the financial position of Canada, which hopes that the present harvest will regenerate all, and hopes, I believe, in vain; but take the case of New Zealand. In spite of Sir Julius Vogel's sanguine anticipations I can see nothing but disaster in store for that colony, unless it receive within the next year or two large additions to its population and to its available working capital. It is now in a position when the least strain might bring on an acute crisis, the effects of which would retard the growth of that fine settlement for a generation, perhaps as an English colony for ever. So with Victoria and most of our Australian colonies in one sense or another. There is abundant room, at least, in all, and where there is room there is need of men. It amazes one to see how apathetic the English Government is to emigration in view of these great necessities. The mere trader's ground is not indeed the strongest which one might urge for a diversion of the superfluous energies and capital of England to her habitable colonies—the colonies, that is, where Englishmen can live and multiply. Of still more importance is the retention by England of a paramount position as a military and naval power, and as the possessor of an unrivalled mercantile marine. More than anything that tariffs can do to hurt us, and than any downward turn in the tide of international trade, do I dread the consequences of the growth of powerful competition on the high seas for the military and naval dominion. Up to the emancipation of Italy and the consolidation of the German Empire we may be said to have been without serious over-sea competition in Europe; and the Civil War in America had thrown into English and Canadian hands almost the total sea-carrying trade of the Union, as well as given our navy complete dominance all over the world. We were, in short, the greatest naval power, and possessed immeasurably the largest and finest mercantile marine in the world. Here and there a feeble and subsidised competition might be kept up against us, and a certain amount of trade might thereby be diverted from our shores and from our merchants, but we did not seriously feel any bad consequences from it. To-day, however, this is very much altered. Not only is France fighting us more keenly, if despairingly, for the China and East India trade, but Germany and Italy are developing powerful competition; and German merchants and traders are penetrating into our old Eastern monopolies in the wake of their steamers—almost beating us in China and fighting us closely in Japan, in Singapore, and even in our own India, for a share of the trade. Towards South America and the States the same competition is in marked progress, and, in spite of defeats at given points, is, on the whole, making way. The dismemberment of Turkey, which is certain to come before long by some means, and the liberation of the Black Sea coast is, as I have said, sure to affect us injuriously in this direction; and, whether Greek or Russ inherit the Golden Horn, we may expect to find new rivalry springing thence, on the Suez Canal route to the East especially, which may be in the long run a greater boon to the reviving races of Central and Southern Europe than to us, unless we direct our energies to the strengthening of positions which the Anglo-Saxon race can hold without perishing off the face of the earth.

This maritime competition is extending elsewhere at present steadily, and in the United States themselves we hold no longer the supreme position which we did five years ago. The Americans have got an ocean line of six fine steamers of their own, and mean, if they can, to build additional ships for it at home as their trade grows. On this side, therefore, our trade is everywhere most keenly touched, such as the tariff war and speculation has left it; and should anything occur to cripple us for a time, we should probably find it gone from us never to return in its old volume, however great the aggregate trade of the world might still be.

Now a naval and, in one sense, a military supremacy is an essential adjunct to a trade supremacy. We must not merely have many and well-appointed merchant fleets, but we must back them, protect them, and clear a way for them, if need be, by an all-powerful navy, and be ready to protect our chief trade centres with abundant troops, surrendering only that trade which we cannot fairly hold. No nation that has ceased to be masterful and strong has ever retained long the leading position in trade; and in some respects, though the British Empire be still the strongest, in others it is one of the most vulnerable on the face of the earth. Witness the clamour over this oft-cited Eastern war, the foaming excitement amongst certain classes, the shouting about 'British interests,' the sympathy with the brutalised Turk and his allies, and the apparently insane hate of Russia. What is it all but an unacknowledged consciousness that we are endangered by Russian success on our vulnerable side? India is, after all, at stake, in a fashion, in this conflict, and that, too, quite apart from any question of Russian invasion. Our Mahometan population there watch the struggle with growing keenness, and watch England's attitude with growing discontent. Our old enemies there, in fact, have all along tied our hands in this business, contributing not a little to drive our Government into the miserable would-and-would-not policy which it has pursued. Yet that creed and race hatred is not the greatest danger of all just at the moment. It lies in the probability that the re-shaping of the East cannot take place without making the maintenance of secure communications with India more costly than it has hitherto been. A naval power in the Eastern Mediterranean would increase that cost and our danger most materially, Egypt or no Egypt, and there is hence a very great stake of ours in this struggle. It affects our weakest part, which is very weak now, and yearly grows weaker still, by the mere increase of poverty in India and by the increase in the tension between rulers and ruled. It would be unwise, no doubt, to withdraw from India before this danger grows into the elements of a new and perhaps disastrous conflict; but we should at least recognise our danger sufficiently to strengthen ourselves where we are already, in one sense, strong, by all the means in our power— in our Colonies. We have neglected them, proud as we may be of them; and instead of running any longer to and fro in the earth, wasting our energies on aims that cannot yield an adequate return, ought now to concentrate our efforts on building up their strength. Nearly all our spare military strength has been concentrated in India, and that one fact reduces us at once to a third-rate military power. In order to hold its populations down, we exhaust ourselves; and the colonies, which might be an enduring element of English strength in all times, are left to provide for their own defence or not as they please, with neither the spare men nor the spare cash with which to make provision. At least let us try to give them population in time, if we have no soldiers to spare from that India where we waste them all in maintaining a sway which our melodramatic Premier has succeeded in making ghastly with his gewgaw of an imperial crown, bestowed when gaunt famine was threatening half the empire with destruction, and which wins us the hate and envy of our neighbours. Trade interests of all kinds hang on such a change of our policy, and perhaps the very existence, in time, of the British Empire, about the real power of which there is now a sort of hysterical, fidgety interest that must make the strong ones around us laugh.

The rise of a new and ambitious power like Germany offers at our very doors powerful reason in this direction. At present Germany has no colonies of her own; but the Germans are an emigrating people, and the tyranny of the Prussian military system is making them increasingly so. Should the ambition of German rulers assume in time a colonising fit as a vent to the home discontent, or as a means of controlling for purposes of imperial aggrandisement the already formidable exodus of discontented and impoverished people, what is there to hinder them from seizing, if not colonies already English, but containing many Germans, at all events points near English colonies which would seriously endanger and damage them and our trade with them? I have already pointed to the dangers which threaten us from a German absorption of Holland, but I must recall them here for a moment because I think they are real and more imminent than most people believe. The Dutch colonies would be the very best medium which the Germans could get for spreading their commercial influence in the East, for overlooking Australia, for impeding the trade of England. We have been so long accustomed to peaceful possession of the high seas that we are ready to laugh at warnings such as these. 'Mere heated alarmists!' we say, and go on our way self-assured. A little time spent in looking the facts steadily in the face, however, will in this instance cure us, I hope, of our boasting confidence. Unless Germany is broken up by internal dissensions—which is a possible but not a probable event—nothing is more likely than that she will turn her attention to extending her dominions abroad. Her very poverty, her internal discontent and large emigrations, her boundless self-confidence and ambition, all drive her towards such a course. No empire that the world has ever yet seen was an empire of peace. It is of the essence of empire to make war : how else would emperors justify their claims to divinity? And Germany is hard at work getting ready for war at sea as well as on land. Her fleet and arsenals are being steadily increased, and she is already in possession of a by no means insignificant navy, while her military chest is unquestionably the best filled in the world. From such contingencies, therefore, I am disposed to regard the dangers of English commerce in the future as much more grave than from all others put together. We are so vulnerable in India and defenceless in our colonies that tenfold our offensive force at sea would not protect us at all points should we drift into war, or should a new marauding power set about preying on us as we have in times past preyed on others. All our colonies might be torn from us—nay, some of them, such as the heterogeneous South African settlements, might elect to go— and the German element in them all might cause us much trouble and anxiety should Germany and we take opposite sides in a quarrel. What we should now do, therefore, is to turn by every means in our power the stream of home emigration towards these places, so that the English element might dominate in all, so that the communities themselves might soon grow able to act in self-defence with effect, and so that our mercantile navy, by having strong fortified ports at leading points in the world, might still hold its own, if not as supreme amongst pigmies, as the greatest amongst many competitors. The defenceless state of our colonies, one and all, is a danger and a disgrace to us; while we perforce keep in India a huge host—a host that strains the military system of England to its utmost in times of peace, and abstracts permanently from our working population some 8,000 men.[1]

This subject is also a seductive one ; but I have already pursued it far enough to earn for myself the title of a prophet of evil, whom no man should listen to, and I shall refrain therefore from particularising further the many dangers which, in my opinion, beset us. I trust that at least I have said enough to justify my pleading for watchfulness, thrift, and forethought amongst our statesmen and merchants, and for a higher,

[1] Recent Australian papers speak of a waking up in the colonies themselves to the necessity of being prepared for the possible advent of war. But how inadequate can their preparations be at best! There are not inhabitants in all Australia and New Zealand exceeding half the population of London, and their work leaves them no time for soldiering. They have a few forts and a few volunteers in New South Wales and Victoria, and talk of getting up corps of them elsewhere and of building an ironclad or two ; but what could they do against a few gun-boats or even a few boats' crews of trained men judiciously directed?

more far-seeing, and prudent colonial policy in our statesmen. Enough has also been said, I know, to demonstrate the extreme difficulty which surrounds the questions which I set myself to answer in this concluding paper regarding the future course of British trade. What affected it in the past we have seen clearly enough; why it has been inflated to so great a pitch, and why it is now suffering from collapse; but its future course we cannot with certainty predict. We may hope that it will rise again and enter on a new course of expansion and speculation; that we shall still, as heretofore, furnish a third of the world and more with the clothes it wears and the tools it uses; but there are many considerations that tend to dash this hope. It is more rational in the face of these to look for a general progress amongst nations in which we shall have, if we take good heed, our full share—a share large enough to compensate us for the loss of great monopolies. This would be indeed an extremely probable outcome of the industrial expansion of the last generation, were we sure that the world would at last consent to beat its swords into ploughshares; but the grim events now happening, and that have happened of late years, are too horribly barbaric and mediæval to permit us to trust in the regenerating effects of modern civilisation. Civilisation, indeed! with Europe all armed, standing expectant by the side of combatants waging war with the most demoniacal weapons of destruction, and in the most fiendish way that the world has ever known since Saul slew the children of Amalek! Civilisation upheld by torpedoes, monster shells, mitrailleurs, breech loaders, revolvers, and all the refined scientific methods of accomplishing murder by wholesale! Dare anyone trust to such a thing? The world seethes with the elements of conflict; nations strain beneath the burden and the curse of horrible despotisms, and long for even the liberty to die fighting; and yet we hope for the peaceful development of a trade rivalry amongst these nations, fold our hands, and leave our great possessions to take care of themselves amid the fire. Alas for the hope! and alas for the world! Not in the signs of the times do I read that peace and brotherly concord are to secure for England her *status quo* through even the near future. The day is coming when we, too, may have to fight, not for supremacy only, as others have fought, but perhaps for dear life; and with that outlook before us who shall predict the course of trade?

All that can be said is what I have already said, that we possess the capacity for work still, the industrial facilities and qualities which will command success; and no doubt when the storms have passed by, and the world has once more settled into a time of recuperation and peace, if we have preserved our empire as we ought and may, we shall pursue our way as we have done heretofore, or at least like a larger

Holland; but I think the storms must pass before that new day of advancement comes.

Europe has been all unhinged by the events of the last twenty years or less. The yeast of the first French Revolution works through its society still. New military powers have come forward, new peoples have risen up to claim their freedom, and old empires find themselves borne on by a tide they try in vain to control. Work will go on still, and people will grow rich or poor, all the world over, whether these clouds break into storms or not. But, whilst they are felt to be hanging over us, it would be idle to predict that we are to have a new rush of prosperity in the near future. Against any individual existing power, and against any single nation, we are still most fit to compete for the trade that is to be done; but even on this supposition, and granting peace restored, the aggregate capacity of working industrial communities is greater now against us than it was five or ten years ago. The desire to measure strength with us in the great markets is also keener, and economic fallacies are fully more powerful for mischief than ever. At the best, therefore, and on any view, I can only say that we shall continue to do a large trade—as against any single country a preponderating trade; but that a new rush of conquest and wealth, like that which the past generation has enjoyed, cannot be looked for. If we do not strenuously develop our Colonies we may even see our commercial prosperity dwindle yet many degrees further, for many countries are deliberately pushing us away from them and thereby endeavouring to make us poorer. Should the long continued cheapness of credit come to an end soon this dwindling may even become a rush, for dearer money will not this time mean ruined trade, as it has always hitherto done, but greater poverty. The low price asked for loans by the banks of this country for the last ten years nearly is so far a sign that the business now done is sound in character, but only so far.

Banking, like everything else, has undergone strange developments of late years, and I am inclined to think that most of the seeming stability which has consoled people in the present time of depression is hollow. Banks, private and corporate, have identified their interests more or less closely with the fathomless masses of public securities in which their customers have become accustomed to speculate and with the trade speculations of private persons, and they endeavour above all things to make business go smoothly. They hide away losses, temporise with difficulties, and, backed by their immense credit, carry on concerns, and sustain values, to an extent which we shall only be able to measure when the day of reckoning comes. We see something of what is done, however, in the extraordinary way in which prices are sustained on the stock exchanges of the world. English railways, foreign loans, sound and unsound, are all more or less at absurdly high prices, and they are maintained at these by the agency of the banks. By-and-by enormous losses will have to be faced somewhere on account of these, and only then shall we be able to realise what the world has lost in the years of depression, how much poorer England has grown. To be sure, a collapse of this kind will afflict all countries where banking is developed nearly alike, but for that very reason we are likely to lose most, and the supervening bankruptcies may cripple trade for a generation. Mercantile credit nowadays hangs everywhere together and through the cosmopolitan agency of banking—an agency which knows no country and which moves the trade of all countries. Should any link in the chain of banking credit which girds the world snap, therefore, we may have money unusually dear, public securities millions in value and concerns of all kinds hurled into bankruptcy. The reckoning day has yet to come, in short, for the business inflation of a generation, and all that cheap money has hitherto meant is that the financiers who did much to create this inflation have hitherto been able to stave it off. Will they be able to do so much longer? Will the world recover itself so as to bridge over its losses with its further accessions of wealth and prevent the necessity for a reckoning? These are the important questions of the immediate future, and according as we answer them shall we hold sanguine views or the reverse. For my own part I do not believe in the recuperative powers of the world to that extent, nor do I think that business can revive in any solid fashion till the reckoning has been made. The swollen credits of all countries must be brought down to the level of the actual facts before confidence which is essential to progress can be restored, and before lending can again become partially wholesome. The profit and loss accounts of the world will prove difficult of adjustment I fear, and it would not be at all surprising to find many fair-seeming institutions, and some few more nations, bankrupt before the adjustment is made. France has not yet paid her war bill; Russia does not know the amount of hers; the debts of Egypt and Turkey have not produced their worst consequences, nor have the United States mastered the evil effect of their lavishness in railway and industrial developments. A promise of a revival of business may indeed be the first thing that will put an end to the hollowness of the entire situation, and whether or not, the increasing poverty of some communities, and the very necessity of coming to a settlement, will force a solution in time. My impression consequently is that a temporary return to peace if nothing else, will in Europe probably be the signal for an outbreak of financial troubles. Everyone waits now and hangs back, but then everyone would be trying to push forward, and the means for doing so would prove to be wanting. Thus at all points we find indications that the world cannot advance anew till storms are over, that the universal habit of trading on credit and progressing under mortgage cannot be renewed till the old accounts are settled. On all grounds in consequence I look for a further depression in the trade of this country, and when I consider how unprepared we are by our habits and social condition for a prolonged time of retrogression, I confess the prospect is to me an alarming one. There is strength enough in the nation to endure it, perhaps, but there may not be strength enough to renew the trade warfare on the same advantageous footing when the time of distress is over. This is not a period like those which followed ordinary panics, in short. It is more likely the beginning of a new era for ourselves and for the world. All the world has come to hang together in matters of trade by a chain of debt. There has been a worldwide issue of irredeemable currency, as it were, in the shape of bonds and banking credits, by means of which prices have been inflated, production unhealthily stimulated, and a feverish activity engendered; and when this inflation has died away all nations will be poorer, many crippled for generations, some perhaps almost extinguished. In the revolution of values which such a recoil will cause we must be heavy sufferers because we have been the most reckless takers of promises to pay, the greatest squanderers of a splendid inheritance, that the world has ever seen.

APPENDICES.

APPENDIX I.

A Comparative Statement of the Total Value of Imports and Exports of Merchandise, including Bullion and Specie, into and from the United Kingdom in each Year from 1858 to 1876, showing also the Percentage Excess of Imports over Exports in each Year.

Years	Imports, including Bullion	Exports			Excess of Imports		Percentage Excess of Imports		Percentage increase or Decrease of			
		British, including Bullion	Foreign	Total	Over British Exports	Over Exports, British and Foreign	Over British Exports	Over Exports, British and Foreign	Imports over preceding year		Total Exports over preceding year	
									Increase	Decrease	Increase	Decrease
	£	£	£	£	£	£						
1858	194,077,022	136,237,632	23,174,023	159,411,655	57,839,390	34,665,367	42·4	21·1	—	—	—	·6
1859	216,252,511	166,100,332	25,281,446	191,381,778	50,152,179	24,870,733	30·1	12·9	11·4	—	20·	—
1860	233,509,059	161,425,995	28,630,124	190,056,119	72,083,074	43,452,950	44·6	22·8	7·9	—	—	·7
1861	236,232,069	145,914,462	34,529,684	180,444,146	90,317,607	55,787,923	61·8	30·9	1·1	—	—	5·
1862	257,373,452	153,318,455	42,175,870	195,494,325	104,054,997	61,079,127	67·8	31·1	8·9	—	8·3	—
1863	278,949,814	173,146,382	50,300,067	223,446,449	105,803,432	55,503,365	61·1	24·8	8·3	—	14·2	—
1864	302,680,448	183,581,353	52,170,561	235,751,914	119,099,095	66,928,534	64·8	28·3	8·5	—	5·5	—
1865	292,534,496	180,928,249	52,995,851	233,924,100	111,606,247	58,610,396	61·7	25·	—	3·3	—	·7
1866	329,577,413	210,556,147	49,988,146	260,544,293	119,021,266	69,033,120	56·5	26·4	12·6	—	11·3	—
1867	299,004,184	195,286,440	44,840,606	240,127,046	103,717,744	58,877,138	53·1	24·5	—	9·2	—	7·8
1868	319,546,203	199,897,826	48,100,642	247,998,468	119,648,377	71,547,735	59·8	28·8	6·8	—	3·2	—
1869	315,961,205	206,331,485	47,061,095	253,392,580	109,629,720	62,568,625	53·1	24·6	—	1·1	2·1	—
1870	332,713,161	218,506,512	44,493,755	263,000,267	114,206,649	69,712,894	52·2	26·5	5·3	—	3·7	—
1871	369,156,307	256,826,833	60,508,538	317,335,371	112,329,474	51,820,936	43·7	16·3	10·9	—	20·6	—
1872	384,301,636	286,593,208	58,331,487	344,924,695	97,708,428	39,376,941	34·	11·4	4·1	—	8·6	—
1873	404,886,603	284,063,888	55,840,162	339,904,050	120,822,715	64,982,553	42·5	19·1	5·3	—	—	1·4
1874	400,461,889	262,411,714	58,092,343	320,504,057	138,050,175	79,957,832	52·6	24·9	—	1·	—	5·7
1875	407,294,366	251,094,003	58,146,360	309,240,365	156,110,361	97,964,001	62·1	31·6	1·6	—	—	3·5
1876	412,208,947	230,103,286	56,137,398	286,240,684	182,105,661	125,968,263	79·1	44·	1·2	—	—	7·4

APPENDIX II.

General Domestic Exports of the United States in Twenty-six Years.

LOW DUTY PERIOD			
Fiscal Years	Raw or Crude Products	Partially Manufactured	Manufactured
1849	$85,853,726	$28,106,978	$17,749,377
1850	90,607,712	21,668,384	22,624,137
1851	128,408,208	22,524,815	27,687,115
1852	106,980,864	21,977,876	25,972,407
1853	130,672,592	28,853,385	30,343,185
1854	128,452,625	48,216,776	37,315,835
1855	117,884,310	35,165,696	39,701,129
1856	171,523,494	53,551,701	41,362,856
1857	186,265,094	49,052,887	43,588,732
1858	169,957,814	39,108,683	42,274,536
1859	197,099,732	34,708,626	46,583,722
1860	224,413,148	39,901,791	51,927,484
1861	104,722,026	50,542,437	49,685,153
Totals	$1,842,851,345	$473,380,035	$476,765,668
Annual average	$141,757,796	$36,413,849	$36,674,282
PROTECTIVE PERIOD			
1862	$75,456,352	$67,664,631	$38,903,885
1863	99,249,116	88,276,256	62,366,064
1864	75,463,144	85,176,267	58,922,226
1865	81,601,107	91,640,548	85,883,408
1866	337,572,897	77,644,663	52,823,343
1867	252,959,905	67,416,036	63,225,175
1868	226,686,087	80,220,222	63,649,429
1869	222,615,504	87,414,017	61,015,628
1870	305,571,539	87,372,543	62,264,259
1871	301,048,092	103,548,993	73,518,207
1872	283,941,261	124,099,942	68,380,275
1873	340,495,286	151,084,296	83,647,435
1874	384,547,951	158,656,238	90,135,179
Totals	$2,987,208,241	$1,270,214,652	$864,734,513
Annual Average	$229,785,249	$97,708,819	$66,518,039

APPENDIX II. 359

'The total exports for the first period were $2,792,997,048, and for the second period, $5,122,157,406, showing an increase in exports of nearly 85 per cent. in the second period over the first. The increase in population in the second period did not probably exceed 35 per cent. It was just 22·6 per cent. in the decade 1860-70. We have thus an increase in our exports, after making due allowance for increase in population, of nearly 50 per cent. in the second period over the first. The great waste of productive power and the serious interruption to commerce, caused by the war in the second period, may fairly be regarded as a sufficient offset to the fact that the exports in the second period are stated in currency values except the exports from the Pacific coast, which are in gold values. Protection, therefore, has increased our exports since 1861, notwithstanding the disturbing influences of a great war, and despite the high prices for labour and all materials and products which that war created.'— *Swank's Report.*

APPENDIX III.

Subjoined is the abstract statement of the debt of Russia, given in the 'Economist' of December 9, 1876, and alluded to in the chapter on Russia. It will be seen that all the floating debt obligations were taken at 29d. per rouble, in my view an untenable mode of reckoning. By admitting it the State would practically be able to release itself in time from all its burdens by merely issuing roubles until they sank to almost no value at all. According to this mode of computing debt the new burdens which the war has imposed are, so to say, neutralising themselves, for as fast as the Government prints and issues new paper the value of the rouble recedes. It is now only 24d., and the following abstract would, therefore, if calculated on that basis, show a reduction of the debt obligations payable in paper of fully 20 per cent. This fact needs only to be stated to show the injustice and even absurdity of thus releasing a State from the letter of its promises to pay. Fairly reckoned, the debt of Russia according to this abstract is close upon 500,000,000l.

Since it was drawn up, however, the war has supervened, and with it has come a new debt of unknown amount. Besides one abortive foreign loan for 15,000,000l. created to serve as security to the Berlin and Amsterdam bankers, who have been engaged this twelvemonth past in supporting Russian credit with their money and by speculation, there have been two internal loans issued for together 300,000,000 roubles nominal, or say, 42,000,000l. The note circulation has also been increased by an indefinite amount which we cannot be exagge-

APPENDIX III. 361

rating in placing at another 300,000,000 roubles, and we have therefore roughly a debt of about 100,000,000*l*. added to the previous burdens of Russia as the result so far of the present horrible war. Created as most of this debt is in that most pernicious of all forms an inconvertible and depreciated paper currency, the deep miseries and credit disorganisation which it must ultimately bring on the Empire will prove to be enormous. Russia will not recover from the financial results of the present war within the next twenty years, even should the period be one of profound peace.

The following is the abstract statement of the debt of Russia on January 1, 1875, as given by the 'Economist.' It does not appear, however, that the 4½ per cent. railway loan for 15,000,000*l*., issued in 1875, has been included in this table:

1. LOANS REPAYABLE IN SPECIE, TAKEN OR CONVERTED AT PAR—

	£
1815-64-66 Dutch and Anglo-Dutch	7,796,083
1864-66 Anglo-Dutch	4,794,700
1846-60 4½ % Loans	8,100,000
1858 Compensation to Denmark	186,489
1830-63-64 4 % Bank bills (metallic) Rs. 50,409,000	
—at 38*d*. per rouble	7,981,425
1820-22-54-55 5 % Loans . . . Rs. 136,500,700	
—at 38*d*. per rouble	21,612,610
1862 Seventh 5 % Loan	15,000,000
1859 3 % Loan (Thomson, Bonar, and Co.)	5,148,700
Total	70,620,007

2. LOANS REPAYABLE IN PAPER CURRENCY— Roubles.

1840-42-43-44-47 Five 4 % Loans	18,600,000	
1864-66 Two Lottery Loans	192,050,000	
1363-69 5 % Bank Bills	23,504,000	
1817 6 % Loans	47,123,773	
1859 4 % Consolidated Stock	153,865,225	
1860 Perpetual Deposits	288,377	
Total	435,431,375	
Converted at 29*d*. per rouble		52,614,622
Total Loans		123,234,629[1]

[1] The totals of these loans have been reduced slightly by sinking fund operations, but the totals are not thereby materially affected, as the sinking funds are small.

APPENDIX III.

3. FLOATING DEBT:

(a) Floating Debt repayable in Paper Currency—

	Roubles.	£
Treasury Bills	216,000,000	
Debt to Credit Institutions (no interest)	118,284,976	
,, ,, State Bank ,, ,,	5,220,797	
,, ,, Redemption Fund ,, ,,	2,317,000	
Banknotes uncovered ,, ,,	566,086,396	
Liabilities in respect to Kingdom of Poland	84,762,852	
Total	992,672,021	
Converted into Sterling at 29d. per rouble		119,947,869
Total Loans and Floating Debt		243,182,498

(b) Liabilities in respect to Railways, in Specie—

	Francs.	£
4 % Nicholas (Moscow) Railway Bonds	571,585,000	
	£	
Converted into Sterling at 10d. per franc	23,816,041	
1870-73 5 % Consolidated bonds	53,882,200	
Total	77,698,241	
Capital of Railway Companies, the interest on which the Government was called upon (1875) to pay under its guarantees 160,000,000 roubles, converted at 29d. per rouble	19,333,333	
Total		97,031,574

(c) Liabilities in respect to Redemption of Peasant Lands . . . . . . 382,425,234 Roubles

Converted into Sterling at 29d. per rouble   46,209,715

(d) Liabilities in respect to Issue of State Bank 5 % Bills . . . . 220,462,250 Roubles.

Converted into Sterling at 29d. per rouble   26,639,188

Total Liabilities almost covered by special resources   169,880,477

GENERAL SUMMARY—   £
1. Loans 123,234,629
2. Floating debt 119,947,869

Total Loans and floating debt . . . 243,182,498

3. Liabilities (at present almost entirely covered)—
Issue of 5 % Bank Bills, in respect to Railways and Peasant Redemption Fund 169,880,477

Grand total of debts and liabilities . . . 413,062,975

APPENDIX III. 363

The following Statement of the Growth of the Public Debt of Russia since the Year 1817 *is also taken from the* '*Economist*' *of the same Date* :—

Description of Debt	1817	1827	1837	1847
I.—LOANS.	Roubles	Roubles	Roubles	Roubles
1. Terminable Loans—Foreign	28,842,000	25,992,000	45,645,250	37,251,121
„ „ Internal	18,408,359	10,225,832	42,471,820	53,714,212
2. Interminable Loans—Foreign (Rente Perpétuelle)	—	70,980,180	105,594,720	160,409,000
Interminable Loans — Internal	46,355,906	74,541,316	72,726,918	73,909,514
Total	93,606,265	181,739,328	266,438,708	325,283,847
II.—FLOATING DEBT AND LIABILITIES.				
1. Debt of Treasury for moneys borrowed from 'Credit Institutions'	—	20,000,000	24,000,000	127,359,000	266,528,000
2. Treasury Bills	—	—	11,428,571	45,000,000
3. Bank Notes (uncovered)	238,857,000	170,221,828	170,221,228	171,686,918
Grand Total	352,463,265	375,961,156	575,447,507	808,498,765

Description of Debt	1857	1867	On 1/13 January, 1875
I.—LOANS.	Roubles	Roubles	Roubles
1. Terminable Loans—Foreign	47,369,000	211,129,500	167,060,600
„ „ Internal	151,530,113	209,130,000	272,021,080
2. Interminable Loans — Foreign (Rente Perpétuelle)	319,434,894	278,925,160	296,170,609
Interminable Loans—Internal		203,863,385	201,277,375
Total	518,334,007	903,048,045	936,529,664
II.—FLOATING DEBT AND LIABILITIES.			
1. Treasury Bills	93,000,000	216,000,000	216,000,000
2. Debt of Treasury for moneys borrowed from 'Credit Institutions'	320,000,000	37,119,000	118,284,976
3. Debt of Treasury on account current with State Bank	—	—	5,220,797
4. Debt of Treasury for Loan from Redemption Fund	—	—	2,317,000
5. Bank Notes (uncovered)	612,458,889	568,467,029	566,086,396
6. Liabilities in respect to Kingdom of Poland	—	—	84,762,852
7. Liabilities in respect to Railways	—	—	703,170,555
8. „ „ Redemption of Peasant Lands	—	216,889,358	¹382,425,234
9. Liabilities in respect to issue of State Bank 5% Bills (1st issue)	—	258,356,000	220,462,250
Grand Total	1,543,792,896	2,199,879,432	3,235,259,724

¹ On 1/13 July, 1875.

NOTE.—The figures for 1817-1867 have been extracted from the *Statistical Review of the Russian Empire*, by W. De Livron, Fellow of the Imperial Geographical Society, St. Petersburg, 1875. The statement for 1875 has been compiled from Russian Official Returns, collated with an article on the Public Debt of Russia, in the *Russische Revue*, vol. ii., 1876.

APPENDIX IV.

THE FINANCIAL POSITION OF EGYPT.[1]

It will be remembered that on the issue of the 1868 loan, Mr. J. W. Larking, in his capacity as agent for the Viceroy of Egypt, stated that the country had a clear revenue of 6,000,000*l.*, and by the last few budgets that revenue has been swollen to about 10,000,000*l.* How has this growth been brought about? If we examine the statements of imports and exports published, we find that last year the figures did not reach so high a point as they did during 1863 and 1864, when Egypt was basking in the prosperity induced by the American Civil War. From 1863 to 1870 inclusive, the exports only twice rose above 9,000,000*l.*, as against 13,000,000*l.* and 14,000,000*l.* in those two years, and the imports fell proportionately low. In 1874 the exports rose, it is so set down, to nearly 15,000,000*l.*, although the English portion of them—say three-fourths of the whole—had fallen to 10,500,000*l.*, but last year they again fell below the figures of the war period. Yet in 1863 and '64 the debt of Egypt was a mere bagatelle, and as late as 1868 the revenue claimed was only 6,000,000*l.*: what then could have made it so much bigger since? Have the loans done it? 'The profits of the Khedive's estates and public works,' some say; but that is an absurd answer, because all these profits are confessed to be quite insufficient for the loans 'secured' on them. Not only so, but these profits are a delusion, so far as the Daira is concerned, if Mr. Cave is to be trusted. He tells us that the whole of the

[1] Extract from an Article in *Fraser's Magazine* for June 1876.

APPENDIX IV. 365

Khedive's property only yields 422,000*l*. a year, or not onethird of the debt charge for which it is liable. This statement has, indeed, been disputed, and a fresh estimate published since, but without reason given ; and if it is considered that the extravagant sugar and cotton growing speculations do not pay, by the admission of the Egyptian officials themselves, the estimate of Mr. Cave may well be accepted as near the truth, if not excessive. Are we to look then to the improved condition of agriculture amongst the people ? We fear not. Take the following description from a letter in the 'Times' of April 15, written by a correspondent not disposed to take a pessimist view of affairs, and judge what improvement Egypt has obtained from the bloated debt that has been put upon her by, I fear I must say, devices as vile as any ever conceived :—

The situation of the town labourer will be acknowledged to be not very enviable. I thought, perhaps, the condition of the cultivators, the fellaheen, the 'sons of the soil,' would be better. Egypt is the most fertile country in the world, produces its three crops a year without exhaustion, and it was only reasonable to suppose that the class who gave their labour to such a reproductive country would, at any rate, secure comfort for themselves. I talked with all classes about them—Europeans, natives, employers, employed, sheiks, fellahs themselves ; but they all concurred in describing the condition of the countryfolk as very miserable. So I went to see for myself. I rowed up the river from Mansoorah, landing here and there at the villages, and thus I saw, not only the homes of the fellahs, but I also obtained an idea of the country which I could not have got in the town. The villages are very frequent, and always in aspect the same—a cluster of brown mud huts, windowless and chimneyless, round a dome and minaret, by way of village church and spire. I landed from time to time to see these human beehives. The walk always lay through great reaches of verdure, along the banks of the small canals which form a vast network over the whole of the Delta. I found everywhere an almost incredible squalor. Let me, by way of example, briefly describe two villages

I saw. I first called on the Sheik-el-beled. He is the headman of the village, responsible to Government for the taxes of the village, its contingent of forced labour, and its contribution of men to the army. If the village is large there are several Sheiks. Nominally the Sheik holds office for life, but the Moudir of the province can practically do what he pleases with him. 'We elect him, yes,' said some fellaheen, 'but the Moudir sends word whom we are to elect.' The Sheik of this particular village was well dressed, in Oriental fashion, had a house of many rooms, and even glass windows. He gave me sherbet and coffee, and then took me round his village. The mud huts are all built one against another, like the cells of a beehive, save where they are divided by the little lanes that run through the village. I chose a hut at random, and asked if I might go in. 'Yes,' said my companion, 'but it is very poor, and there is nothing to see.' We went to the entrance, these huts having, as a rule, no doors. An old woman—at least, she looked old, but the women are old at forty—barred the way. I offered money, but that was not enough to overcome her feelings that her house was her castle, where no Christian should enter, and the Sheik had to insist. One small room—mud walls, mud roof, mud floor—was all we found. Four bricks made a small fire-place, but there was no fire. A small basin of maize, five water jars, an earthen pot for artificial hatching of chickens, a cock and three hens, a small heap of sacking by way of bed-clothes, constituted all the furniture of the house. Four yards by five was the extent of the house, and this was partly taken up by a raised dais of mud, which serves as the family bed in every fellah habitation. A family of four lived in this space. The head of the family was considered pretty well-to-do by the fellah world, as he is the owner of five feddans (acres) of land. I tried another house, taken similarly at random. It was still smaller and more pitiful than the last. The mud bed occupied half the space. Three yards by one was my measurement of the rest. A water jar and a reed pipe were all the signs of habitation. There were no boxes or cupboards in which other goods and chattels might be hidden. A family of three, labourers on the lands of others, lived here. I have seen pigs better housed in England. . . . Excess of population is not the cause of the misery I saw. Five millions are not too many for the country. . . . Corn, formerly 8s. the ardeb, is now 18s. Eggs, once twelve a penny, are now a halfpenny each. Fowls, which used to cost a piastre, are now worth four or five. Cotton, the staple of the country, has fallen in price from 55 dollars the cantar, which it fetched during the American War, down a gradually declining scale until it has reached 11½ dollars, and now it hardly repays the cost of cultivation. While the source of wealth has thus decreased, the number of workers is diminished by the conscription in a way that almost recalls the days of Mehemet Ali, when, for a long series of years, the country was drained of its best men by the demands of military service. Forced labour is another cause of misery. It may not be unreasonable that districts should labour in common to maintain the roads and canals. But it is hard that fellahs should have to give their time to works of no benefit to their district, and even to works of no public utility at all, however high in position may be the person who demands it. Last, but by no means least, comes the burden of taxation, which the Government, with its costly schemes of internal development and external conquest, has increased year by year.

These extracts give a picture worth pondering over. Egypt, instead of being richer by all this money, has, it is clear, become poorer than ever, till, for the majority of the wretched people, existence is not worth having. If the revenues of Egypt have increased, therefore, it has been by a burden of taxation, such as this which I cut from the same letter :—

I give the following list of charges per feddan of good cotton land actually paid by a cultivator in the Delta, between July 31 and December 29, 1875 :—

'Maintenance of Nile banks, 19 piastres 10 paras; two-twelfths of an ardeb of wheat (said to be collected to enable Government to fulfil contracts made in Alexandria), 20 piastres; Moukabaleh (annual sum paid in redemption of half land tax), 172 piastres 20 paras; National Loan (a forced loan of five millions at 9 per cent.), 108 piastres; irregular expenses (unexplained what expenses), 5 piastres; Amour de la Patrie (thought to be a war tax), 38 piastres 20 paras; one-third Moukabaleh for the coming year, 60 piastres —total 423 piastres 10 paras.'

Ninety-seven and a half piastres are equal to a pound sterling. The value of good land has fallen. What was formerly worth 30*l.* is now only worth 20*l.* Some of the poorer land, where water is not easily obtained, has even been abandoned. Other land of better character has been sold in payment of taxes. Great quantities of produce have been seized and sold for the same purpose. The people themselves do not run away, as families, friends, and even villages are held responsible for unpaid taxes. No reduction is made for a bad crop or low prices. Considering that the average produce of land is now only worth, on an average (taking cotton, which can only be planted once every three years, wheat or maize, and clover together) about 9*l.* per acre, and that out of that taxes and cost of irrigation have to come, there is not much left for the peasant proprietor. It is not surprising that they are selling their lands, and coming into towns, where, if they do not earn a fortune by their labour, at any rate they escape much of the heavy taxation.

A flourishing state of things, truly; but not even all this grinding taxation and abject misery suffices to wring out of a population of over 5,000,000 a revenue of 10,000,000*l.* The budget, and budget surplus, and definitive accounts of the Egyptian Government are utter deceptions upon this point, as can be easily shown.

For example, the second and improved budget for 1873–74 exhibited a surplus of over a million, and the definitive account of the income and expenditure for the year or fifteen months in 1874–5 showed an almost exact balance; while the budget for 1876, published as an appendix to Mr. Cave's Report, exhibits a surplus of over 1,700,000*l.*, which the Egyptian Government has, as usual, the hardihood to point out as sufficient to pay the charge on the floating debt. According to these figures, disjointed though they be, the Egyptian Government should now have little or no floating debt at all; for, although the 1873 loan is said to have only netted 20,000,000*l.*, and, therefore, left 9,000,000*l.*

or 10,000,000*l.* to be carried on, that should have, with these surpluses, been lessened rather than increased. The Egyptian Government has itself, however, knocked down all support to this pleasant fiction. As was well pointed out by the 'Daily News,' the lumped-together statement of revenue and expenditure between the years 1864 and 1875 (given in Mr. Cave's Report), when compared with a similar statement issued two years before, shows that, even with an income of 10,000,000*l.* per annum and a paper surplus, the last two years must have involved a deficit of 8,243,628*l.* per annum. The figures come out thus—income of the two years, 1874 and 1875, 21,348,838*l.*; expenditure, 37,836,094*l.*; deficit on the two years, 16,487,256*l.* The detailed budgets are, therefore, entirely illusory by the confession of Egypt itself, and, as the 'Economist' says, drawn up only with a view to deceive. The doubts which such comparison induces as to the budgets naturally extend to the revenue itself. If there was no source but increased taxation on an already impoverished people from which to draw an augmented revenue, how could it possibly be raised from under 5,000,000*l.* in 1864 to 6,000,000*l.* in 1868, and to 10,000,000*l.* in 1874? Previous to 1864 it had, as stated in Mr. Cave's Report, taken thirty-four years to augment 1,600,000*l.* Does not this mysterious growth suggest that these large figures were merely put down to look as well as possible beside the swelling debt charges? There are few direct means of answering the question, but some approach towards its solution is gained by examining (1) what has become of the money that was raised on the various loans, and (2) some of the items of the budgets and accounts in the light of the explanations of Mr. Henry Oppenheim and others, as well as of the Government itself.

First as to the loans. Egypt, as we have seen, began to borrow in 1862, and, including the floating debt, taken at

Mr. Cave's estimate, and adding to it, for the sake of a correct account, the 4,000,000*l*. got from England, has, within fourteen years, borrowed an average sum of nearly 6,500,000*l*. per annum. What has become of this money? Mr. Cave says that Egypt has nothing to show for it except its Suez Canal, which is in itself an absurd statement, seeing that the Canal is leased to a Company, and that Egypt gets at present loss rather than gain from its existence. Still it is true that the money which has not gone into that undertaking has gone mostly to keep the ball of loan-concocting rolling merrily, and to gratify the whims, improving and other (mostly other), of his Highness the Khedive. The Canal, according to a calculation of Mr. R. H. Lang, a gentleman acquainted with Egypt, had cost the Viceroy 17,423,178*l*., including interest up to the end of 1873, and the railways 11,899,411*l*., also including interest, money having been raised at 27 per cent. Beyond these sums and the other interest and sinking fund charges there is nothing to show for the whole 80,000,000*l*. or 90,000,000*l*. that have been nominally squandered. Of course, it must not be forgotten that that big sum is probably more than double what the Khedive ever received. All his loans were issued at a greater or less discount, and those of 1870 and 1873 were never thoroughly 'absorbed' by investors. He paid exorbitant rates for short advances at times, and always very high ones, so that, altogether, if he got 40,000,000*l*. or 50,000,000*l*. out of the gross sum owing, he did well. We can put the net receipts at about 45,000,000*l*. But that makes no difference to the Egyptian liabilities. When we come, moreover, to analyse the import figures of Egypt, we find that the utmost that could have been spent on works of utility is about 1,000,000*l*., per annum, against a borrowing that latterly much exceeded 10,000,000*l*., and that has averaged over 6,500,400*l*. per annum. In one shape or other, therefore, the bulk of the

APPENDIX IV. 371

money received has gone to make good revenue deficits; and as these deficits grew rapidly larger after each new loan, it is but fair to infer that they did so because legitimate revenues did not augment with the rapidity that has been set forth. That inference is the more likely when we consider that the most favourable period in the commercial history of modern Egypt was 1863 and 1864, when the revenue was set down at only some 5,000,000*l.*, and that since then poverty and misery have been steadily on the increase amongst a population that stagnates at about 5,250,000.[1]

The most important item in the Egyptian revenue is, of course, the land tax; and it is also the most difficult to get any just conception of. In the first budget of 1873-74 it was set down as yielding 4,579,000*l.*, exclusive of the date-tree tax, tithes, and the Mokabala. When the amended budget came out, however, this sum was altered to 4,185,000*l.*, and Mr. Henry Oppenheim puts it down at 3,368,000*l.*; while Mr. Cave says in his Report that in 1871, the year before the Mokabala arrangement came into force, the land tax yielded, 'as nearly as we can judge,' 4,793,459*l.* a year. According to the highest estimate for 1873-74, therefore, this item of income would appear to have diminished rather than increased. How, then, has the total revenue grown to 10,000,000*l.* ? In 1871 Mr. Cave says it was only 7,377,912*l.*, and in 1873-74, according to the first budget, it was only 7,000,000*l.*; so that,

[1] The account may be made up thus :—

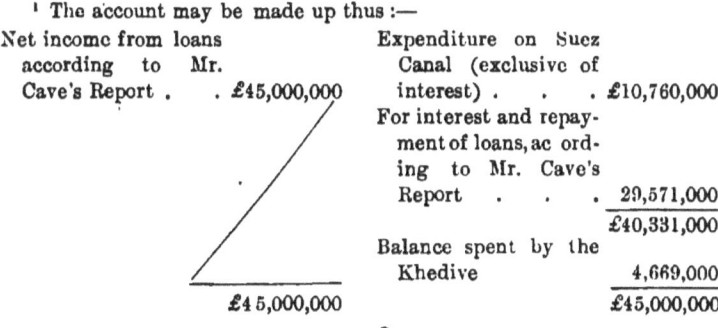

Net income from loans according to Mr. Cave's Report	£45,000,000	Expenditure on Suez Canal (exclusive of interest)	£10,760,000
		For interest and repayment of loans, ac ording to Mr. Cave's Report	29,571,000
			£40,331,000
		Balance spent by the Khedive	4,669,000
	£45,000,000		£45,000,000

B B 2

on any showing, its growth since has been sufficiently striking. Part of the answer to this conundrum is to be found in the magic word 'Mokabala.' When the amended budget came out in 1873, that mysterious item stood for 1,576,000*l*., which had not appeared in the previous one, although deductions had there figured on its account to the amount of 699,000*l*., which, in the new fabrication, dwindled to 132,000*l*. What, then, is the Mokabala? It is an arrangement whereby the Khedive forces double contributions from the landholders over nominally a term of years, on conditions which are thus described at page 5 of Mr. Cave's Report:—

The revenue of Egypt has increased from 55,000*l*. a year in 1804, 3,300,000*l*. in 1830, and 4,937,405*l*. in 1864, the second year of the Khedive's administration, to 7,377,912*l*. in 1871, the year previous to the changes caused by the law of Mokabala. Under this law all landowners could redeem one-half of the land tax to which they were liable by the payment of six years' tax, either in advance in one sum or in instalments. Those who paid down this contribution in one sum received an immediate reduction of their tax; those who elected to make the payments in instalments receive a discount of $8\frac{1}{3}$ per cent. on their advance, and the reduction only takes place on the completion of their contribution. The extreme term for the entire redemption of each contributor's tax was at first fixed for six years; but as the law was either not properly understood, or the small owners were unable to make so heavy a payment annually, as their land tax plus its amount minus $8\frac{1}{3}$ per cent., the term was extended from six to twelve years, two years after the first promulgation of the law, so that it has now ten more years to run, during which the contributing landowner has to pay land tax plus one-half the tax (6-12) and minus $8\frac{1}{3}$ per cent. of the same. It is most advantageous to the landowner who can afford the present sacrifice, as, in addition to the advantage of securing in perpetuity the redemption of half his tax by a payment of five and a half times its present amount, to which it is reduced by the discount allowed ($8\frac{1}{3}$-100·$\frac{1}{2}$ × 12=$\frac{1}{2}$), he secures an indefeasible title to his land, the tenure of which is at present of an uncertain character. To the State the arrangement is a ruinous one from a fiscal

APPENDIX IV. 373

point of view, as the Khedive has bound himself in the most solemn manner not to re-impose the redeemed moiety of the tax in any shape whatever, and he has thus sacrificed for all time 50 per cent. of revenue from this source in order to realise eleven times the annual amount remitted during a period of twelve years. The original intention of the law was to realise at once, or in a few years, sufficient capital to pay off the floating debt, but by extending its operation the sum raised annually has only sufficed to pay the interest on it.

In other words, for the first year the landholders paid their tax twice over, less 8⅓ per cent.; for the second twice over, less 16⅔ per cent., and so on until, at the end of twelve years, they are released from half the burden of the old permanent tax for ever. By this means, we are told, the Khedive hoped to pay off his floating debt. He has failed to do that, however, and, instead, this is what happens. For a few years—supposing every landholder able to pay the tax, which he is whipped to do—the land revenue is excessively swollen, and then it gradually drops away, until, according to Mr. Cave's calculations, it will amount, at the twelve years' end, to 1,805,131*l*. Mr. Cave was first told that Mokabala would only involve an ultimate loss of 1,531,118*l*., but afterwards the Khedive confessed to him that it would actually come to 2,500,000*l*., while in 1873 an anonymous estimate, generally attributed to Mr. Oppenheim, counted it at 3,022,000*l*.: but their estimate of the original land revenue differs so much that these other discrepancies ultimately come together in almost the same result as regards the final issue. By this means, then, the land revenue was temporarily raised, according to the amended budget of 1873, to 5,629,000*l*., and it will sink in 1886 to less than 2,000,000*l*. Nay, by virtue of the cumulative discount, it is becoming less every year, and never would have sufficed to make 5,000,000*l*. into 10,000,000*l*. And what is

there to fill up the gap now yearly on the increase? The upholder of Egyptian finance could only find two sources of consolation, and only one of compensation. Before the Mokabala is lost the permanent charge of the Egyptian debt would, they say, be lessened by the liquidation of several of the short loans. That would be most satisfactory were there not new debts growing, and had not the recent decree of consolidation swept these hopes entirely away, for no loans are to be paid off now for sixty-five years. The second consolatory and compensatory consideration lies in the augmentation of land revenue from new cultivation brought under taxes. Mr. Cave says that 620,000 feddans may be expected to yield revenue soon, and he estimates that revenue at 320,000$l.$, or about 10$s.$ per feddan, which, contrasted with the 20$s.$ and 21$s.$ per feddan said to have been got from the old acreage before the imposition of the Mokabala, excites reflections. At that rate the whole land registered as cultivable, and amounting to 1,098,000 feddans, would not, were it brought into cultivation now, suffice to make good what would be lost in 1886 by a couple of millions sterling. But there is little chance of any such good fortune. Land is rather going out of cultivation than coming in. The people are too experienced in oppression to be eager to open new ground on which taxes could be laid. All things considered, therefore, there is much force in the observation with which the anonymous pamphleteer aforesaid sums up his favourable review of the Mokabala arrangement:—
'It must not be forgotten,' he says, 'that, although the remission of the land taxes promised as a return for the Mokabala instalment is absolute, the income of the taxpayers is increased by the remission, and would be available to the State in some form or other if necessity should arise.' No doubt it would. The hint is a most suggestive one; and if one may judge by the list of burdens borne by the poor fellaheen given above, it

has not been lost on the astute, conscienceless ruler of Egypt. But the taxation that increases poverty, that causes cultivators to sell land rather than bear the burden imposed for five years' purchase, does not augur well for the productiveness of this source of fresh income. Mr. Cave forgot these views of the situation when he expressed the hope that the Mokabala remissions would give an impulse to cultivation— the more is the pity. And the new unifying decree which has been applied to the debts actually announces the abandonment of the entire arrangement. The Mokabala is to be no more, and the land revenue will return to its old footing. Those who paid double tax in the hope of obtaining remissions and a fresh title to their land must renounce their land and pay again as best they can.

So much for the land tax, which we think it would be hard to fix the actual yield of amid the confusion of budgets. The item next in importance is the receipts from the railways, and here again we have nothing but conflicting data to go by. In the four documents which condescended to loose particulars regarding Egyptian finance, viz. the two budgets of 1873–4, the 'definitive account' of 1875, and the budget of 1876, we have their net receipt set down thus—first budget, 750,000*l*., second ditto (for the same year), 878,000*l*., 1875 account, 966,066*l*., and the 1876 budget, 990,800*l*. No details are given of the working of these railways, except an account published in 1873, which shows that they are worked at about 40 per cent. of their gross receipts, and that it only costs 107,722*l*. to keep over 1,000 miles of railway and telegraph lines in repair. It is remarkable, too, that this should have been accomplished while the Khedive considers that he has the same right to use his railway for nothing in the carriage of freight and soldiers and for pleasure, as he has to goad his people under the lash to work without compensation on his estates. So far as I know, no other system of railways in the world could yield such extraordinary results under these conditions. And if the loss of Indian transit traffic, as well as the decrease in Egyptian trade through the opening of the Suez Canal, be taken into account, the enormous amount of the receipts becomes striking beyond the capacity of human credulity. The net receipts of these railways were, moreover, set down as only 282,853*l*. in 1864–5, and at a still less sum the year before, when Egypt was in the full tide of its fitful cotton prosperity, and while it had an enormous transit trade to and from India. Where in the world, therefore, has the sudden increase come from since? I do not believe that it exists. The increased mileage has not brought increased profits; but if the truth were told, the reverse, as a moment's consideration of the falling prices, reduced trade, and general situation will make evident. If the railways yield a net revenue of a quarter of a million, they do better than many of our Indian lines that are quite as well situated for traffic, and not so burdened with the caprices of unreasoning despotism, or with the weight of money borrowed at 27 per cent.

Almost equally difficult to believe is the statement as to Customs receipts, although Mr. Cave says that they appear to have been under-estimated last year, the income from the whole Customs being taken at 17,500*l*. less than an independent authority has set down, on 'imperfect data,' for Alexandria alone. The sum ranges from 528,000*l*. to 624,000*l*., and we will let it pass with this remark only, that it was levied on about five and a half millions of imports in 1875, according to the official statement, of which at least a fifth passed in free for the Khedive's account, while a good portion of the remainder was simply goods in transit; and, further, that the English Board of Trade returns show that the

Egyptian imports from this country have fallen from 8,829,000*l*. in 1870 to 3,674,000*l*. in 1874. How could it be otherwise with a population hardly able to buy the necessaries of life? It is only the Khedive and his Court and the Europeans in the country who can afford to import duty-paying luxuries. Everything is, however, so loose that relates to Egyptian trade, that we find a wide disagreement in the import and export figures published two years ago and those given in Mr. Cave's Report. For example, the old figures stated the total exports of the period 1852 to 1861 at 27,386,000*l*., and the imports at 21,755,000*l*., showing a surplus on the right side of 5,631,000*l*. Mr. Cave, on the other hand, gives a table for the same period in which the exports are set down at 29,870,000*l*. and the imports at 24,763,000*l*., which shows a larger total and a smaller sum on the right side. Matters are still worse when we come to the period from 1862 to 1875. The old table which comes down to 1871 states the gross exports at 123,241,000*l*. and the imports at 52,682,000*l*., while Mr. Cave's table, which comes down four years later, shows a gross export total of only 145,939,000*l*. and an import total of 61,940,000*l*. This gives an import for the last four years of 22,698,000*l*., or only 5,675,000*l*. per annum, and an export of 9,258,000*l*., or only 2,315,000*l*. per annum. It is not so set down in the tables of course, being accounted for by a general cutting down of figures over the years embraced in the period; but all the same this is how the totals work out, and we have to conclude either that the table issued in 1874 was grossly exaggerated, or that both statements are a mere haphazard guess, prompted, in the case of the figures furnished to Mr. Cave, by a desire to make things look a little like the totals in the English home accounts. On the whole we may, therefore, leave the Customs revenue as an undiscoverable quantity, which, whatever it be, does not tend to grow bigger. Nor does our quest for big revenues get clearer when we deal with such items as the salt monopoly, which figures in the original budget for 187,000*l.*, and in last year's accounts for 299,000*l.*, although consumption is necessarily about the same. The tobacco duty is equally puzzling. In 1873 the inspired anonymous pamphleteer had many reasons to give why this item, which did not figure for a farthing in the first 1873 budget, should be made to show in its duplicate or amended version for 500,000*l.* He said 1½ lb. per head was no extravagant consumption of tobacco for the poor people, and 1*s.* 6*d.* per lb. no heavy sum to pay as tax; and, in short, proved to his own satisfaction, that the tax was the most sure in Egypt—admitting, however, that it might yield but half the estimate just at first. His sanguine anticipations have not, unhappily, been fulfilled; the tax has yielded, by the comparison of succeeding documents, only from 250,000*l.* to 260,000*l.* Once more, receipts from provincial governors figure in the first budget for only 223,000*l.*, but in the 1875 accounts they have been swollen to 703,000*l.*, including municipal receipts, which do not figure in the first budget at all. In the 1876 budget they are higher still. In one budget the miscellaneous receipts of the Ministry of Finance do not appear at all, in another they figure at 272,000*l.*, and in yet another at 455,000*l.* General miscellaneous receipts, octroi, &c., stand in the first budget for 167,000*l.*, and in the 1875 account for 493,000*l.*, and so on; it is hardly necessary to go through all details. All that can be said of some of these is that they represent illegal 'squeezes' and 'backsheesh' on which no reliance can be placed as regular revenue. Enough has been said in the mere recapitulation of these figures to show the utterly untrustworthy nature of every statement regarding the income and trade of Egypt, and to prove that any

APPENDIX IV. 379

just estimate of what the revenues really are is almost impossible; all we can assert is that they are lower than officially set forth. We must perforce fall back on general considerations, and, remembering that the revenue was confessedly under 5,000,000*l.* in 1864, think whether in the interval Egypt has 'progressed' so as to be able to double it. Her trade is by official statements smaller now than it was then and much less profitable, the population by all accounts poorer, the yield of soil not greater; the private ventures of the Khedive do not pay, his 'new provinces,' with the possible, but only possible, exclusion of the Soudan, entail loss; where then is this augmented revenue to come from?

How is a poverty-stricken population subject to *corvées*, hardly able to get bread, whose goods are liable to be sold at the bidding of the ruthless tax-gatherers, who must pay 'squeezes' to every corrupt official in order that he may get speedily rich—how are these to pay 2*l.* per head in taxation, young and old, infant and imbecile, or 8*l.* per family, if we suppose each family to consist of four persons? Worked to death, often hurried off to the Khedive's foolish wars, driven to build the Soudan Railway under the eye of an English contractor who ought, because he is an Englishman, to be ready to cut off his right hand rather than touch such work, where are these wretched creatures to find every year such sums of money?

The question hardly needs putting to reveal the absurd impossibility of realising this preposterous revenue. All the financial statements of Egypt are illusory. If the revenue was under 5,000,000*l.* in 1864, when Egypt was comparatively prosperous, not all the squeezing of the Mokabala exactions can have forced it beyond 7,000,000*l.* now, and I doubt if it has ever really exceeded six. How could it possibly do so when the civil administration lives by plunder?

Let anyone conceive what it would be to wring 10,000,000*l*. sterling out of a population of some 5,000,000 souls, all but a few thousands reduced to a state of poverty more abject than that of the dwellers in the bye-lanes of Soho, Seven Dials, or Drury Lane, or than that of the Irish labourers before the potato famine, and that it is, moreover, wrung out of these people at a cost of from 20 to 30 per cent. additional, which goes as 'backsheesh,' and tax-farmer's profit, after approved Turkish fashion, and he will have some idea of what the budgets of Egypt must mean. The parrot cry always rises when this view is advanced, 'But Egypt is a very fertile country, and its people need little to live on beyond a few dates.' Yes, Egypt is fertile; but of what use is fertility when there is neither capital nor security to enable that fertility to bear its due fruit? Mr. Henry Oppenheim estimates the yield of this fertile country at from 4*l*. to 6*l*. per acre, and the 'Times' correspondent says it averages 9*l*. Compare these estimates with what a Scotch farmer contrives to get out of his bleak moorland or bare hill-side, and then talk of the fertility of Egypt as much as you like. It will be found to be but one more Egyptian dream.

People will, it is to be hoped, not forget, when these glittering empty schemes are paraded before them, the budgets which have always shown a surplus and have lied systematically in so doing; that the 'floating debt' was, like Moses's burning bush, inconsumable—always about to be extinguished by the newest loan, always reappearing bigger and more importunate than ever. Yet there is no telling what mankind may do. Where the temptation of gain is large, men grow blind to all risks and to all iniquity too. I can hardly conceive of a man with a conscience in his bosom sitting down and looking calmly at the state into which the miserable loan-dealing of adventurous rogues has brought Egypt without being awakened to pity, and, if he has been partaking in the gains, to remorse; and yet such men are often to be met with. They have become accustomed to look on these matters as merely so much per cent., and the agonies of the wretched slaves of Egypt reach not the peaceful luxuriousness in which these percentages enable them to dwell. By the toil of those weary millions these people have grown rich, and to them riches are more than humanity, an easy life better than the refusal to live by the sweat of another's brow, the slow draining of another's blood. I meet such men often, and wonder and fear also that with a new bait there will be a new rush after the gold, and a new impetus given to an oppression that has already mounted to an agony crying to heaven for vengeance. It is a gamble after all with the mass of those who join such ventures, and 'devil take the hindmost' their cry. These people, the majority of them—men and women of all classes, sober priests and professed gamblers, one-idead shopkeepers and jewelled dwellers in palaces—can only be kept away by fear of loss, and hence I have iterated and reiterated the utterly baseless character of Egyptian financial statements. I appeal to prudent greed rather than to the hearts and consciences of men. If people will believe that on any terms the Egyptian fellaheen can find means to pay the charges on the present funded debt alone, and will lend further money to Egypt on that belief, they deserve their fate. But I would fain hope yet, and after all said, for humanity's sake, that the end of this modern system of fraud and oppression has come so far as Egypt is concerned; that neither the English Government nor the English people will any more associate themselves with crimes so great as those that have been perpetrated there under the name of progress. Whether from doubt of gain to be had or from an awakened consciousness of the harm that has been done, let us hope that our part and lot in the affair is over. The more what has been done in the past is looked at the uglier will it seem. It is melancholy that the wealth of England should ever have been turned to such a use. That the wealth so employed should be lost may prove to be the lightest part of our retribution.

THE END.

www.ingramcontent.com/pod-product-compliance
Lightning Source LLC
Chambersburg PA
CBHW022334230426
43664CB00040B/482